Collective Decision Making

Collective Decision Making

Applications from Public Choice Theory

Clifford S. Russell, editor

published for RESOURCES FOR THE FUTURE
by The Johns Hopkins University Press
Baltimore and London

Library of Congress Catalog Card Number 79-16614
ISBN 0-8018-2320-X
Library of Congress Cataloging in Publication data will be found
on the last printed page of this book.

Resources for the Future, Inc.
1755 Massachusetts Avenue, N.W., Washington, D.C. 20036

Resources for the Future is a nonprofit organization for research and education in the development, conservation, and use of natural resources and the improvement of the quality of the environment. It was established in 1952 with the cooperation of the Ford Foundation. Grants for research are accepted from government and private sources only if they meet the conditions of a policy established by the Board of Directors of Resources for the Future. The policy states that RFF shall be solely responsible for the conduct of the research and free to make the research results available to the public. Part of the work of Resources for the Future is carried out by its resident staff; part is supported by grants to universities and other nonprofit organizations. Unless otherwise stated, interpretations and conclusions in RFF publications are those of the authors; the organization takes responsibility for the selection of significant subjects for study, the competence of the researchers, and their freedom of inquiry.

The papers in this volume were presented at a forum held January 17–19, 1978 which was sponsored by Resources for the Future and funded by the Rockefeller Foundation. Clifford S. Russell is head of the institutional research unit at Resources for the Future. The book was edited by Ruth B. Haas.

RFF editors: Joan R. Tron, Ruth B. Haas, Jo Hinkel, Sally A. Skillings

Participants

PETER BOHM
Department of Economics, University of Stockholm, Stockholm, Sweden

EMERY N. CASTLE
President, Resources for the Future, Washington, D.C.

JOHN R. CHAMBERLIN
Department of Political Science, University of Michigan, Ann Arbor, Michigan

EDWARD H. CLARKE
Woodrow Wilson International Center for Scholars, Smithsonian Institution, Washington, D.C.

CHARLES CLOTFELTER
Institute of Policy Sciences and Public Affairs and Department of Economics, Duke University, Durham, North Carolina

JAMES T. COLEMAN
Department of Sociology, University of Chicago, Chicago, Illinois

RALPH K. DAVIDSON
The Rockefeller Foundation, New York, New York

JOHN FEREJOHN
Division of Humanities and Social Sciences, California Institute of Technology, Pasadena, California

MORRIS P. FIORINA
Division of Humanities and Social Sciences, California Institute of Technology, Pasadena, California

A. MYRICK FREEMAN III
Department of Economics, Bowdoin College, Brunswick, Maine

EDWIN T. HAEFELE
Department of Political Science, University of Pennsylvania, Philadelphia, Pennsylvania

RUSSELL HARDIN
Department of Government and Politics, University of Maryland, College Park, Maryland

JEFFREY HART
Department of Politics, Princeton University, Princeton, New Jersey

HELEN M. INGRAM
Department of Political Science, University of Arizona, Tucson, Arizona

ALVIN K. KLEVORICK
Yale Law School, Yale University, New Haven, Connecticut

EDWIN S. MILLS
Department of Economics, Princeton University, Princeton, New Jersey

ROBERT CAMERON MITCHELL
Institutional Research Unit, Resources for the Future, Washington, D.C.

DENTON E. MORRISON
Department of Sociology, Michigan State University, East Lansing, Michigan

DENNIS C. MUELLER
Department of Economics, University of Maryland, College Park, Maryland

MICHAEL NICHOLSON
Richardson Institute, London, England

WILLIAM NISKANEN
Ford Motor Company, Dearborn, Michigan

ROGER NOLL
Division of Humanities and Social Sciences, California Institute of Technology, Pasadena, California

MANCUR OLSON
Department of Economics, University of Maryland, College Park, Maryland

CHARLES R. PLOTT
Division of Humanities and Social Sciences, California Institute of Technology, Pasadena, California

PAUL R. PORTNEY
The President's Council on Environmental Quality, Washington, D.C.

DANIEL L. RUBINFELD
Department of Economics, University of Michigan, Ann Arbor, Michigan

JON C. SONSTELIE
Department of Economics, University of California, Santa Barbara, California

RICHARD B. STEWART
Harvard Law School, Harvard University, Cambridge, Massachusetts

RUSSELL TRAIN
The Conservation Foundation, Washington, D.C.

GORDON TULLOCK
Center for Study of Public Choice, Virginia Polytechnic Institute and State University, Blacksburg, Virginia

ORAN R. YOUNG
Department of Government and Politics, University of Maryland, College Park, Maryland

Table of Contents

Acknowledgments

Many people helped to make each step in the long process from original idea to this proceedings volume pleasant and instructive. Louise Russell first suggested to me that a conference on these lines could be a useful indication of RFF's serious interest in the field of applied public choice. I was encouraged to pursue this idea by Emery Castle of RFF and Ralph K. Davidson of the Rockefeller Foundation; and the latter was all important in obtaining the grant that made the event possible. In planning the conference, I received valuable help from Mancur Olson, Oran Young, Paul Portney, and Edwin Haefele. The actual event went smoothly under the watchful eye of Margaret Parr and with the efforts of Nick Gavin of Brookings. The participants represented here and several others listed in the back of this volume all contributed to two very exciting days.

In preparing my introductory essay I was helped by comments from my colleagues, Robert Cameron Mitchell, Helen Ingram and Emery Castle. In addition, in making final editorial changes and rewriting my essay I was stimulated by the very challenging official reviews prepared by Vernon Smith, Joe Oppenheimer, and Edgar Dunn and by the informal comments and questions of Jerry Kelly. These reviewers, each coming from a different direction, as it were, helped me to rethink the fundamental questions at issue. I hope they will find that I profited from their careful critiques, but I cannot, of course, leave them with any of the blame for remaining inadequacies in my writing or editing.

Finally, there is no doubt that the RFF editor, Ruth Haas, made many improvements and deserves the reader's thanks as well as mine.

August 1979   C.S.R.

Charles J. Hitch

Introductory Remarks

When I came to RFF I believed strongly that institutional factors were of preeminent importance in shaping resource and environmental policies, as well as in determining what actually happens in implementing those policies, and hoped that the thrust of RFF's research could be modified to reflect the true importance of institutions.

It proved to be much harder than I expected for a number of reasons, some of them adventitious; others, I expect, fundamental. We probably did not have on the research staff enough people with the interest and experience to deal effectively with institutional problems, and financial constraints on hiring and growth made it impossible to change the character of the staff substantially in the short run. We found it very difficult to obtain grants for institutional studies, which reinforced these constraints. Foundations and granting agencies had an image of RFF as solely an *economic* policy research organization: it was not obvious to them that we could contribute to the analysis of intergovernmental relations, the sociology of decision making, or the role of the courts, to cite a few relevant examples. In short, we had an "image" problem with potential sponsors.

But the obstacles were not all externally imposed. We had genuine self-doubts about the state of the art of institutional analysis; a feeling that current tools are far from satisfactory for predicting and assessing the effects of suggested institutional changes. Let us take a relatively simple example.

President Carter believes, as I do, that institutions matter. Specifically, he believes (more strongly than I do), that the organization of the executive branch of the federal government matters a great deal. His Office of Management and Budget has appointed a series of task forces in various areas to come up with recommendations for reorganization. One of these groups is dealing with natural resource and environmental functions of the federal government, now widely dispersed among departments, bureaus, and regulatory agencies, allegedly frequently at odds with each other, and inadequately coordinated. The "public" has been solicited by the task force for comments on questions such as the following:

1. How important is regulatory independence? Independence from what?

2. Where and how should advocacy be built into the system? How about the responsibility for resolution of conflicts?

3. Is the federal role with respect to public and private land and related resources so different as to permit or require separate organizations? Conversely, are the objectives and problems so similar as to permit or require that they be joined under a single management?

4. Are decision making and implementing responsibilities in natural resource management and environmental protection assigned to best advantage among levels of government (federal/regional/state/local)?

5. Should we create a formal body, perhaps called the Natural Resources Council, to develop policy and oversee its execution by the operating agencies?

6. Should all natural resource functions be consolidated in a new department of natural resources, leaving environmental regulations in a separate Environmental Protection Agency? Alternatively, should both be consolidated in a department of natural resources and the environment?

7. What specific federal functions are unnecessary, outmoded, unjustified, or actually counterproductive?

My opinions have been solicited (along with those of thousands of others) but I really do not know how to go about answering those questions, with the possible exception of the last. There I do have the assistance of the economics of externalities, which helps me to distinguish types of decisions which should and should not be left to the market. As far as the first six are concerned, I have only anecdotal types of evidence on the success or failure of various types of governmental organization—but no body of theory, or even an insightful historical analysis. (Here I may be unfair; I am not familiar with the whole body of public choice literature, and it may well contain something helpful of which I am unaware.)

What can we say about the desirability of large conglomerate government departments? (Question 6 above.) The conventional wisdom is that the Department of Defense (DOD) is a modest success but that Health, Education and Welfare (HEW) is ungovernable. Even if this is so, why is it so, and how could HEW be made a modest success?

I emphasize that these are simple institutional problems, concerned only with the organization of the executive branch. Of course, institutions interact. One plausible explanation for the relative success of DOD is that Congress reorganized its committee structure to match the new executive structure, whereas in the case of HEW it did not.

But generally, as we leave the field of executive reorganization, the problems become more difficult. Here are a few which occur to me; no doubt the reader can supply many others.

• We have not devised a good method for reconciling, or even reaching a compromise on energy and environmental objectives. Both Congress and the executive seem to be organized to avoid facing up to the resolution of such tradeoffs.

• As a result, a tremendous burden, which they are ill equipped to bear, has been thrown on the courts—not merely in applying policy to particular cases, but in making policy. An egregious example is what the courts have made of the National Environmental Policy Act, going far beyond what anyone thought was congressional intent, resulting in delays stretching into years for project after project, and introducing major and debilitating uncertainties in a large area of governmental and industrial planning.

• Institutional problems and closely associated distributional problems are at the heart of our inability to enact or implement a rational energy policy.

• There is the problem of devising institutions which, in the absence of market mechanisms, will conserve water in high-value uses and divert it from low- to high-value uses.

• All of our "sunshine" laws and public interest interventions have failed to give the consumer/taxpayer an adequate voice in public decisions. Howard Margolis (1977) introduces the concept of "political externalities" to describe costs or benefits of political actions accruing to parties not involved in the decision. He argues that the auto emission standards enacted by Congress in 1970 represented an implicit deal between leading environmental groups, which were not interested in costs at all, and the automobile industry, which was interested only in costs to the industry and not total costs, to the exclusion of the public, which must pay all the costs. The standards saved the industry from its one real nightmare, the threat of being required by the government to adopt radically new engines.

• How, with government responsible for controlling or regulating high technology industries, can it attract staffs that understand the industries they are regulating? I was concerned that at the Department of Energy (DOE) very few of the top officials—division directors and up—had had any industrial experience, and the new and tougher conflict-of-interest rules applying to DOE may well make the situation worse. I don't think we are counting the costs of slamming that "revolving door." I think that one of the great strengths of our system in the past—despite its occasional scandals—has been the free movement of persons among government, industry, and academia, and the existence of institutions such as the contractor-managed National Laboratories, combining elements of all three.

The question for this forum is whether public choice theory offers promise of providing a firmer foundation for applied institutional research and for institutional innovations which could contribute to the solution of some of these problems. To play devil's advocate, there is a lack of evidence that this is in fact the case; as you know well, there is widespread skepticism about the potential of the theory. Public choice theory has its own "image" problem: it is perceived by many, including those in foundations and other granting agencies, as the highly theoretical plaything of a few intellectuals. Of course, this was the way the theoretical physics of Einstein, Bohr, and Oppenheimer was perceived in the 1930s; the analogy may or may not be apt.

In any event, I hope that the papers in this forum identify productive research opportunities in social institution and group decision making. I do not care at this point whether the opportunities are to be seized by RFF or someone else; I would like to see some funding sources convinced that the opportunities are there and that they are real, if they are.

In this regard, I want to thank the Rockefeller Foundation for what may be a leap of faith in making this forum possible. I very much hope that these papers confirm that faith.

REFERENCES

Margolis, Howard. 1977. "The Politics of Auto Emissions," *The Public Interest*, no. 49 (Fall).

Collective Decision Making

Clifford S. Russell

Applications of Public Choice Theory: An Introduction

This book contains a set of papers and accompanying discussions which were presented at a Resources for the Future forum on applications of public choice theory. The forum was held to explore the promise of this line of study in helping to solve the very serious institutional problems that crop up whenever we attempt to deal with specific substantive policy issues such as those of interest to RFF (energy, resources, and pollution). Beyond this broad aim, it seemed potentially valuable to bring together in one place examples of a growing but still quite fragmented literature. If, however, the collection is to appeal to those not currently working in public choice, it is desirable to provide some background and to put the papers into perspective against that background. These are the aims of this introductory essay.

Public choice is concerned with the mechanisms by which human societies make decisions about their collective lives.[1] It is distinguished from the older disciplines of "government" and political science by matters of substance and style. And, though many of its practitioners have come to it from economics, its interests are not the same as those of traditional economics, even that part dealing with such government concerns as the theory of public finance. Public choice is a new field. Its birth is usually dated from 1951, the year Arrow's pathbreaking *Social Choice and Individual Values* was published, but many earlier scholars

[1] Some people do and some do not recognize a distinction between "public" and "social" choice as names for the field. To the extent a distinction is recognized, it seems to be that public choice indicates a broader field, and that is the term I use. Two other terms (at least) are apparently also used to denote the same general field: "collective choice" and "the new political economy." I have left the other authors' usage untouched.

contributed to its development, especially in the area of voting systems
and their properties.

Let me be more specific about the content of the field without attempting to duplicate the existing review articles (such as that of
Mueller, 1976). It seems to me useful to think of public choice theory
as having two major distinct, yet occasionally intertwined threads. The
first of these is the study of rules (institutions) for arriving at a collective choice or ranking of alternatives (which may be individual issues
or comprehensive combinations of such issues) on the basis of the
choices or preferences of the individuals making up the collective unit
(committee, neighborhood, state, or nation). Such choices are made all
the time by actual governments as, for example, when by one means or
another we decide how much pollution to tolerate, how much national
defense to provide, and how much to tax ourselves to pay for the desired
"outputs." Arrow's contribution was a very powerful and mildly depressing impossibility theorem in this area. He showed that there is no
mechanism for aggregating individual preferences that satisfies certain
quite plausible and even innocuous-sounding conditions. It would not be
unfair to say that a large fraction of the energy of public choice theorists
since Arrow has been devoted to qualifying, expanding, and interpreting
this fundamental theorem, an enterprise which has involved the use of
set theory, symbolic logic, and other mathematical tools that have
given the field a special flavor of abstraction.

This part of public choice theory begins with the assumption that
the individuals making up the collective have well-defined (and, almost
always, rational) preferences among the alternatives to be ranked or
chosen from. Participation in the preference aggregation exercise is
assumed and usually, but not always, it is further assumed that each individual's true preferences are what get aggregated.[2] The central question may be thought of as: What properties will the aggregated or social
preference have under different sets of assumptions about the individual
preferences and the aggregation technique? (For a superb review of the
work in this field written with a minimum of mathematics and a maximum of motivation, see Plott, 1976.)

The other major thread to the theory begins at a different point
and asks quite different questions. Here the interest has been to insert

[2] This is not the case, however, in some of the literature about vote trading
as part of the voting aggregation procedure. There, falsified ("insincere") information on preferences may be generated by the trading activity as individuals strive to
better the results they obtain with truthfulness (sincere voting). See, for example,
Haefele (1973).

into the actual world of collective choices the homo economicus who is so useful and familiar in the world of private, market choices, and to see how the creature behaves. Because in real life the market and political worlds are linked at innumerable points and many people are active in both simultaneously, it may seem odd to think that a special theory should grow up around the application of economic concepts to the study of politics and public decisions. But it is really not so strange, for there is a strong tradition in our political theory that people ought to act differently when engaged on public business *and* that they in fact do act differently. Public choice theory says: Let us assume that people act as rational maximizers of their own well-being whether they are deciding which shirt to buy or which candidate to vote for—or, indeed, whether to vote at all. Put these self-interested people into the real contexts of public life, as voters, candidates, bureaucrats, and so forth, and see how they behave. Are the predictions of the theory borne out by experience? Do they help us to understand what happens better than the more traditional view?

These questions have prompted public choice research on the motivation and behavior of legislators (e.g., Fiorina, 1977), bureaucrats (e.g., Niskanen, 1971), the interaction of the two (e.g., Fiorina and Noll, 1978a), and even judges (e.g., Landes and Posner, 1975). The message of this research generally is that the self-interested public actor will behave in ways quite different from those anticipated in the conventional wisdom of our political culture. Legislators will not be motivated to master issues, but rather to help constituents and contributors in dealing with the federal government. Bureaucrats will aim at maximizing their power (budgets, staff, etc.), not at making socially optimal decisions. Judges will interpret legislation according to the original intentions of the writers because it is in the judges' self-interest to do so (Landes and Posner, 1975).

As these predictions have the ring of accuracy, at least when the empirical test is the casual variety based on current events, it is tempting to think that the theory has got hold of a key that has eluded the traditional approaches. The task now should be to use this powerful insight to redesign our institutions to take explicit account of the self-interested behavior of those who will run and staff them. There will be no more assumptions that those in public service will act to serve "the public interest."

A general impression of accurate prediction is not, however, the same thing as careful empirical examination of the theory, and it is the latter that should be available before we go very far in redesigning our institutions. When such a careful examination is done, we find that there are problems. Consider, for example, the area of collective life in which the two threads identified above are most obviously tangled: the activity of voting, whether for candidates for legislative or executive office or in referenda on specific issues. Voting is far and away the most commonly used method of aggregating individual preferences to arrive at social decisions, and all conceivable voting systems suffer from the basic infirmity captured by the Arrow theorem. At the same time, the process of voting for candidates and in referenda is as close as most people get to politics and public decisions and so provides the major opportunities for us to behave either as selfish maximizers or selfless public citizens. A problem for public choice theory is that when the rational pursuit of self-interest is taken to be equivalent to the maximization of the expected value of an action, it can be shown to be irrational for individuals to vote at all whenever more than a handful of other voters are involved. This is because the probability that a single vote will affect the outcome is always so small that even large prospective differences in well-being that depend on the election outcome will not outweigh the small costs of actually casting a ballot (Downs, 1957). However, even public choice theorists know that people vote, so we must obviously look closely at the theory that leads us to this false theorem. On the other hand, the part of the theory (axiomatic social choice theory, as it is called) that looks at the *process* of arriving at decisions through voting, given participation, has had considerable success in predicting outcomes under particular structures. (See, for example, Plott's paper in this volume and Plott and Levine, 1978.)

Therefore it seems clear that "application" of public choice theory must involve two distinct kinds of activities. First, there must be efforts to probe the reliability of the theory through empirical testing of its implications. Second, if we gain confidence in the theory, its lessons may be used to critique existing institutions and to design new ones. This book contains examples of both kinds of work, and though only one of the papers (that of Ferejohn, Forsythe, and Noll) actually includes integrated theory, testing, and design elements, the papers which deal principally with testing can give us some basis for judging how seriously to take the essays in criticism and design that were also part of the forum.[3]

---

[3] Other papers, for example, those of Tullock, and Portney and Sonstelie, also include elements of testing and design, so the dichotomy used in the text implies more tidiness than actually exists.

Before going on to look at these papers it will, however, be worthwhile to pause and consider some fundamental difficulties. First, when we test a theory we match its implications (theorems) against empirical data. If a particular implication is not shown to be false, that does not mean that the theory is "true." One swallow does not make a summer; indeed, in this case no number of swallows (failures to falsify) is enough to make a summer (a conclusion that a theory is true). If, on the other hand, the implication is shown to be false, then, assuming the deductive logic employed has been correct, we know that one or more of the assumptions of the theory are false. But by the time we have arrived at a testable deduction, the theory has probably become quite complex since the fundamental assumptions have usually been embellished with auxiliary assumptions and identifications of parts of the theory wtih real-world items, and we don't know what part (or parts) of the construction is (are) false.

Thus, in the voting example mentioned above, the failure of the deduction in empirical test may mean any (or all) of several things. The fundamental assumption of self-interested maximizing behavior may be wrong. Or the identification of "interest" with measurable gains attributable to the election *results* may be wrong. Or, finally, the identification of "maximizing" with maximization of the net expected value of the act of voting may be the culprit. Therefore, before we throw out the most fundamental assumption, we may want to check the other features of the theory. For example, perhaps people obtain a reward from the act of voting itself, so that self-interested behavior leads to voting, whatever the prospective gains from the outcome, so long as the costs of voting are not too high (Riker and Ordeshook, 1968). A problem with this postulate is that we have really not explained much with our new theory. Until we can predict which people (or at least how many people) will vote in a particular election, we have really only said that people vote because it is in their self-interest to do so. When they don't vote, it must be in their self-interest to abstain.

Perhaps, on the other hand, we should modify the rule adopted for the pursuit of self-interest, that is, the maximization of net expected value. This is the line pursued by Ferejohn and Fiorina (1974 and 1975) who show, for example, that if an individual uses a more conservative strategy (minimax regret) he or she might well rationally choose to vote even when the probability that his or her vote would break a tie is approaching zero. This is because the strategy takes account of how wretched the prospective voter would feel on the morning after the election, having decided not to vote and finding that his or her position lost by one vote or that there had been a tie in votes cast. (A tie is assumed to lead to a decision based on the toss of a fair coin.) The prospective voter can, with certainty, avoid this wretchedness simply by voting.[4]

Another possibility, perhaps more difficult to model, is that the prospective voter looks beyond the winner-take-all nature of elections and referenda and is concerned with the size of the difference between majority and minority. An overwhelming majority may be seen as a mandate for important policy shifts; or a healthy minority vote may be seen as a stabilizing force, restraining the ego and ambitions of the winner. Whatever the specific view, the implication would be that every vote mattered, whether or not it caused or broke a tie. Thus, the act of voting would be uncoupled from the knife-edge events occurring when voting sentiment is neatly, but improbably, split in half. On the other hand, this approach raises as many problems as it solves, for within it any self-interest calculation must involve much more subtle considerations. And the theory to be constructed must still explain abstention. Of course, any theory that allows for subjective evaluation of the probabilities of events—whether of cliffhangers or of routs—must inevitably lead to a certain irreducible indeterminacy unless the process for forming those probabilities out of experience is specified. If in addition, it is allowed that different people may adopt different rules for pursuing their self-interest, the difficulties in the way of prediction or post hoc explanation are formidable indeed. It may, in fact, be the difficulty of constructing sufficiently subtle formal theories that lies behind the contrast to be found in this volume between the apparent success of public choice theorems when faced with the tests of casual empiricism and the difficulties discovered when greater specificity is required and actual data are confronted in a rigorous way.

This discussion of voting as an example of testing and probing public choice theory raises two other important issues. First, because no theory can ever capture the world completely, a continued program of testing

[4] It is interesting to note in this connection that the 1978 business meeting of the American Economics Association in Chicago provides an example in which one presumes there was much morning-after regret. A motion to move the 1979 meetings from Atlanta, because of Georgia's failure to ratify the Equal Rights Amendment, failed by one vote, and the total votes cast were a very small fraction of the 2,800 or so registered conference participants, nearly all of whom were presumably eligible to vote. Clearly many economists now have a new appreciation of the minimax regret criterion applied to voting. They might nonetheless adopt the same strategy again, as the cost of voting was very large, consisting of being forced to listen to a three-hour debate lasting until after midnight!

each available alternative will inevitably lead to the falsification of every one. How then can we decide which theory is "best"? On which one is it best to base predictions or, in this case, institutional design recommendations? Miller (1975) provides a depressing answer: There is no way of comparing false theories that will answer the question on the basis of the total results from each. We seem to be left then, at this fundamental level, with the unsatisfying idea that we can and do specify in advance the boundaries of the problems of interest to us and then judge competing theories on how well they perform in the restricted area we have defined. All of which does not really save us much grief, for we surely cannot contemplate with contentment a theoretical approach to politics that may require a completely different structure of axioms and identifications for each sub-area of interest.

What if we could develop a public choice theory based on the rational, self-interested individual that we could not seem to falsify? How would we use it? One important way would be to begin with a set of properties that we would like a collective choice institution to satisfy as, for example, Arrow did and Ferejohn, Fiorina, and Noll do in their paper in this volume. Then, on the basis of our theory, we would construct an institution satisfying those requirements. I find it extremely interesting, however, that the Arrow impossibility theorem finds an echo in the Ferejohn, Forsythe, and Noll paper. All their requirements, each reasonable enough (and all described below), cannot be satisfied at once.

One important implication of this result is, it seems to me, that in many areas where we might want to do this kind of "institutional engineering" (the phrase of Ferejohn and coauthors) we shall find ourselves in a difficult constitutional bind. While it may be possible to obtain agreement—even unanimous agreement on a set of principles or characteristics we want our new institution to satisfy, these may often turn out to be inconsistent. When they do, we face the much more difficult task of trading off one principle for another or one set for another set. The implicit values attached to each principle by each voter or citizen then become important, and the possibility of unanimous choice must decline sharply.

It is also interesting to observe the key role in the impossibility results just mentioned that is played by strategic behavior, which is nothing more than a consequence or manifestation of self-interested behavior. Arrow's principle of "independence of infeasible alternatives" (to use the terminology adopted by Plott, 1976) is, as Plott shows, simply a statement that people will behave strategically. That is, people will reveal their preferences incorrectly or insincerely when it is in their self-interest to do so. Ferejohn and his coauthors want to construct a process in which there will be no incentives for strategic behavior and which will satisfy certain other conditions. But they find that their efficiency and nonstrategic requirements are inconsistent. Thus, there seems to be a sense in which self-interested maximizing behavior is a fundamental problem for human societies collectively—a conclusion which, if justified, is very different from the conclusions of microeconomic welfare theory for market systems.

This last tentative observation suggests to me a possible answer for a challenging question asked by one of the reviewers of an earlier draft of this chapter: How does one account for the conservative tone of much of the public choice literature? If "conservative" is roughly equivalent to "market-oriented," it may be a sense of these contrasting implications of our "original sin" of selfishness that encourages those in the field to prefer markets. On the other hand, of course, this interpretation may be entirely too simpleminded, for markets have their own imperfections, many of which stem from physical laws at least as immutable as any "law" of human nature. Perhaps the study and critique of process is simply the handiest and most effective club with which to attack habits of thought and action that have led over the past thirty or forty years to "regulatory excess," the "welfare mess," and other results opposed by many of those active in public choice. After all, the architects of the regulatory mechanisms and fiscal policies that are the focus of such heated public debate today (1979) were not called upon to justify their work by rigorous models of individual behavior. But whatever the explanation of this intriguing feature of the field, it will be well to turn to a discussion of the papers themselves.

I.   TESTING PUBLIC CHOICE THEORIES

Tullock, in the overview to this volume, reports very briefly on a number of studies that confront public choice theory with the results of natural experiments presumed to be relevant to testing the implications of the theory. The studies described include efforts to find evidence of "political business cycles." These are predicted when the theory is applied to national leaders facing reelection battles who have access to the power to stimulate the economy through fiscal policy. The assumption is that voters vote against unemployment. While Tullock is skeptical of the evidence confirming this deduction, Fiorina points out that a new book by Tufte (1978) shows quite convincingly that presidents and congresses do pump up the economy in quadrennial election years. Perhaps the most interesting question here is why the electorate appears to be influenced by it. If the economy can be pumped up in one year, only to go into recession the next (or to take off on an inflationary burst leading to a delayed but more severe recession), then it can presumably be managed in other ways as well, at least some of which ought to be preferable for a majority of the voters. Apparently politicians perceive their constituents as willing, time after time, to attribute the boomlet to good stewardship rather than cynical manipulation, or to care very little what is behind it, but to vote their *current* pocket books only.

This question is related to another deduction from the theory, on which Tullock reports little disagreement. He points out that self-interested voters have almost no incentive to inform themselves on the issues, and that indeed ignorance seems to be the rule. There is an interesting link here, which Tullock does not mention, to the implications for voting behavior with which I began. Clearly, if there is no incentive to vote, there is none to inform oneself so as to vote intelligently. It appears, however, that many people do vote, but without spending much effort at becoming informed.[5]

Tullock further mentions work purporting to show that ideology influences votes, where the underlying argument is that ideology functions as a substitute for information, given that the effort to become informed is irrational. While the proposition has some intuitive appeal, the tests described by Tullock are so devastatingly criticized by Fiorina in his discussion that one can hardly say there is any evidence for it.

Empirical work touches close to the vexing matter of voting behavior again when the question is the rational choice of activities by elected representatives. If the electorate does not bother to be informed on the issues, then a self-interested strategy for reelection should hardly concentrate on mastering the issues. Rather, it should put effort into giving individual voters a real incentive to prefer the incumbent. In brief, it should concentrate on service to the folks back home. This does appear

---

[5] One reviewer of this essay pointed out that this statement (that voters lack the incentive to become well informed on the issues) is, as it stands, a vacuous one because it offers no criteria for deciding what "well-enough-informed" would be. Voters are not as well informed as the specialists and zealots who may dominate the agenda, but that is not saying very much. On the other hand, the very success of the political business cycle theory suggests that there are areas in which greater information would be worth something, so that the incentive to gather and digest such information must be of some interest.

to be how representatives apportion their time (Fiorina, 1977; Fiorina and Noll, 1978a, b).

Finally, Tullock mentions in passing a number of studies by his colleagues, Crain and Tollison, which involve tests of a variety of implications of the theory. These have apparently been successful—that is, have not shown the theorems to be false. In sum, the paper and accompanying discussions report a mixed bag of empirical results, certainly not very powerful ammunition to use in converting the heathen.

While Tullock's summary indicates the kinds of results to be found in the empirical public choice literature, by its nature it cannot give the reader a feeling for the methods used and difficulties faced in particular projects. As an example of such a study, however, the paper by Portney and Sonstelie, "Super-Rationality in School Tax Voting," fills this gap. This paper also demonstrates some of the large conceptual and empirical obstacles standing in the way of such tests.

Portney and Sonstelie begin with the rationally self-interested house owner/voter facing referenda on changes in the levels of public services and property taxes to be provided by the jurisdiction within which his house sits. They hypothesize, and test in passing, that the valuation of the annual flow of public services (along with property taxes) which "go with" a house is capitalized in its value. They assume that homeowners act as if they knew how a prospective change in public services and taxes would change their net house values. Most important of all, they assume that using this information, the homeowners vote their pocket books, *ceteris paribus*. In Portney and Sonstelie's terminology, they are "super-rational."

The data for the test of this theorem come from a county in California and consist of information on the characteristics and prices of individual houses, measures of local service levels relevant to each house, and precinct-by-precinct returns for a single school tax referendum in 1970. The results of the regression runs provide some support for the hypothesis of superrational voting but certainly not enough to settle the question even temporarily. The data suffer, as what data do not, from a heavy dose of multicollinearity, and the variations in precinct returns appear to be influenced by factors other than property values, some of which are not reflected in their data.

Once again, the implications of public choice theory, while refreshingly testable, are not impressively supported. This is perhaps especially disappointing here, for Portney and Sonstelie have gone beyond theorizing to suggest that if their reasoning is correct and if it is supported in other regression tests, then it should also be possible for local governments to devise service and tax packages that will be unanimously favored by the (homeowner) voters. On the other hand, disappointing though the lack of strong positive evidence might be, it is hardly surprising, for these authors have picked an especially knotty problem to tackle. To begin with, there is the problem of abstention. Is it not irrational to make the effort to vote in these referenda even though large changes in net wealth positions may be involved? Why do people do it? Until we can answer this question, it seems quite bold to think that we can explain how those people who do vote pick one side of the question or another. (It should be noted that Portney and Sonstelie believe they can sidestep this issue.) Then there is the "as-if" assumption. The calculation they require the homeowner to mimic at some intuitive level is itself not all that well defined. It is not a case of acting as if one knew one's own marginal rates of substitution between various market goods. Instead, one must act as if one knew the market's (other people's) evaluation of marginal changes in unmarketed services. Finally, there is the practical difficulty of translating property value changes based on individual houses into aggregate precinct vote shares. For example, a large aggregate increase in value concentrated in a few houses would not produce a big yes vote.

Before turning to the other empirical papers with their different methods and styles, this is a convenient point at which to consider more generally the status of testing public choice theories against evidence from real-world events. There were some key general points made by the discussants that deserve emphasis here by way of caution in the design of future research. First, it is important that the nuts and bolts of the specific problem and system be thoroughly understood in order to reduce the chance that silly variables will be chosen for the tests. Second, while there are obvious reasons for concentrating on income and wealth effects, political decisions also involve issues that cannot be reliably translated into dollars—for example, war, abortion, street violence. If people are rationally self-interested about public choices, they will be so about these issues, and leaving them out of our calculations will be very damaging, while bringing them in will be extremely difficult. Finally, the long-run credibility of the entire exercise would be boosted by an effort to identify, formalize, and test alternative theories side by side with the products of the rational self-interest postulate.

In the paper "National Environmental Lobbies and the Apparent Illogic of Collective Action," Robert Mitchell describes a different kind of empirical research project aimed at testing part of the body of public choice theory. In this case the motivation comes from Mancur Olson's *Logic of Collective Action* and the apparent contradiction between the argument found there and the dramatic growth over the past decade of the national environmental "public interest" groups.[6] Briefly, Olson shows that rational, self-interested individuals will not bind together to achieve production levels of public goods that would be of benefit to all because the free rider problem makes it profitable for each person to "abstain." Such groups as do lobby for public goods desired by the membership are, according to Olson's argument, held together either by the cement of private benefits (group insurance, travel packages, publications, and the like) or by coercion (such as state licensing laws), making them closely akin to governments. How then can we account for the million people or more who are members of at least one national environmental public interest group?[7] Surely these groups are seeking quintessentially public goods.

To explore the possibility that Olson's theory may be modified to embrace this phenomenon while remaining consistent with the rational self-interest hypothesis, Mitchell uses data from a massive mail questionnaire, probing the motivations of group members, in combination with the results of telephone interviews with a random sample of U.S. citizens. While at this writing the data gathering has only just been finished, so no results can be reported, it is interesting to note that a critical thrust of Mitchell's argument extending Olson's theory has to do with imperfect information that is shown by individuals imperfectly understanding the importance of their contributions. That is, the potential member, solicited by a mail appeal, may really believe that the dollars he or she might send in will be critical to the organization. This approach has some similarities (not surprisingly, because of the similarity of the incentives faced) to that suggested earlier for dealing with the voting behavior paradox. That is, individuals might join a group to avoid the regret they would feel if the group(s) in question failed for want of a few dollars, or if a major cause was lost (a species extinguished, for example) because there was no money to pay for filing a law suit.

---

6 The national groups include: National Wildlife Federation, Audubon Society, Sierra Club, Wilderness Society, Environmental Action, Environmental Defense Fund, Natural Resources Defense Council, and Friends of the Earth.

7 There exist an enormous number of local groups, usually focusing their energies on one issue, such as a proposed dam or nuclear power plant. The problem of incentive is in principle the same for these local groups.

It is interesting to note in this connection that Frolich and Oppenheimer (1970) provide a different sort of argument about free riders and voluntary association to provide public goods. They show, by an argument closely akin to mathematical induction, that the size of the group is irrelevant, for if it is not a problem at group size $n - 1$, it will not be at n. Nothing in the individual's decision problem (whether to give or not, or how much to give) changes with the addition of other members, if we confine ourselves to the assumption of rational self-interest. Additional assumptions about information and transactions costs are necessary to show that free riding is a greater problem in large than in small groups. Notice that Mitchell has, in effect, made those assumptions the centerpiece of his investigation.

Mitchell's argument has other facets as well, including an effort to build up an expanded catalog of goods and bads being sought, and stress on the way direct mail appeals reduce the total cost of contributing. Certainly if the act of contributing produces significant returns through feelings of virtue or avoidance of anticipated guilt, the logic of collective action loses its compulsion. But, as with the intrinsic rewards to voting, we have not really explained much, since we are left without a way of predicting which individuals will react to such appeals by giving.[8] And, of course, reductions in the cost of contributing do not really come to grips with the self-interest implication, because *no* cost should be incurred voluntarily where the goods concerned are really public in nature.

It is only fair to note, however, that Hardin, in his discussion of the Mitchell paper, puts the whole enterprise in a different perspective. First, he reminds us that in fact the total memberships and action budgets of these organizations are really rather small fractions of the U.S. population and pollution-related expenditures.[9] While many would stress that these figures are proof of great effectiveness, Hardin makes a different point. It may not be very important to fit such a small fringe of people and expenditure into a scheme which no one believes could explain every action of every person. Why not relax, then, and accept the

[8] The direct mail experts may not be able to explain what is going on, but they seem implicitly to be acting on this theoretical approach, for they know (or think they know at least) that a person who answers one such appeal is much more likely than the average new prospect to answer another. Thus the importance of swapping mailing lists.

[9] For example, Hardin roughly estimates that the national groups spend about 0.07 percent as much on their action programs as the nation spends on pollution abatement alone; and one million is less than 0.5 percent of the population.

fact that not everyone is rational all the time?[10] This, of course, puts large parts of observed behavior beyond the reach of theory and, moreover, begs the question of when we shall allow ourselves to fall back on this pillow. How many people, behaving in a "peculiar way," can be excused as the "irrational fringe"? As a second caution, Hardin notes the blurred line that separates a perceived moral imperative (I should support such efforts if I expect others to do so) from a misunderstood causal relation (if I do not support these groups then no one else will). In the second case, which Hardin guesses is a widespread way of thinking, one is, in a sense, creating and opting for the nonrational path out of the resulting prisoners' dilemma on the bet that enough other similarly placed and conditioned individuals will also, so that something can be accomplished. It is almost as though each individual strove by force of will to keep all those "others" from taking the obvious next strategic step. (But if everyone else will give, then I don't have to.) I hope the results of Mitchell's empirical work help us sort out this fascinating behavioral puzzle. (For a related development, see Guttman, 1978.)

Yet a third line of empirical research into the validity of deductions from the axioms of public choice theory is represented by the laboratory experiments described by Charles Plott in "The Application of Laboratory Experimental Methods to Public Choice," and by Ferejohn, Forsythe, and Noll in "Practical Aspects of the Construction of Decentralized Decision-making Systems for Public Goods." These papers are perhaps the most exciting of the forum, for they open up, to those of us previously uninitiated, entirely new possibilities for inquiry. There is an appealing elegance about a method which controls the background conditions and thus eliminates the considerable noise in natural-experiment data. The fact that such elegance is obtainable, albeit at a cost, may not surprise psychologists, but will be a revelation to many economists and political scientists.

Plott's paper sets out the rationale for laboratory methods in public choice, explains briefly how the relevant individual preferences are induced and thus controlled, and reports on the results of a number of specific experiments. For the most part these do not involve tests of the self-interest hypothesis. Rather, they were designed to test alterna-

---

[10] It seems to me significant that Hardin's point applies with particular force to the groups that offer none of Olson's private goods—no magazines, field trips, classes, or other enticements to membership. These are much the smallest part of the movement; indeed there may be no more than 100–200,000 individuals willing to make contributions to these operations.

tive deductions from the theories about majority rule decisions (given participation) or to show the importance of specific institutional features in determining how individual preferences actually get combined.[11] Thus, for example, Plott is interested in comparing the core of an n-person game against alternative predictors of the decisions reached by small groups asked to decide on a point in 2-space by majority vote and using Roberts Rules of Order. While the results support the core against its challengers, the greatest interest for many of us may be the further experiments which show how important the specific parliamentary procedures are in determining the outcome. Shifting from Roberts Rules to very different alternatives destroys the dominance of the core—a forceful reminder of the importance of thorough knowledge about the system we are trying to examine in our theories as well as our empirical work. (See also Plott and Levine, 1978.)

As the discussant of Plott's paper points out, it would be a mistake to think that experimental methods represent a miraculous cure-all for the frailties of public choice research. On the one hand, there are questions about the extent to which the method of protecting experimental (internal) validity by excluding reality destroys the perceived, and even the actual, validity of the tests in relation to real institutional problems. For example, the tests described here involve choices over outcomes which have been purged of meaning except for that most congenial to the self-interest hypothesis, money returns. There is a possibility that the emotive nature of real issues means that individual behavior is different depending on which issue is being decided. That is, certain issues may call up conditioned altruistic responses in at least significant fractions of the collective. (But see also the rejoinder by Plott and Smith.) It is also possible that actual outcomes affect subsequent preferences, or at least the way preferences get expressed. The latter possibility was subjected to some testing by Plott. He compared predictors of outcomes of individual experiments with the outcomes of similar experiments run in sequences, thus giving some scope for the operation of dynamic models that predict the evolution of coalitions. Plott's experiments gave no support for the dynamic models, but it would be very rash to say that we can reject the possibility in general. In a less rarefied situation, of course, outcomes might affect the expression of preferences in such a way that apparently nonrational, altruistic behavior was observed, as, for example, through the operation of a guilt factor about the

---

[11] The one test in which Plott probes the dominance of selfish behavior involves a market rather than a public choice setting.

collective results achieved via self-interested action. It is even possible that the underlying preferences might change as a result of the outcomes, but this might be very difficult or impossible to disentangle from the effects just discussed.

Ferejohn and his coauthors report on some other laboratory experiments in a fascinating paper which carries us from real problem to theory to "institutional engineering" to empirical testing. Because their desire to design better institutions is coupled with efforts to test alternative designs, this paper can serve as a convenient bridge between the "testing" and "design" papers in this volume.

The specific problem attacked by Ferejohn, Forsythe, and Noll is that faced by public television stations when each year they have, as a group, to decide how programming budgets will be allocated among the ideas competing for funds. Because the programs, once produced, can be distributed at essentially zero cost to all stations, the group of stations faces a problem of deciding on the production of a bundle of public goods, and each of the members faces a situation in which concealing true preferences may be optimal behavior.

The method actually being used by the PBS essentially treats each program as a private good in the production of which there are economies of scale. This is achieved by allowing a program to be shown only by stations which "vote" for it in the final round and thus agree to pay a specified share of the cost of its production. The choice process is iterative, with the cost shares resulting from station choices in round k being published and forming the basis of station choices in round $k + 1$. Because the programs could in fact be distributed to all stations at close to zero cost once produced, the results of this choice process will in general be inefficient ex post, for some stations (viewers) could be made better off at no cost. But the discipline of the process requires that these opportunities not be seized.

In exploring for preferable alternatives for handling such problems, the authors began by developing a set of desirable properties the choice institution ought to possess. Their list has five items, and it is not easy to quarrel with any of them.

Bankruptcy of individual agents cannot be possible.

In the aggregate, the system cannot agree to spend more than the total budgets of the agents.

The choice made should be efficient in that it should not be Pareto dominated by another possible choice.

The choice procedure should be fast and easy to use (e.g., not require many expensive iterations or the services of specially trained operators). There should be no incentives for strategic behavior (the concealment of true preferences) by agents during the choice process.

This list, as has been pointed out, faintly echoes the set of conditions imposed by Arrow on acceptable social choice processes (Arrow, 1963) and what the authors have proved (Ferejohn, Noll, and Forsythe, 1978) echoes the Arrow paradox: that the efficiency and nonstrategic requirements are inconsistent. Given this fundamental result, the problem becomes one of trading off the degree to which particular properties are satisfied by alternative processes. To some extent this can be explored formally, but more can be learned from actual operation; and this is where the laboratory experiments come in. In those reported here, a close mimic of the existing public broadcasting choice method is compared with alternatives derived from the public choice literature:

A bidding procedure representing the multialternative version of the incentive scheme which, in its more familiar two-alternative version is widely known to induce agents accurately to reveal their preferences (an "incentive compatible" tax).

An auction procedure without the incentives for sincere preference revelation of the above tax, but in which the agents are assured of non-bankruptcy and the system of nondeficit operation.

To summarize all the results of these tests in this introduction would be pointless, but it is worth noting that the existing public broadcasting procedure comes out looking very good in comparison with the others. While it satisfies the first two criteria by design and is simple and quick in operation, it also turns out to be surprisingly efficient and free from strategic behavior.

The most interesting of the questions raised by discussants to my mind center on information needs and possibilities. Clotfelter wonders how widely applicable the institutional design implications are, given that, for the system to work, each agent must have knowledge of his or her preferences among the alternatives in question. This requirement seems to limit the procedure to situations involving small groups of highly motivated people—a limitation which does not bother Ferejohn, Forsythe, and Noll, who in private communication with Clotfelter explicitly reject the possibility that the methods hold promise for making national decisions requiring the involvement of all citizens (Noll, 1978).

Clarke, whose name is frequently linked to the incentive compatible tax mentioned above, is interested in the possibility that the apparent complexity of the multialternative case could be reduced by cooperative sharing of information, to the extent that a single round of bidding and incentive-tax calculation would be sufficient. This would allow capture of the nonstrategic property of the Clarke tax without the high cost of operation reported by the authors for its analog. This is an interesting possibility, though not one I would bet heavily on; and Ferejohn, Forsythe, and Noll show in their reply that the incentive compatible tax has the additional disadvantage of allowing bankruptcy of individuals.[12]

II.   DESIGNING INSTITUTIONS

Before turning to the two papers concerned entirely with institutional design, it will be necessary to turn back to Tullock's overview, for he suggests several possibilities for actions in the real world which are based on his reading of the theory. The first of these amounts to a reversal of the trend toward centralization of governmental decisions and functions, which is a feature of U.S. experience at least. Tullock suggests the dispersal of functions to lower level jurisdictions, indicating by his examples that he would carry this even below the traditional local level, to neighborhoods. His second suggestion is to introduce elements of competition among the providers of public goods, essentially by rewarding efficiency with that which warms the cockles of the bureaucratic heart: expansion of mission, budget, and power.

The first of these suggestions touches on an enormously difficult but fundamental problem—the choice of jurisdictional boundaries, or of who gets to participate in the decision-making process. While I have neither the space nor the expertise to discuss this matter in depth, it is worth pointing out several things. First, it has been shown by Gary Miller (1976) that it is impossible to justify on efficiency grounds any move from the status quo in the matter of metropolitan organization. Both the fragmented and consolidated settings are Pareto optimal and

---

[12] In this context it is interesting to note that large numbers of players are said to reduce incentive taxes to zero, but at the same time this clearly increases the mechanical difficulties of organizing the process. (Coalition formation incentives and opportunities may or may not be systematically related to number of participants.) Removing the threat of bankruptcy also destroys the incentive-compatible nature of the process.

"one cannot change the institutional setting without changing the distribution of resources in someone's favor and at someone else's expense" (Miller, 1976, p. 205). The choice between greater fragmentation and greater centralization involves distributional change and is therefore inherently political—not a matter to be settled by public-choice analysis. Second, the trend toward central government action has not been entirely, or perhaps even primarily, the product of self-interested actions by central government politicians and bureaucrats. It grew out of and continues to be fueled by a widely shared perception that state and local governments are unresponsive to the preferences of their constituents. Third, it must be remembered that there are complications on the supply side as well. While it may seem clear that a particular service should be produced at a very local level and another at a somewhat higher level, there may be links between the two services that would lead to inefficiency if decisions about them were separated. Finally, in the business of communication between a government and its constituents, there is no guarantee that smaller is better, for, even though they are impersonal, modern communication technologies, with their considerable economies of scale, have the ability to transmit more, and more accurate, information over a given time period than do the small-scale methods of face-to-face discussion, mimeographed newsletters, and the like.

Tullock's second suggestion, on increased competition, sounds rather chilling when he refers to the Internal Revenue Service as a prime candidate, since one can only speculate how greater efficiency would be achieved and measured in such a system, the interpretations and actions of the existing monopoly seem too harrasing now. But Fiorina, in his discussion, points out that there exist some examples of actual competition in the federal bureaucracy now (for example, among the dam builders in the Corps of Engineers, the Bureau of Reclamation, and the Soil Conservation Service), and suggests that research might thus precede action.[13]

The final two papers in the volume continue the theme of institutional design on the basis of the lessons of public choice theory. Richard Stewart, in "The Resource Allocation Role of Reviewing Courts: Com-

---

[13] Tullock makes one other suggestion for actual institutions which might be called purposeful experiment, in the real world. It involves the possibilities for trying electronic referenda voting and other innovations in South American countries facing prospective transitions from military dictatorships to more democratic regimes. This is, to say the least, visionary and was, I think, offered with tongue more firmly in cheek than is clear from the printed page.

mon Law Functions in a Regulatory Era," advocates a greater role for the courts in passing on the substance of decisions about provision of public goods rather than on the procedures leading to the decisions. His argument, which he applies particularly to environmental questions, rests on such problems as:

The behavior of legislators dominated by concern for reelection and influenced therefore by interest group contributions and bloc voting.

The desire of bureaucrats for greater budgets and staffs and the perverse incentives this creates in the decision process affecting implementation and enforcement of laws.

The phenomenon of regulatory capture, in which the guardians of the chicken coop are persuaded that their interests lie with the foxes.

Beyond these arguments against relying on legislatures and bureaucracies for the efficient provision of public goods, Stewart makes some positive points about the special place of environmental public goods in the scheme of society's rights and duties. These points are designed to demonstrate that the courts have a place in ascertaining how well particular policies protect those rights and apportion those duties.

The questions raised by Stewart are not the kind susceptible of either logical or empirical settlement, for they involve the deepest sorts of constitutional issues and the trading off of attributes that are neither measurable nor even expressible in agreed-upon units. On the other hand, public choice has been at least partially responsible for raising the questions and ought to have something to contribute to the debate. That contribution might be measured against an ideal that would amount to the Ferejohn, Forsythe, and Noll institutional engineering approach writ large. Fundamental criteria for institutional design would be the subject of theoretical inquiry from which one could expect some new inconsistency theorem leading to the exploration of tradeoffs embodied in alternatives. The final step would be testing the alternatives by using historical data, laboratory experiments, and perhaps inquiries into existing preferences. How easily said and how immensely difficult in practice! The compensating observation is that each stage in such an enterprise would be valuable in itself. For example, the very activities of devising and debating criteria would carry us beyond the current situation in which institutions are judged on the desirability (usually defined in terms of efficiency and some particular version of equity congenial to the judge) of actual or prospective outcomes.

Oran Young, in the final paper of the volume, extends the forum's scope to the international arena by examining alternative institutions for the management of natural resources which share the problem that they are not obviously the property of any single state. The difficulty here, of course, is that even the possibility of an enforceable constitutional framework cannot be taken for granted, so that procedures which are perceived to be fair, but which may, in specific decisions, result in costs for some actors and benefits for others, may never develop. Since the losers are sovereign states, they may simply opt out when they would suffer costs, and the entire process must usually be visualized as bargaining among unequally endowed participants. Therefore much of the wisdom of the theory cannot be applied straightforwardly. But one can still ask what minimal sets of mutually agreed-upon rules might be viable and what sorts of incentives would exist within that institution. This Young does for seabed minerals.

III. RESEARCH CHALLENGES AND OPPORTUNITIES

The final session of the forum was a panel discussion of future research on applications of public choice theory. The two articles by panelists which are found in this volume present two very different challenges to those who would make a contribution to the field. Haefele invites us to look back over our history with a view to interpreting events in the light of theory, to understanding what has been lost (and gained) in the evolution of our institutions, and perhaps to setting the stage for recouping some of the losses. Coleman asks us to look out, beyond the usually perceived boundaries of public choice inquiry, and to attempt to come to grips with collective actions such as panic, riot, fashions, and the avoidance of collective action where it seems obviously called for. These are not usually thought of as products of choice by rational actors, but Coleman speculates that they do reflect rational and unilateral decisions by many individuals to transfer control of their own actions to others.

Other important challenges which are to be found, implicitly or explicitly, in the papers and discussions in this volume include improving our methods for defining who has a voice in a particular issue and for eliciting preferences among alternative bundles of public goods. The jurisdictional design problem is raised explicitly by Tullock, Young, and Stewart, and lies in the background of Mitchell's study, but is not the subject of any of the empirical work. Tullock, as already noted, advocates experiments in the real world involving decentralization of decisions, accepting, however, the geographic basis of definition which is the current standard. Another line of inquiry might well be a search for promising alternatives to geography as a base for jurisdictional boundaries. One such possibility, for example, would be the institution of contracts in which individuals desiring a voice in a particular decision bound themselves to take part in a demand revelation process, to abide by the results, and to pay the resulting costs and incentive taxes (if any). There are obvious problems: income limitations which would restrict participation and individual motivation; and devising mechanisms for the actual demand revelation and adjustment, to name only two. At the simplest level, however, one might imagine experimental work designed to compare arbitrary jurisdictional definitions (choices of players) with procedures of choice involving free contracting based on willingness to bear some of the costs of the choice made.

This possibility is linked in an obvious way to the second large set of research opportunities—the exploration of the alternative demand revelation processes themselves. Ferejohn and his coauthors have taken an important step along this road, but the enthusiasm of Tullock and Clarke, no less than the skepticism of others, suggests that much more ought to be done. For example, the advocates of the incentive compatible taxes are inclined to minimize the problems posed by multidimensional choices, the threat of participant bankruptcy, and the possibility of coalitions destroying the incentive compatible feature of the system. It would be interesting to see what happens when fairly large groups are asked to play such a game under experimental conditions, using induced preferences on "bloodless" spaces. Such expensive and difficult but contained efforts might pave the way for extension of the method to some real-world situations or might show it to be impractical. Competitors such as the program choice system of the PBS, though having certain theoretical shortcomings, might be found to have great promise for applications beyond their current confines.

Hints of other research opportunities abound in the papers and discussion. An attempt to identify them all would carry this already long introduction much too far. Consider, however, two examples. First, the exchange between Tullock and Fiorina suggests the potential importance of competition in the supply of public goods and the possibility that existing duplication of function in governments at all levels may provide some useful natural experiments on this question. Second, the unsatisfactory state of our understanding of voting *participation* and the ubiquitousness of related phenomena identify this set of issues as potentially fertile but currently barren ground.

IV. CONCLUSION

There is, in short, no lack of major challenges for those who would make a contribution through the application of public choice theory. These challenges include empirical testing of the theoretical structure, analysis of existing institutions, and design of alternatives to established ways of making collective decisions. The prospective payoff is there, for we find wide agreement that specific public policy problems, ranging from energy through pollution and medical care to inflation and unemployment, are not being addressed adequately. Indeed, they may be caused or at least exacerbated by our current public choice arrangements.

Whether or not public choice theory can really help us with these difficult problems remains, as I stressed above, an open question. More seriously, it will almost certainly remain an open question for a long time because the necessary research is difficult and time consuming. There will be few payoffs along the way, though Ferejohn and his colleagues have demonstrated that some very real payoffs are possible where problems have manageable boundaries, and able researchers can devote significant time and effort. Typically, however, the would-be applier of public choice theory cannot promise short-term help with the problems so widely perceived; and the proposals coming from this field may not seem particularly responsive to the pressures felt by suppliers of research funds, both public and private. This is not, of course, a dilemma unique to public choice. It is really only a slight variation on the "basic" versus "applied" research debate which receives periodic airing in *Science* and the daily newspapers. The pendulum of consensus on the relative weights of near and certain as opposed to distant and speculative payoffs has moved steadily toward the former over the past decade. Its appropriate position is a public decision, though not one subject to a well-defined choice process, and claims from interested parties must be viewed with skepticism in this as in other debates. Nevertheless, one can hope that the evidence in this volume serves, among other things, to make more widely known the promise and prospects as well as the unsolved problems in public choice research.

REFERENCES

Arrow, Kenneth. 1963. *Social Choice and Individual Values* (2nd ed., New York, Wiley).

Downs, Anthony. 1957. *An Economic Theory of Democracy* (New York, Harper & Row) pp. 265–273.

Ferejohn, John, and Morris P. Fiorina. 1974. "The Paradox of Not Voting: A Decision Theory Analysis," *American Political Science Review* vol. 68, no. 2 (June) pp. 525–536.

———— and ————. 1975. "Closeness Counts only in Horseshoes and Dancing," *American Political Science Review* vol. 69 (September) pp. 920–925.

————, R. Noll, and R. Forsythe. 1978. "An Experimental Analysis of Decision-making Procedures for Discrete Public Goods: A Case Study of a Problem in Institutional Design," in Vernon L. Smith, ed., *Research in Experimental Economics* vol. 1 (Greenwich, Conn., JAI Press).

Fiorina, Morris P. 1977. *Congress: Keystone of the Washington Establishment* (New Haven, Conn., Yale University Press).

———— and Roger Noll. 1978a. "Voters, Legislators and Bureaucracy: Institutional Design in the Public Sector," *American Economic Review, Papers and Proceedings* vol. 68, no. 2 (May) pp. 256–260.

———— and ————. 1978b. "Voters, Bureaucrats and Legislators," *Journal of Public Economics* vol. 9, pp. 239–254.

Frolich, Norman, and Joe A. Oppenheimer. 1970. "I Get by with a Little Help from My Friends," *World Politics* vol. 23, no. 1 (October) pp. 104–120.

Guttman, Joel M. 1978. "Understanding Collective Action: Matching Behavior," *American Economic Review, Papers and Proceedings* vol. 68, no. 2 (May) pp. 251–255.

Haefele, E. T. 1973. *Representative Government and Environmental Management* (Baltimore, Johns Hopkins University Press for Resources for the Future).

Landes, William M., and R. A. Posner. 1975. "The Independent Judiciary in an Interest Group Perspective," *Journal of Law and Economics* vol. 43, no. 3 (December) pp. 875–911.

Miller, David. 1975. "The Accuracy of Predictions," *Synthese* vol. 30, pp. 159–191.

Miller, Gary A. 1976. "Fragmentation and Inequality: The Politics of Metropolitan Organization," unpublished Ph.D. dissertation, The University of Texas at Austin.

Mueller, Dennis C. 1976. "Public Choice: A Survey," *Journal of Economic Literature* vol. 14, no. 2 (June) pp. 395–433.

Niskanen, William A. 1971. *Bureaucracy and Representative Government* (Chicago, Aldine-Atherton).

Noll, Roger. 1978. Letter to Clotfelter, 18 May.

Olson, Mancur. 1965. *The Logic of Collective Action* (Cambridge, Mass., Harvard University Press).

Plott, Charles R. 1976. "Axiomatic Social Choice Theory: An Overview and Interpretation," *American Journal of Political Science* vol. 20, no. 3 (August) pp. 511–596.

——— and M. E. Levine. 1978. "A Model of Agenda Influence on Committee Decisions," *American Economic Review* vol. 68, no. 1, pp. 146–160.

Riker, William H., and Peter C. Ordeshook. 1968. "A Theory of the Calculus of Voting," *American Political Science Review* vol. 62 (March) pp. 25–42.

Tufte, E. 1978. *Political Control of the Economy* (Princeton, N.J., Princeton University Press).

Gordon Tullock

Public Choice in Practice

I. INTRODUCTION

It is a little hard to define "public choice" specifically, but, in any event, we can reach agreement on the early works in the field. It is notable that all of them were strictly theoretical and, until *The Calculus of Consent* (Buchanan and Tullock, 1962), there were no significant recommendations for actual government policy. It is true that Anthony Downs endorsed simple majority voting (1957), but this was, in the first place, acceptance of what he obviously thought was the status quo and, second, essentially *obiter dicta,* since it did not follow from his theory.

The absence of practical recommendations is striking, particularly since Arrow's general impossibility theorem was one of the early contributions (1951) to public choice theory. One would have thought that it would have led to a vigorous search for alternative forms of government, but, as a matter of fact, it did not. Indeed, as far as I can see, almost all the students in the field, including Arrow himself, simply disregarded his proof when they turned to policy matters. Policy recommendations tended to be based on much the same reasoning as that of standard economists, with public choice having very little effect.

This occurred in the very early days when public choice theory was a rare specialty and only a part-time concern of a few people. The situation changed with the publication of *The Calculus of Consent* which, although it basically supports the Constitution of the United States, nevertheless implies that a considerable number of changes in democratic practice are desirable. Its recommendations, however, are obviously the kind that are not likely to be applied in any short period of time. Indeed, the only application of which I am aware was to the constitution of a coeducational dormitory at the University of Rochester, where a Riker student succeeded in convincing his colleagues that reinforced majorities, and various other things drawn from *The Calculus of Consent,* were desirable.

It is no criticism to say that the early scholars in the area were primarily concerned with understanding the function of government and developing a theory and *not* with making specific improvements. Since the mid-1960s, however, suggestions for improvements and changes have been quite common in the public choice literature.

There has been another change in public choice literature recently. It was originally essentially theoretical. In recent years, a good deal of empirical work has been done which has, in general, validated the basic structure of the public choice approach and has produced specific data where only general assumptions existed before. As usual, it has produced both new information and new problems.

Although both of these developments are important, and I will turn to them in a moment, I should like to discuss first what I believe is the most important effect public choice has had on both economics and the actual functioning of government.

II.   CHANGES IN ATTITUDE

Role of Government

In a recent book published by the Brookings Institution, Charles Schultze (who is generally regarded as a liberal economist) said, "In all cases the comparison should be between an imperfect market and an imperfect regulatory scheme, not some ideal abstraction" (1977, p. 38). A little further on he says, "The suggestion that the political debate be confined to ends, while technicians and experts design the means once the ends have been decided, is facile and naive" (1977, p. 89).

The change in general attitude is illustrated not only by the fact that Schultze said this, and by the particular place that he said it, but also by the suspicion that few readers would regard the statement as in any way extraordinary. Twenty years ago, this would have been an extremely radical statement.

This recognition that government is also imperfect, and that proof of imperfection in the market does not indicate that one must turn to the government, is relatively recent. It is a view that would be familiar to

Adam Smith and Ricardo, but in the 1950s many economists who proved that some particular private activitiy was not perfect—that is, the market "failed"—deduced from this that government action was necessary. The realization that government action, too, is imperfect, although fairly obvious, was slow in coming.

I was once showing a distinguished European visitor around the University of South Carolina. He remarked about the difficulties of getting to Columbia, S.C., by air. I said that under Civil Aeronautics Board (CAB) regulations, only two airlines were then permitted to serve the Columbia airport, and both of them had monopolies of specific routes to Columbia. I added that what we needed was to get the CAB out so that we would have some competition. He looked at me in shock and horror, and said, "What we need is to get the government to come in and insure competition." We rarely encounter that attitiude now.

Today we think of the decision as to whether something should be regulated by the government, or made part of the government, or left to the market, as a choice among instrumentalities, none of which is likely to be perfect. Thus, evidence that one instrument does not function perfectly is not, in general, regarded as sufficient reason to turn to the other. Interestingly enough, the only examples I have recently encountered in which the old argument was used involved the new anarchists of the right. Although the leading members of this small school rarely make this mistake, some of their followers will demonstrate (and it is usually easy) that the government performs some function imperfectly; they deduce from this that the function should be returned to the market. Clearly, this is as bad as the contrary reasoning of the 1950s.

In my opinion, this change in attitude is the most important impact of a practical nature that public choice theory has had on policy in the United States. So far, it must be admitted that the impact is less strong on policy than on the intellectual community, and it also has to be admitted that, as usual, only part of the intellectual community has absorbed the lesson. But I would still expect little objection to the claim on the part of my readers.

I could be criticized, however, on other grounds. It could be argued that the recent general reduction in confidence in the ability of government to solve problems is the result of the Vietnam War and the general upsurge of leftism in the 1960s. I do not think this is so, but I have to admit that my argument is based on personal impressions. First, all of the leftists I knew during that period were very much annoyed by the government; but, in general, they regarded the market as worse. Basically, what they wanted to do was to reform the government. The new reformed government was to have even greater scope than the old government.

One of the reforms the members of the New Left did push was one which resembled the public choice position. This was a desire to move government, as the New Left would have put it, closer to the people—that is, use smaller governmental units for many issues. But public choice and the New Left differed very sharply, not on the desirability of the use of smaller governmental units for many areas, but on the view as to what these smaller units should do. Members of the New Left seem frequently to have had totalitarian ideas as to the scope of control of these local governments. Communes, for example, commonly not only attempted to insulate themselves from the other governments— that is, to become a very small local government—but also attempted to regulate the personal behavior of their members through collective decisions. No one with a public choice background would have been likely to do this.

It is also notable that the desire to move government "closer to the people," which was shared by the New Left and a great many public choice scholars, has so far been implemented very little and, indeed, seems to have largely dropped out of the general public's political discussions. In fact, the general trend toward movement of government functions to higher and higher levels continued more or less unimpeded through the 1960s and the 1970s, although I hope that we will be able to do something about it in time. But this is a case in which public choice has unfortunately not been applied. Let us leave it aside for the time being and turn to another area where I think our work has had at least some effect on practical policy.

Self-interest and Government

As in the previous case, what I am now talking about is essentially a change in attitude, but one that originated in the public choice literature. As in the previous case, also, it is hard to prove whether it actually was public choice that led to the change. I have a fairly strong opinion on the subject, but this may be professional bias rather than the result of dispassionate observation.

In any event, there has been a change in attitude toward the motives of government, whether we think of the government as the whole organization or simply individual officials. The traditional view of government has always been that it sought something called "the public interest" or, in Leo Strauss's words, "right action," or, possibly, "benefiting the people" or something of that sort. Historians will recall that most of the discussion of economic matters before 1700 was essentially ethical. Businessmen were either assumed to be attempting to generate good for their customers or they were lectured on the desirability of doing so. It was realized that many businessmen did not have as high moral standards as might be desired, but this was thought to be a defect, and the system was thought to operate on essentially good motives.[1]

Many political scientists, until very recently, took this same attitude toward government. The public interest was the goal of government action, and this depended upon "good men" in government. Once again, there was usually some realization that individual government officials did not meet these moral standards, but the only remedy suggested was more careful selection of personnel and moral lectures. With public choice, all of this has changed. We tend to think of bureaucrats and politicians as no better, but also no worse, than businessmen. The voter is thought to make decisions not in terms of the public interest but in terms of his own interests, just as he does when he is in the supermarket.

It is important here not to oversimplify, since most human beings do have at least some concern for other people, and therefore they are not entirely egoistic in their decisions. Indeed, within the family they are extremely altruistic; but outside the family, they are largely (although not completely) egoistic (or perhaps "familistic"). This applies both in the private market, where such private enterprise systems as charities and churches exist, and in the public market, where individuals do in part vote for the public good or to help the starving citizens of Bangladesh, and so on. Nevertheless, in both areas individuals are basically self-seeking rather than interested in maximizing the public interest.

This realization, which is only gradually creeping over the community of people involved in policy, can have immense effects. No doubt practical politicians have always really thought that most of the people with whom they have personal contact were basically self-seeking. They have, nevertheless, operated under a theoretical structure

---

[1] Ed. note: For a discussion of the historical background, see Hirschman (1977).

which involved devotion to the public interest and have felt compelled in their public utterances to give lip service to this theory. Further, many of them seem, quite honestly, to have thought that the people with whom they had difficulties were exceptions to the rule and that the average person was driven primarily by moral considerations. Indeed, in many cases, the politician does not seem to have been able to distinguish motives; he noticed that the farmers in his constituency favored high price supports for their crops, but somehow he saw this as part of the public interest.

It seems likely that this misapprehension must have had negative effects on politics. It had very strong negative effects on the professional students of politics, whether they were economists, political scientists, or sociologists. They were compelled either to simply misunderstand what was going on or to disapprove of it. Further, proposals for reform very largely took the form of moral lectures.

The realization that politicians and bureaucrats were not solely interested in the public good once again could be attributed to the New Left, which also denounced these groups for poor moral standards. However, I think in this case the difference between the attitiude of the New Left and public choice scholars was much more radical than in the previous one. The New Left denounced the politicians and bureaucrats for being no better than vicious reactionary capitalists. Public choice students said that the bureaucrats, politicians, and voters were really very similar to businessmen and private citizens, but they did not condemn anyone for this. The emphasis in public choice was the design of institutions which would lead self-seeking bureaucrats or politicians to generate public welfare in the same sense that the market leads some self-interested businessmen to produce a social surplus.

Thus, the businessman produces a good product at moderate price because he thinks he will make more money that way than from trying to sell a poor product at a high price.[2] By the same token, the politician should anticipate reelection from good policies at a low tax price. Unfortunately, the institutional structure for putting politicians under this type of pressure is a good deal harder to identify than that of the marketplace.

The area in which changing attitudes toward self-interest are having the greatest impact today is probably that of regulatory reform. Proponents of restricting the power of regulatory agencies, a major drive

---

[2] Needless to say, there are cases where the poor product with the high price will make more money, but they are, fortunately, rare.

at the moment, often discuss the activities of the regulatory agencies as efforts to acquire private gain, primarily for the regulated industry, but to some extent for the regulators. The opponents of the reforms do not really contest this, although they normally also do not admit it. For example, when progressive industries such as the airline industry are arguing against the abolition or restriction of the CAB, they turn to traditional arguments. They point out that a large industry has developed under the shelter of regulation and that, for some reason or other, continued regulation is necessary for the industry's survival. They do not specifically argue that regulation is not largely controlled by private rather than public motives. Indeed, they even sometimes accuse at least some of the people who are in favor of deregulation of private motives. This is, for example, the argument advanced by opponents of deregulation as an explanation of United Airlines' enthusiasm for getting rid of regulation; that is, the opponents allege that United Airlines would be able to drive a large number of small companies out of business. This is clearly an allegation that at least some people engaged in public debate are motivated by private rather than public interest.

Of course, the public interest point of view still informs many statements by public figures and the more old-fashioned students of politics. President Carter has never, and I predict never will, concede that he decided to become president because he thought it was a good job. It is notable, however, that when Barbara Jordan decided to retire from Congress she did not offer any public-interest argument but simply said that she was tired of the job. I doubt that her remark involved any deep knowledge of the public choice literature, but it is at least conceivable that we observe here the result of some slight and very indirect influence on a general climate of opinion.

If, however, we look for specific actual changes in government policy which can be directly attributed to public choice activity, I think we would find that there are none. This is not surprising. The public choice approach is still new, and it is still rather undeveloped. It will be recalled that Adam Smith's basic ideas had little impact on actual politics until about fifty years after the publication of *The Wealth of Nations.* It was no doubt true that, in the years immediately after the publication of Smith's book, there was a considerable indirect effect in the form of changes in the general climate of opinion. This effect was, however, comparatively modest, and the great period of enactment of reforms recommended by Smith took place well into the nineteenth century. I hope that reforms in this generation will not be delayed so long, but it is not surprising that so far there are no direct detailed applications of public choice theory comparable to the reforms of the nineteenth century in England.

However, we are beginning to see some progress. Large-scale empirical studies have been undertaken to test the validity of the theory or to develop parameters and detailed measurements of political variables. This type of study has made it possible to make more detailed recommendations for reform in government procedures, and, at the same time has improved the arguments for reform. After a brief summary of the empirical work, I will turn to a set of practical proposals of a fairly concrete and not very radical nature, which I think might begin to have practical effects in the not-too-distant future. I will then close with what the diplomats call a *tour d'horizon*, which in this case will be a summary of some extremely radical proposals which I would not suggest we urge on politicians today, but which may be important for tomorrow.

III.   EMPIRICAL RESEARCH

The Political Business Cycle

The first area of empirical research I would like to discuss (and, indeed, it is one of the earliest) is a rather discouraging one: the relationship between government policy and depression and inflation. I am not going to talk about the economics of this issue, which has, over the past thirty years, been a major field of investigation by economists. What I am interested in here is the politics of it, that is, the relationship of voter dissatisfaction to unemployment or inflation, the expression of it in their votes, the politicians' perception of this dissatisfaction and, hence, the type of policies they are likely to adopt.

I should perhaps begin by warning that the empirical evidence seems to indicate that, in terms of government policy, the issue is nowhere near as important as it has been in economics. Indeed, during the preparation of this paper, the government of Australia, which (upon assuming office) had changed its economic policies to sharply increase unemployment, went to the people on a platform of continuing with these policies and won by a landslide. This is merely one observation, of course; but, as we shall see, the empirical evidence seems to point in the same direction. People do, indeed, dislike unemployment and inflation; politicians know this and fear for their votes, but it appears that there are other things that have much more effect on politicians and voters than these two matters.

The pioneering work on voter response to unemployment or inflation was done by Gerald Kramer (1971) and, with the exception of the correction of a computational error, his basic research design has been followed more or less by all of the considerable number of people who have worked in the field. He regressed the vote for the parties against a number of variables, of which the rate of inflation and unemployment were important. Taking not his results, which were vitiated by the computational error, but the later reworking of the same procedure, it appears that the voters do penalize the party in power for either unemployment or inflation; but the penalty apparently is fairly small. Indeed, in the various studies it hovers around the significance level.

This led George Stigler (1973) to develop a special theory as to why this penalty should be either small or nonexistent. He pointed out that the voters presumably can remember over a period of several years, and therefore they are not too much affected by the results in just the short period before the election. But, more important, they are aware of the fact that the political parties do not want unemployment; as he put it, only sadism would lead a political party to deliberately cause unemployment or refrain from actions which would reduce it, unless there were great costs to these actions. Thus, the voters assume that the party in power is doing its best and that the other party would be unable to do better. Stigler suggested, and we will discuss this suggestion later, that politics, then, would mainly be concerned with distributional matters—who gets what rather than about whether we should have depressions or booms.

The research since Stigler gave his paper on this matter has, on the whole, come up with the same results as he and his predecessors. The voters do not seem to give extremely high weight to unemployment or inflation, although they give a somewhat higher weight to inflation than to unemployment.

Looking at the matter from the other side, we could ask whether politicians are motivated to manipulate depressions and booms in such a way as to maximize their continued chances of employment by way of reelection. Here the theory is simple and straightforward, and it will be found very commonly in the popular press. It is alleged that incumbent politicians would prefer to have elections take place during boom periods. It would, therefore, be in their interests to create booms just before elections. Unless it is possible to run a continuous boom, this would mean that there would be some nonboom periods. Whether they would be depressions or not would depend on the definition, and the incumbent politician would presumably prefer that these periods occur right after elections rather than right before, so that the voter will have had time to forget them by the time the next election rolls around.

Politicians attempting to provide booms just before elections could generate what is called the "political business cycle." Except for a silly article written in the 1930s by Kalecki (1943), the actual discussion of this point starts with a series of articles by Bruno Frey and various coauthors (1976). They quickly discovered, as anyone looking over the data will also quickly discover, that, in its pure sense, the political business cycle either does not exist or, perhaps if one accepts Nordhaus' demonstration (1975), is only a very minor phenomenon. That is, there may perhaps be some small tendency for a movement in this direction.

Frey, however, is an ingenious man and he had excellent collaborators, with the result that he complicated his model and got some really quite good results. He made use of public opinion polls showing support for the government, and he argued that governments have utility functions, in which desire to get reelected is only one argument, although a very powerful one. He felt that if support of the government, as shown by the opinion polls, was large, it could pursue the nonreelection parts of its utility function and would only turn toward specific efforts to manipulate the economy if its popularity fell. Using this model and making some not unlikely assumptions about the utility function of the government and the point at which it begins worrying about lack of support, he was able to produce some good fits on both American and West German data. Further, using his equations, he was able to project forward (predict future movements in German economic conditions) with greater accuracy than the more standard methods of prediction. Unfortunately, the latter part of the empirical testing of this model has only run for a couple of years at the moment.

However, the Frey method seems to work much better in Germany than anywhere else. In particular, in the United States it is necessary to make a number of special assumptions about individual presidents to make it work. Since it seems likely that American presidents are in fact very different from each other, this is not a statement that the model is false, but merely that it is hard to say for certain whether it is picking up the real variables in the United States.

In all of these models, however, including the Frey model (or Frey models), the effect of economic conditions is in fact modest. The politicians' ability to manipulate the business cycle seems to be relatively poor. This led Richard Wagner (1977) to suggest a radically different theory of the political business cycle. Wagner gives up on what we might call "macro variables," alleging that politicians are not too much interested in them, but he points out that politicians are decidedly and strongly interested in distributional variables.

He suggests that politicians may concentrate their distributional activities in the period before elections, and these activities, as a sort of by-product, affect the macro variables. Basically, these efforts by politicians to redistribute wealth from their opponents and their friends to the marginal voter disturb the economic system and lower its total efficiency; also, because they tend to be concentrated before elections, they may introduce a political cycle. Once again, this cycle does not seem to be very strong, although the facts that politicians do redistribute wealth, and that they do tend to concentrate it in the periods just before elections, are, I believe, easily validated.

Altogether, however, the results of these investigations raise some questions about standard economic histories of recent years. It appears that the economists, who devoted so much time to advising the governments as to how to avoid depressions and booms, were not only having technical difficulties in economics (no one looking at stagflation today —whether he is a monetarist or a Keynesian—can doubt the existence of such difficulties) but were also offering advice to politicians on an issue that apparently did not greatly concern the politicians.

Recently, two public choice scholars, James Buchanan and Richard Wagner (1977), have suggested (forcefully) that the basic effect of all of this discussion of macroeconomics was simply to convince the politicians that they did not have to balance the budget. Granted the politicians' desire to transfer wealth to various citizens, and their aversion to taxation, this could lead to substantial changes in government behavior and the general inflationary level we observe in most western countries today.

Micro Issues

So much for macroeconomics. Let me now turn to a large number of "micro" issues on which the public choice workers have recently developed empirical evidence. Before discussing these micro issues, however, there is one important general proposition that has to be kept in mind. For many generations, students of democracy have noticed that the people do not seem to be very well informed, and they have initiated various programs, either educational or preaching, to do something about it. Almost from the beginning of public choice work (indeed, from Downs's book), public choice scholars have realized that this general ignorance was indeed rational from the standpoint of the average voter. Granted the extremely small effect on him if he improves the quality of his vote by learning more about the issues, the cost–benefit analysis would almost uniformly indicate that he should not try. Thus, a rational voter, unless politics happened to be a hobby, would be quite ignorant of political issues.

The empirical evidence that voters are in fact ignorant is now overwhelming, although the bulk of it has been generated, not by public choice scholars, but by ordinary public opinion surveys carried out by more conventionally educated political scientists or sociologists. As an experiment, the reader might ask a number of his friends and neighbors the name of their congressman. Unless they are an unusual collection of friends and neighbors, one will find a surprising amount of ignorance, even at this basic level.

As a special application of this ignorance hypothesis, Richard McKenzie (1976) wrote a study in which he theoretically deduced that people who are compelled to take courses in political science, sociology, or economics in college, to improve their ability to vote intelligently, would forget about these courses as soon as they had passed the final examination. Having developed this theoretical proposition, he then proceeded to empirical testing, and found that it was true. As an ironic by-product of his study, he found that philosophy majors were slightly better than economics majors in assessing the effects of government economic policy.

In theory, we would expect this kind of ignorance to be a little less for special interest groups, that is, we would anticipate that on such a matter as the milk program, milk producers would be better informed than the average citizen. As far as I know, there is no formal empirical test for this proposition, but it is probably true. It is a case in which information may have perverse effects rather than beneficial ones.

This general lack of information may be one of the reasons why we observe such poor correlations mentioned above between macroeconomic policy and voting outcomes. Indeed, when the average U.S.

citizen does not know which party controls Congress, it is a little difficult for him to penalize the politicians for bad economic performance.

But, to turn to our micro issues, we might begin with a body of empirical research generated by Crain (1977), Crain and Tollison (1976, 1977a, b), and Crain, Deaton, and Tollison (1977), based mainly on American state data. These authors have tested an immense collection (they are averaging something over ten articles a year) of basically rather simple hypotheses. All of their hypotheses could be taken as specialized application of the general position that people are engaged in politics for their own interests rather than the public good. So far, not only have their tests failed to refute that hypothesis, but the authors have been able to provide explanations for a large collection of specific patterns of behavior that we observe in local governments. These range from the salary of governors and legislators to the frequency with which different states resort to the amendment process rather than simple legislation.

Note that here, too, the R^2s are frequently rather small, even if the results are significant. Further, sometimes the bulk of the R^2s come from some standardizing variable rather than the one of interest. The reason for this is simple. The private interest theory of politics will always lead to small R^2s, simply because different individuals have radically different private interests. Thus, any particular private interest hypothesis—let us say, that legislators would prefer higher to lower salaries, everything else being equal—is no doubt true; but the impact of that particular argument on the individual legislator's utility function will vary greatly depending on what else is in the utility function. Since normally there will be a great many other arguments, we should anticipate fairly low R^2s on most such tests. This is, indeed, what we do get. The micro work to which I refer (and a high percentage of this comes from Tollison and Crain) is not important so much for the specific discoveries, although a number of them should be taken into account if we are designing reforms, but for the triumphant validation of a general attitude and approach to politics that can no longer be regarded as just a matter of theory.

Two additional bits of micro politics might be mentioned here. First, Paul Rubin and James Kau (1976) have been investigating the prospect that votes are determined in part by ideological factors. Note that voting in terms of ideology is, in general, an expression of ignorance. The individual uses the ideology as a sort of rule of thumb rather than looking at each individual issue.

Naturally, it is very hard to get proxies for ideology, and Rubin and Kau have been forced to fall back on such things as membership in Common Cause, but they have demonstrated fairly convincingly that ideology does have an effect. A recent and interesting example is their demonstration that people who are basically liberal are apt to vote against science, while people who are basically conservative are in favor of it. No doubt this is merely a statement about the current attitude toward scientific progress held by the two groups, not the attitude held ten years ago or the one which will be held ten years in the future.

The second point I wish to discuss is the proposition originally presented by William Niskanen (1975) but which, once again, seems to have survived empirical testing (Fiorina, 1977). Niskanen pointed out that a congressman who invested an hour in constituent work obtained a direct gain from it, whereas if he had invested the same hour in supervising the function of the government (for example, by reading a proposed new law or cross-questioning the secretary of defense on the actual necessity of having an orchestra at a headquarters on a small island in the Pacific), he would be generating a public good, both for the country and for his colleagues. Niskanen, therefore, hypothesized that congressmen would tend to devote relatively little time to their nominal duties and a great deal of time to constituent service. Needless to say, constituent service involves a lot of contact with the bureaucracy, not with the intent of convincing the bureaucracy to adopt good general principles, but to get them to make exceptions to the principles they are enforcing.

Indeed, it appears that many congressmen are devoting so much attention to their constituents—spending four-day weekends at home, and so on—that a specialized type of congressional assistant, who reads at least part of the bills and tells the congressman how he should vote, has become very important on Capitol Hill. Thus, we have an odd reversal. Today congressmen are mainly engaged in supervising the executive branch. On the other hand, the executive branch, through the rise in importance of regulations, has become our principal lawmaking body. This is the exact opposite of what the founding fathers intended, but that does not prove that it is inefficient.

To repeat what we have said before, this large volume of detailed work has so far not led to anything very detailed in the way of reform proposals. Taking away a congressman's office staff and requiring that a complete transcript of any conversation between a congressman and any bureaucrat or other member of the executive branch be published might have some effect, but then again it might not.

IV. SUGGESTIONS FOR CHANGE

Decentralization

I promised above, however, to suggest two areas in which I do think that public choice could be applied without too much *political* difficulty. The first of these two is the movement of many government functions to a more decentralized level—transferring national functions to the state, state functions to the local government, and local government functions even further down.

For the past six or seven years, I have lived in what can only be described as small private governments. In one case, it was a colony of townhouses that owned its own lighting system, street system, and so on, and that performed a number of public services which are not performed by the average municipality, such as mowing everyone's lawn, repairing roofs, and painting the outside of houses. My current residence is in a somewhat more posh example of the same kind of thing, in which there are single-family dwellings located on lots that are all larger than an acre in size. It also owns its own street system, provides lighting, and exercises considerable control over the external appearance of houses. These local governments, of a *very* local nature, can achieve certain efficiencies that cannot be achieved by larger government units, although whether they should be universalized is another matter. Still, it is encouraging that very small governmental units are being created through the private operation of the real estate market. Naturally, I recognize that officially they are not governmental units but private contracts.

In general, the transfer of powers to lower units has had rather bad press in detail, although frequently it is favored in general terms. So far as we can tell, both from theoretical and empirical studies, our present governments are much too centralized. For example, the great centralization of school districts, which has occurred over the past twenty-five years, has led to an increase in school costs and a rise in salaries (particularly of school administrators) but also to either no change or a decline in the amount the students learn. Similarly, the movement for metro governments characteristically leads to a rise in tax level and either no change or a deterioration in the quality of services. In this connection, the works of the Ostroms are particularly important. (See, for example, Bish and Ostrom, 1973.)

Politically the drive for "new federalism" seems to have petered out; present trends are for further centralization. Apparently, centralization is encouraged by the fact that, if the federal government taxes money and then disperses it by way of local governments, there is only one political cost in the form of the tax, but there are two political gains: first, by the congressman and, second, by the local official. Such "double counting" of credit would be a reflection of poor voter information about the real incidence of costs, and it may not be the correct explanation of the phenomenon.

If the present trends are in the direction of greater centralization, it still seems to me that it would not be very difficult to reverse them, and I believe this is an area where practical gains of a sizable nature can be made.

If we push in this direction, we will not in a real sense be pushing against the American tradition, but against a lot of work done by social scientists in the past fifty years which we now regard as perverse. The view that one could always improve efficiency by centralizing control was widely held throughout the learned professions, and no doubt it had considerable effect on the actual outcomes. We now think that this was a mistake, and it seems to me that it should be possible to have influence in the other direction.

Competition in Bureaucracy

My second basic proposal for applying public choice is that we try to inject a certain amount of competition into the bureaucracy. Currently, efficiency experts almost always attempt to eliminate what they call "duplication." Another way to say the same thing is that they try to organize cartels in government. Congress, facing a monopolistic supply of government services, is in almost as bad shape as the customer of a monopolistic supplier of goods and services in the private market.

Introducing competition is not only sensible, it is fairly easy. The American national government, after all, is larger than the average national government in the world. If the British treasury can collect taxes efficiently in England, it is likely that seven or eight different Internal Revenue Services, each dealing with a part of the United States the same economic size as England, could do a good job, too. Further, this will permit Congress to make comparisons of relative efficiency and to reward efficiency by expansion of area and penalize inefficiency by reduction.

This is by no means the only method to introduce competition. We could permit bureaus to make proposals to Congress for performing duties that are normally performed by some other bureau. They would have to allege that they would do a better job, and this might or might not be true. It is certainly true, however, that the existence of this competitive threat would keep the individual bureau continuously on its toes.

The decentralization of government which I mentioned above goes well with this kind of competition. I happen to live in a part of southwest Virginia in which there are a number of small towns. I was surprised when I arrived to discover that there is a well-functioning competitive market for government services. Individuals decide to enter the job of being city manager or police chief; they start in a small town and, if they are successful, move to a larger one. If they are unsuccessful, they are removed or, in any event, moved down the ladder. The situation is radically different from the civil service, but, most assuredly, it is markedly more efficient.

The extreme method of introducing competition, of course, is contracting out government activities to private agencies. There does not seem to be any particular rule for those things that are contracted out and those that are not. All of our actual guns are produced by government arsenals, but aircraft and electronic equipment—to say nothing of transport equipment—are purchased in the private market. We build our roads and our government buildings by contracts with private producers, but we maintain them, in general, by bureaucracies. I could go on with this list of essentially unrationalized choices between government production and government purchase almost indefinitely.

In general, it seems sensible to move toward the government purchase side. There is more competition here and stronger pressure to cut costs and provide a good product. Note, however, that although I have no doubt that this is the right way to go, we should not expect too much from it. What is sometimes called the military-industrial complex produces, on the whole (with some exceptions), excellent military equipment; but there seems to be no doubt that the costs are a good deal higher than they have to be. Still, we would improve competition by this method, and I am sure we would get some improvement in efficiency.

The two suggestions above are, I think, within relatively easy reach politically. By this, I do not imply that we can make the change tomorrow by sending a delegation to talk to a few congressmen. I do think, however, that it is an area where we could push for improvement with a fair chance of obtaining some results. Thus, in addition to the areas where I feel public choice has had some effect, these are areas where I think it can have some effect in the near future.

Changes in Voting Procedures

These are all cases of efficiency improvement, but they are not really drastic improvements. Students of public choice have recommended a number of fairly revolutionary changes at one time or another. As is well known, I was (and, for that matter, still am) associated with a proposal to make the normal voting majority something on the order to two-thirds to three-quarters. I am also in favor of the European type of proportional representation, and recently I have argued for dispensing with democratic procedures and using the demand-revealing process in their place. I regard all of these policies as sensible, but I do not think we are likely to apply any of them in the next year or so.

I should perhaps say that these proposals, and such other proposals as radical changes in the nature of voting through the introduction of instant referenda using cable TV with the capability of feeding back responses from viewer/voters, might be sensible right now on a small scale in certain parts of South America. At any given time, there are a number of South American dictators who are beginning to get worried about the permanency of their control; but they would prefer to lose control by way of setting up, peacefully, a government that will continue to protect their property rather than being overthrown by some other dictator. These people may sometimes be motivated, then, to establish an ordinary democratic government, but presumably they would be interested in experimentation in new methods—if for no other reason than that it would tend to give them a legitimate excuse for delaying the election by a year or so. Still, I know little about Latin America and perhaps this suggestion is totally impractical. I would like to see some experimentation on demand-revealing processes and electronic voting by almost any means, including their use in the gradual easing out of a dictator; but, once again, I have no great hopes for immediate implementation.

My main theme has been applications of public choice. When I first contemplated this paper, I was thinking largely of simply surveying the now quite voluminous empirical literature on the subject. My decision instead to mainly look at cases where public choice either has had some effect on active political life, or where it appears that it might have, may have been a mistake. Nevertheless, I am a reformer at heart and hope that public choice will in time lead to better government.

Morris P. Fiorina

Comments

My general reaction to Tullock's paper is that he has adopted too restrictive a focus. One almost has to have an affiliation with a Virginia university to receive mention (the latter condition is only necessary, not sufficient—two Virginia PhDs who went on to become president of the Public Choice Society are conspicuously absent from Tullock's survey). In addition to the neoclassical economists from the old Confederacy mentioned by Tullock, I would include two other groups in any discussion of public choice research. First, there is a group typically referred to as "axiomatic social choice theorists" who study the formal properties of existing and proposed decision processes. Too often the contributions of this group are dismissed as not practical, but I think that judgment reflects more on those who make it than on the contributions themselves. (For a detailed survey which points out many practical implications, see Plott, 1976.) Second, there is a growing political science research group variously referred to as positive theorists, formal theorists, or "rational choice types" who have made significant strides in developing theories of elections and legislatures (for a survey of early work see Ferejohn and Fiorina, 1975). Perhaps I appear testy by emphasizing these omissions from Tullock's survey, but I am regularly reproached by mainstream political scientists dismayed by some public choice "contribution" they have come across, and if I must share the blame, I want to share the credit as well.

Let's turn now to what Tullock includes rather than omits. In his introduction he writes that "the most important effect public choice has had on both economics and the actual functioning of government" is the recognition of government imperfection (p. 28). He quotes approvingly Charles Schultze's dictum that we should compare imperfect markets with imperfect governments, not with perfect regulatory schemes, and notes that academics no longer regard a market imperfection as a sufficient justification for government intervention.

It seems to me that Tullock too quickly dismisses the impact of recent policy failures. But I agree with him that public choice has made at least some contribution to the current rhetoric of lowered expectations. I would go further and argue that the nature of that contribution is not merely popularization of the perception that governments are imperfect, *but that they are inherently so!*

Political science as a discipline has historically accepted the fallacy of positive correlation: all good things go together. The general presumption is that good people operating in good (i.e., "democratic") processes necessarily produce "good" outcomes. The fallacy has been so widely accepted that until recently few political scientists even looked at government outcomes, simply presuming that they were as satisfactory or unsatisfactory as the processes which produced them. Whenever an especially egregious policy failure or process inefficiency has surfaced, the immediate reaction has been to propose structural reform (to eliminate overlapping jurisdictions, divided authority), or moral improvement ("an agency is only as good as the people who run it").

But consider what the contributions of public choice tell us. The social choice people have disillusioned us about majority rule and its variants. Democratic political processes simply have no optimality properties, even in the simple models analogous to those of classical economics which generate the "hidden hand." The rational choice people have pointed out the importance of prisoners' dilemma situations in common political processes. (For an explanation, see Luce and Raiffa, 1957. For evidence of importance, see Aranson and Ordeshook, 1977; Fiorina and Noll, 1978; Weingast, 1978.) I would like to dwell on this latter point a moment. The prisoners' dilemma is probably one of the most important intellectual discoveries of the twentieth century. In decentralized situations ordinary people like us, acting in perfectly natural fashion, may produce rotten collective outcomes. No conspiracies of evil people need be posited, just each of us acting as we find natural. American politics would be less strident if we could get this simple point across to various environmentalists, political process reformers, and Naderites.

A second widespread attitudinal change which Tullock attributes to the influence of public choice research is the increasing acceptance of the self-interest axiom. Again, I concur in the existence and importance of this attitudinal change, but fear that Tullock goes a bit far in claiming the central premise of the economic paradigm as a public choice contribution. In this case I definitely think the well-publicized policy failures of the 1960s and '70s may have more to do with increasingly cynical views of human behavior than do the academic writings of either economists or public choice people.

When it comes to specific policy applications of public choice research, Tullock is cautious: "If we look for specific actual changes in government policy which can be directly attributed to public choice activity, I think we would find that there are none" (p. 33). Caution in such matters is advisable, but the situation is not so barren as Tullock suggests. Elsewhere in this volume, Ferejohn, Forsythe, and Noll report on their continuing efforts to develop and implement a demand-revealing mechanism for the Public Broadcasting System (PBS). Noll has also worked with the Federal Communications Commission (FCC) on the allocation of television stations among cities, and Plott with the Department of Transportation on methods of setting barge rates. I daresay that policy makers in the education arena have seen Jim Coleman's research, that those who work on campaign and electoral law reform have occasionally run across a public choice analysis of some aspect or another, and that advocates of reform and/or reorganization of the bureaucracy may have chanced upon books by Downs, Niskanen, or even Tullock. Granted, these are probably instances where a public choice contribution has affected internal debates and perhaps a proposal or two, rather than an entire bill with numerous titles, but let us take satisfaction in that and not sell ourselves shorter than we have to.

Rather than specific policy contributions, Tullock chooses to concentrate on the empirical public choice literature. This is a bit like dwelling on the rushing accomplishments of Joe Namath. The empirical public choice literature is very uneven. On the one hand, most economists receive a tolerably good training in statistical method, so they are capable of producing analyses which have the appearance of thoroughness and sophistication, but on the other hand, their lack of contextual knowledge leads them to rely on naive model specifications. Often, too, public choice empirical studies utilize outrageous indicators for crucial theoretical variables (e.g., Settle and Abrams, 1976), a failing for which I have no plausible explanation.[1]

---

[1] The editor has requested that I elaborate on this remark. The Settle and Abrams paper tests something called the "rational theory of voting behavior" by means of a multivariate analysis of a time series (1868–1972) of turnout in presidential elections. Settle and Abrams measure the latter as the percent voting among the *voting age population*. During the third party system (Civil War to Bryan), turnout consistently hovered at around 90 percent of the *eligible electorate* (i.e., males over 21, mostly white) or at something above 40 percent by Settle and Abrams' measure. The decline in male turnout at the turn of the century produces a less pronounced dip in their measure, which then jumps sharply after the passage of the

Let us consider three of the empirical research areas Tullock discusses. First there is the large and growing body of work on the political business cycle (now a light industry in Europe as well as the United States). George Stigler suggests that the entire literature is without foundation, that only malevolent parties favor inflation or unemployment, and that sensible voters realize that. Thus, fluctuations in the state of the economy should have no electoral effects. Here is one of those rare occasions when an economist sounds like a political scientist. The question is not whether a party wants unemployment or inflation, a typically political science way of asking the question, but rather how the parties stand with respect to the tradeoff between the two phenomena— a distinctively economics way of thinking. Maybe not everyone accepts the idea of such a tradeoff today, but several generations of economists have convinced government officials and the informed public that such a tradeoff exists. Moreover, survey evidence indicates that voters have clear ideas of where the parties stand when it comes to such a tradeoff. Whether Stigler likes it or not, there is ample basis for presuming the existence of the incentives which might generate a political business cycle.

Of course, governments may be too decentralized or too incompetent to produce a marked cycle, a proposition for which I hold considerable sympathy. But we should remember that small economic fluctuations which produce small electoral fluctuations are not necessarily small in importance. A private firm may be relatively insensitive to a drop in market share from 51 percent to 49 percent, but elected officials tend to be sensitive to small variations around the 50 percent

---

nineteenth amendment (1920). Bear in mind, then, the shape of the dependent variable: a flat line at 40 percent from 1868–96, a decay until 1920, then a new steady state at around 60 percent thereafter, with some decline in recent years. Moving on, one of the hypotheses tested and "verified" by Settle and Abrams is that turnout increases with the availability of free information about the candidates. And how is the latter measured? Settle and Abrams use the proportions of households containing radios and televisions. Consider briefly the shape of these measures: a flat line at 0 until the 1920s (radio) or the 1940s (television), followed by a sharp upward trend. Any variable with this general shape would relate strongly to turnout as defined by Settle and Abrams (television usage with its later break point relates less strongly than radio). My personal suggestions for two variables which would correlate even more strongly with turnout would be the number of 1917 30-06 Springfield rifles manufactured, and the amount of fuel consumed by American prop-driven military aircraft. Not only do these variables have take-off points at approximately the right time, they also capture the post-New Deal decay in turnout.

The simple fact is that presidential participation should be measured as the percentage of the *eligible electorate voting*. This series shows a general decline since 1868 and will correlate *negatively* with *any* time series which captures technological advancement (radios, television, rifles, airplanes, even deodorant), the rational theory of voting behavior to the contrary notwithstanding.

mark. Stigler and Wagner speculate that politicians really do not manipulate macro variables but concentrate various distributional efforts prior to elections, efforts whose weak reflections may show up in macro indicators. This is a very good hunch I think, primarily because a political scientist, Ed Tufte, has already documented it (1978).

Next Tullock turns to a number of "micro" studies which focus on voting, acquisition of information, the behavior of officeholders, and so on. Such studies run the gamut from quite interesting to quite awful. Though I hesitate to name names (as a rational choice type I believe in making enemies only if the benefits exceed the costs), one study mentioned by Tullock does illustrate some of the weaknesses too often found in public choice empirical research, so it might be worthwhile to examine it in detail.

In an unpublished manuscript, Rubin and Kau (1978) conclude that liberal congressmen oppose science while conservatives favor it. An interesting contention, certainly, but should we believe it? The explanatory variable, liberalism, is measured by the Americans for Democratic Action (ADA) index. Since the roll call votes that compose the latter are presumably functions of party and constituency as well as ideological influences, it is difficult to treat the summed score as a measure of liberalism alone, but Rubin and Kau show no great concern over this. Their explanatory model also includes such variables as constituency age and race distributions. The relevance of these variables to support for basic science is not completely obvious to me. But all this is of small import compared with the indicator of support for science, the dependent variable. Rubin and Kau have discovered a roll call vote on an amendment to an appropriations bill which would have expanded the National Science Foundation administrator's discretionary authority to reprogram funds. Democrats opposed the amendment, Republicans favored it. Democrats tend to have high ADA scores, Republicans low ones. Possibly this single roll call is an excellent indicator of support for basic science. But only in the Public Choice Society would the proposition be given nontrivial probability.

Finally, Tullock takes note of Niskanen's observation that

> a congressman who invested an hour in constituent work obtained a direct gain from it, whereas if he had invested the same hour in supervising the function of government . . . he would be generating a public good, both for the country and for his colleagues . . . therefore, . . . congressmen would tend to devote relatively little time to their nominal duties and a great deal of time to constituent service (p. 40, this volume).

I share Tullock's judgment about the accuracy and importance of the preceding argument. But I should point out that it was rescued from the political science descriptive literature and systematized by me (1977), and extended in papers with Roger Noll (1978a, b).[2]

Toward the end of his paper Tullock proposes two areas that might provide targets for applied public choice: decentralization of government functions, and competition among government bureaucracies. As he notes, we hear a lot of favorable rhetoric about decentralization, but see rather little of it in practice. The situation with competitive bureaucracies is similar. I wonder, though, if the world has not already given us some reasonable quasi-experiments with competitive bureaucracies which only need scholarly examination. There have been comments and complaints for many years about conflict (i.e., competition) between the departments of interior and agriculture, the Bureau of Land Management vs. the Forest Service. Similarly, we have the Army Corps of Engineers, the Bureau of Reclamation, and the Soil Conservation Service competing for projects and programs. Has anyone examined such agencies from the standpoint of public choice questions rather than those traditionally posed by public administration? I would not be surprised if our governmental system contains an interesting sample of public choice applications even if no one intended them as such.

[2] Niskanen has graciously declined to accept the credit Tullock offers.

Dennis C. Mueller

Comments

As Gordon Tullock mentioned in the delivery of his paper, it is a most difficult paper upon which to comment. I shall focus my remarks, therefore, more upon the empirical public choice literature than upon Tullock's paper. My remarks pertain to the latter only where it discusses this part of the public choice literature.

The methodology of empirical model building in public choice can be most usefully discussed, perhaps, by contrasting it with the methodology of model testing in traditional, "private" choice economics. The basic behavioral postulate underlying both the private and the public choice literature is, of course, that individuals maximize their own utilities. To get testable predictions from this assumption, however, one must further restrict the arguments of the individual's utility function to a few variables. Indeed, it would be nice if there were but one argument in the individual's utility function, for then one could get really clean empirical predictions! As soon as two arguments are assumed, tradeoffs can occur, and the possibility of income effects swamping substitution effects arises with the resulting predicted sign ambiguities. The number of variables included in an individual's utility function for the purposes of empirical testing has been, therefore, typically small—more often than not, only two.

The left-hand side of table 1 lists the key actors in private choice economics and the most important variables assumed for each actor's utility function. Although these models have had a fairly wide dispersion in their success (measured by, say, their R^2 statistics), at explaining the behavior they purport to explain, a consensus has arisen, at least within the profession, that the basic economic approach to explaining this behavior has been vindicated. This conclusion has emerged despite the fact that these models have never been tested against any others formulated upon an alternative behavioral foundation, as for example against

TABLE 1. Private/Public Choice Models

Private choice models		Public choice models	
Actor	Utility function arguments	Actor	Utility function arguments
Consumers	Private goods	Voters	Public goods, income, wealth
Factor owners	Income, leisure, risk	Politicians	Income, ideology
Managers of firms	Profits, sales, growth, quiet life	Bureaucrats	Budget size, security

a sociological model of the corporation. What testing of alternative models has taken place, and this has been rare enough, has been within the economics paradigm, as when the profits maximization assumption is tested against the sales or growth maximization hypotheses.

Economic model building in public choice has begun to develop along the same lines the private choice models have followed. A few key actors are distinguished—the voter, the representative, the bureaucrat— and the utilities of these actors are assumed to be functions of one or two variables (see table 1). Although this approach is reasonable enough, and to be expected, given the heavy predominance of economic training among public choice scholars (which is particularly conspicuous in the empirical literature), it seems even less legitimate here than in the private choice economics area. The public choice field has an obvious alternative methodological approach against which to judge itself, and an obvious alternative set of hypotheses to examine—those existing in political science. Yet very little, if any, work has been done which derives both a public choice and say, a political science model, and tests the one's predictions against the other's. This is particularly unfortunate, since the empirical public choice literature, at least at this early stage in its development, seems far more replete with implausible results and unsolved riddles than its more venerable, private choice brother. These factors combined make it difficult to evaluate the achievements of the empirical public choice literature at this time. But let us see what we can infer about the behavior of its key performers from the results to date. Here I begin to draw more heavily on Tullock's paper.

Anthony Downs (1957) first pointed out that rational behavior on the part of voters required a limited gathering of information on public issues and a low turnout at the polls. The former prediction seems supported by public opinion surveys showing widespread voter ignorance of issues, candidate positions, and even candidate identities. The latter is contradicted by the relatively large turnouts at national elections, however. A large theoretical and empirical literature has now arisen trying to explain this *voter's paradox,* but the paradox remains a continuing challenge to the empirical public choice approach.

Given that the voter does vote, however rational or irrational this may seem, what determines the way in which he votes? Here there appear to be two schools of thought emerging as discussed by Tullock. The one we might call the Chicago–Virginia school as represented by the empirical work of Stigler, Crain, Tollison, and Wagner. Characteristically these papers have focused on micro variables in explaining candidate elections. Voters are motivated by the changes in private income and wealth that follow political victory, by direct and indirect income transfers. The pork barrel is put forward as the underlying hypothesis explaining candidate and voter behavior.

On the other side, we find what might be called the Keynesian school of empirical public choice, which focuses on macro variables. Here we have the work of Frey, Kramer, MacRae, and Nordhaus. The key determinants of voter behavior are the macro variables, unemployment and inflation. Parties compete by manipulating or promising to manipulate the macro policies affecting these variables.

Although the differences between these two approaches are obvious and important, perhaps even more significant is their one basic similarity. They both focus on the income and wealth effects of government policies. This is important from the perspective of public choice, because all of our theoretical models of voter behavior assume that the voter's utility function is defined over the basket of public goods he consumes, as the consumer's is defined over private goods, and that it is government policies on the allocation of public goods that determine the voter's vote. But, from the empirical public choice literature one gains the impression that the decisions of the allocation branch, to use Musgrave's terminology, do not matter. It is only the work of the redistribution and stabilization branches that affects voter decisions. To read the bulk of the empirical public choice literature, one would never think that issues such as the Vietnam War, the environment, and crime in the streets were of any interest to voters.

Perhaps they are not. But the verification of this hypothesis requires more than just a statistically significant F-statistic for an equation omitting these other variables. A convincing demonstration that only these income and wealth variables matter requires testing these models against others that take into account positions on traditionally defined public goods. Interestingly enough in this context, one of the few public choice-type studies that has found public good issues important in explaining voting behavior was by someone trained as a political scientist. John Aldrich (1975) found the Vietnam War and crime in the streets to be the most salient issues in explaining voter choices in the 1968 U.S. presidential election.

Models of politician behavior again build on the work of Downs. The politician is assumed to choose platforms to win votes. Although the salary of an elected official may exceed some candidates' opportunity costs, this seems unlikely for most candidates, given their professional backgrounds. Thus, getting elected can be only a means to some other end for most politicians, and the need arises to posit some other argument in the politician's utility function, some additional pecuniary or nonpecuniary income. The Frey models assume the pursuit of a nonpecuniary goal by politicians once their popularity gets high enough so that they feel secure in office. The pecuniary goals are taken as givens, however, revealed by the actions of the politicians in office. The Crain–Tollison model posits a form of spoils system of government in which the politician appears to be maximizing his legal and extra-legal permanent income. Neither type model has been formulated in such a way so as to allow easy testing against alternative behavioral assumptions. Much work obviously needs to be done.

The most systematically developed model of bureaucracy is Niskanen's model of the budget-maximizing bureaucrat. This model has obvious behavioral similarities to the Baumol and Marris models of sales and growth maximization in the firm (see Williamson, 1966, for a review), and the evidence which exists in support of these models may be regarded as indirect supportive tests of the Niskanen hypothesis. No direct tests of the hypothesis exist to my knowledge, although it is frequently cited along with tabulations of data on the growth of government. A fairly large literature on the regulated firm and nonprofit institutions now exists, and this might be regarded as part of the empirical literature on bureaucracy. But none of this systematically develops a general behavioral model of the nature of Niskanen's and confronts it with alternative sets of data. Instead, a particular objective function is posited for the bureaucrat given his specific position, and evidence is presented that he has pursued this objective. The only general conclusion that it seems safe to draw from this literature is that, given discretion to pursue goals in conflict with the objectives of their constituents, bureaucrats do take advantage of this discretion and pursue these conflicting goals.

Thus, the empirical public choice literature does not appear to have progressed all that far up to this time. This need not be regarded as particularly surprising or disappointing, since it has existed for only about a decade. Much promise remains, and therefore much opportunity and justification for future research.

REFERENCES

Aldrich, John. 1975. "Candidate Support Functions in the 1968 Elections: An Empirical Application of the Spatial Model," *Public Choice* vol. 22 (Summer) pp. 1–22.

Aranson, P. H., and P. C. Ordeshook. 1977. "A Prolegomenon to a Theory of the Failure of Representative Democracy," in Richard Auster, ed., *American Re-Evolution* (Dallas, Criterion Studies) pp. 23–46.

Arrow, Kenneth. 1951. *Social Choice and Individual Values* (New York, Wiley).

Bish, Robert L., and Vincent Ostrom. 1973. *Understanding Urban Government: Metropolitan Reform Reconsidered* (Washington, D.C., American Enterprise Institute).

Buchanan, James M., and Gordon Tullock. 1962. *The Calculus of Consent* (Ann Arbor, University of Michigan Press).

———, and Richard E. Wagner. 1977. *Democracy in Deficit: The Political Legacy of Lord Keynes* (New York, Academic Press).

Crain, W. M. 1977. "On the Structure and Stability of Political Markets," *Journal of Political Economy* vol. 85 (August) pp. 829–842.

Crain, W. M., and R. Tollison. 1976. "Campaign Expenditures and Political Competition," *Journal of Law and Economics* vol. 19 (April) pp. 177–188.

——— and ———. 1977a. "Legislative Size and Voting Rules," *Journal of Legal Studies* vol. 6 (January) pp. 235–240.

——— and ———. 1977b. "Attenuated Property Rights and the Market for Governors," *Journal of Law and Economics* vol. 20 (April) pp. 205–212.

——— and ———. (forthcoming) "The Influence of Representation on Public Policy," *Journal of Legal Studies.*

——— and ———. (forthcoming) *Monopoly Aspects of Politics* (Leiden, Martinus Nijhoff).

———, T. Deaton, and R. Tollison. 1977. "Legislators as Taxi-Cabs," *Economic Inquiry* vol. 15 (April) pp. 298–302.

Downs, Anthony. 1957. *An Economic Theory of Democracy* (New York, Harper & Row).

Ferejohn, J. A., and M. P. Fiorina. 1975. "Purposive Models of Legislative Behavior," *American Economic Review, Proceedings and Papers* vol. 65, no. 2 (May) pp. 407–414.

Fiorina, M. P. 1977. *Congress: Keystone of the Washington Establishment* (New Haven, Conn., Yale University Press).

———, and R. G. Noll. 1978a. "Voters, Legislators and Bureaucracy: Institutional Design in the Public Sector," *American Economic Review, Proceedings and Papers* vol. 68, no. 2 (May) pp. 256–260.

———, and ———. 1978b. "Voters, Bureaucrats, and Legislators," *Journal of Public Economics* vol. 9, pp. 239–254.

Frey, Bruno S., and H. J. Ramser. 1976. "The Political Business Cycle: Comment," *Review of Economic Studies* vol. 42 (October) pp. 553–555.

————, and Friedrich Schneider. 1976. "An Empirical Study of Politico-Economic Interaction in the U.S." Discussion Paper No. 76, University of Konstanz.

Hirschman, Albert O. 1977. *The Passions and the Interests: Political Arguments for Capitalism Before Its Triumph* (Princeton, N.J., Princeton University Press).

Kalecki, Michal. 1943. "Political Aspects of Full Employment," *Political Quarterly* vol. 14, pp. 322–331.

Kau, J. B., and P. H. Rubin. 1976. "The Electoral College and the Rational Vote," *Public Choice* vol. 27 (Fall) pp. 101–108.

Kramer, Gerald H. 1971. "Short-Term Fluctuations in U.S. Voting Behavior, 1896–1964," *American Political Science Review* vol. 65 (March) pp. 322–331.

Luce, R. Duncan, and Howard Raiffa. 1957. *Games and Decisions* (New York, Wiley).

McCormick, Robert E., and Robert D. Tollison. 1978. "Legislatures as Unions," *Journal of Political Economy* vol. 86, pp. 63–78.

McKenzie, Richard B. 1976. "Politics, Learning, and Public Goods Literacy," *Frontiers of Economics* (Blacksburg, Va., Center for Study of Public Choice).

Niskanen, William A. 1971. *Bureaucracy and Representative Government* (Chicago, Aldine-Atherton).

————. 1975. "Bureaucrats and Politicians," *Journal of Law and Economics* vol. 18 (December) pp. 617–643.

Nordhaus, W. D. 1975. "The Political Business Cycle," *Review of Economic Studies* vol. 41 (April) pp. 169–190.

Plott, C. R. 1976. "Axiomatic Social Choice Theory: An Overview and Interpretation," *American Journal of Political Science* vol. XX, no. 3 (August) pp. 511–596.

Rubin, Paul, and J. B. Kau. 1976. "Voting by Congress on Appropriations for Science," unpublished manuscript.

Schultze, Charles L. 1977. *The Public Use of Private Interest* (Washington, D.C., Brookings Institution).

Settle, R. F., and B. A. Abrams. 1976. "The Determinants of Voter Participation: A More General Model," *Public Choice* vol. XXVII (Fall) pp. 81–89.

Stigler, George J. 1973. "General Economic Conditions and National Elections" *American Economic Review* vol. 63 (May) pp. 160–167.

Tufte, E. 1978. *Political Control of the Economy* (Princeton, N.J., Princeton University Press).

Wagner, Richard E. 1977. "Economic Manipulation for Political Profit: Macroeconomic Consequences and Constitutional Implications," *Kylos* vol. 30, fasc. 3, pp. 305–410.

Weingast, B. 1978. "A Rational Choice Perspective on Distributive Policy Making." Working paper number 27, Center for the Study of American Business, Washington University, St. Louis, Mo.

Williamson, John. 1966. "Profit, Growth, and Sales Maximization," *Economica* (February) pp. 1–16.

Paul R. Portney and Jon C. Sonstelie

Super-Rationality and School Tax Voting

Students of public choice have long been fascinated with what has come to be known as the Tiebout model of local public expenditure. The central feature of this model, we may recall, is the ability of a household to select as a place of residence in a metropolitan area the community offering the mix of public services and tax price that best suits the household's tastes and budget. The appeal of this conception of residential choice lies in the possibility that such "shopping" among local governments will result in an efficient allocation of resources to the provision of local public goods. This is especially important since the possibility of free ridership was thought to make the honest revelation of preferences for these goods otherwise unobtainable.

As we have pointed out elsewhere (Sonstelie and Portney, forthcoming 1979), the Tiebout model has not gone unnoticed by students of empirical local public finance. Beginning with Oates (1969) and continuing to the present, empirical studies have questioned almost exclusively one implication of Tiebout's hypothesis; namely, does the price of a house reflect not only its structural or physical characteristics but also the quality and cost of the public services provided by the community in which it is located? Almost without exception the many tests of the Tiebout hypothesis have answered this question in the affirmative. Hedonic estimation reveals that better public services, however measured, do exert a positive and significant influence on property values, other things being equal. Higher property taxes, on the other hand, reduce property values when service quality is held constant. Thus, housing prices do serve as a register of the demand for local public services.

However, to imply that household mobility is the only avenue through which households express their preferences for local public services would be to ignore an essential feature of local political economy—the popular referendum. Households vote far more often with their heads and hands than with their feet. Last year alone, local governments in the United States held thousands of referenda, each of which gave voters the chance to express their feelings about proposed changes in the quality or quantity of a wide range of public services, including school expenditures, police and fire protection, and parks and recreation expenditures.

These referenda have also provided grist for the empirical mill. Between 1960 and 1972, for example, more than a hundred studies were completed that undertook to relate the outcomes of local school tax and bond elections to a host of variables ranging from the religious background of the electorate to the times of year at which the referenda were held. While a number of these studies included "economic" factors among the explanatory variables, or even purported to be tests of Downs' "rational voter" model, one fact stands out. (For a review, see Piele and Hall, 1973.) In not one of these studies was it recognized that alterations in either the menu of public services offered by a community or the cost at which they are provided will affect, perhaps significantly, the value of that community's housing stock.

In other words, housing prices have been decomposed to reveal the implicit prices placed on a variety of local public services as determined by residential mobility and choice. Yet no one has considered that the *supply* of these services will thus be influenced by the preferences initially expressed through voting. This possible dependency suggests an interesting feedback from individual preferences—expressed through residential choice—to the public good supply decisions of local governments as determined through their political processes. First, individuals choose a community in which to live so that housing prices reflect local public goods. Then, if homeowners vote in referenda with an eye toward the effect public services will have on property values, the supply of these services will be determined by the preferences expressed through referenda. Thus, voting by ballot can be thought of as a complement to, rather than a substitute for, voting with one's feet. Indeed, voting by ballot might tie together residential mobility and the supply decisions of local governments, a possibility which heretofore has gone unnoticed. In this paper we address this lacuna in the literature on local public goods and referendum voting.

In section I of this paper we briefly review earlier studies that have attempted to explain the outcomes of local school tax elections. These are almost without exception what we will call aggregate analyses. That is, they use as units of observation school tax referenda in different communities at different times. The outcomes of these referenda are then linked to the socioeconomic characteristics of the voters in the respective communities (their income, education, occupation, religion, ethnic background, and parental status), the specific features of the election itself (type of school district, size of the proposed tax change, and existing tax rate), as well as certain other explanatory variables. We also review a recent study by Rubinfeld (1977) that utilizes data on individuals' characteristics and their (reported) votes in two consecutive school tax elections.

In section II, we introduce the notion that voting by homeowners in such referenda might be motivated at least partially by the expected effect of the outcome on residential property values. Individuals who behave in this way we refer to as "super-rational"; we do so for the simple reason that the less grandiose term "rational" has been preempted to describe voters who weigh the increased property taxes they will bear if school spending is increased against the benefits they will enjoy from "better" schools—where these benefits depend almost exclusively on whether they have children in the schools. In section II we also discuss the conditions under which we might expect super-rationality to prevail and conditions under which it will be quite unlikely.

In section III, we combine data on precinct voting in a 1970 South San Francisco, California, school tax election with our estimates of the changes in property values expected to result there from passage of the referendum. This enables us to test the super-rationality hypothesis. In section IV, we discuss the implications of our results and the direction that future work might take.

One final point bears mention. Throughout our discussion we will be concerned primarily with the decisions of those who choose to vote in school tax elections. We make only brief mention of why individuals do or do not vote and, hence, ignore the controversy surrounding the rationality, or lack of it, of voting at all. For our purposes it matters only slightly if an individual votes because the symbolic value of so doing exceeds the expected value of his or her vote (i.e., the change in wealth from a favorable outcome times the probability that the vote will determine the outcome) (Riker and Ordeshook, 1968); or, whether individuals vote because they wish to avoid the remorse they would no doubt feel if they failed to vote in an election in which their vote would have made a difference (see Ferejohn and Fiorina, 1974). In short, we are concerned with outcomes rather than participation.[1] (See Barkume, 1976, for an analysis of participation and outcome.)

I. PRIOR VOTING STUDIES

As we pointed out above, aggregate studies of the determinants of school tax elections are numerous, so much so that an entire book has been devoted to summarizing them (Piele and Hall, 1973). In addition, Hamilton and Cohen (1974) have surveyed the literature on the referendum process itself and, in doing so, have discussed studies specific to particular referenda. In view of the number of such studies, we will discuss here only the general methodology behind them, referring to specific studies when appropriate.

One possible determinant of school tax referenda outcomes that has received considerable attention has to do, not with the characteristics of the individual voters, but rather with their sheer numbers. That is, it has been hypothesized that large school districts, on account of their complex organizational structures, will be far removed from the voters and hence will have a more difficult time passing school tax increases. However, while there are exceptions to this finding, the majority of studies report that school district size is unrelated to the likelihood of passage (Piele and Hall, 1973, p. 75). Alexander and Bass (1974) did find that unified school districts—those in which elementary and secondary education are administered together—had a significantly lower success ratio than districts that were exclusively elementary.

On the other hand, the evidence is overwhelming in support of the proposition that larger turnouts are associated with smaller percentages of favorable votes. It appears to be the case that those voters who come to the polls only infrequently do so to vote *against* proposed increases in school taxes and expenditures. Finally, results seem to indicate that the timing of a school tax referendum has no influence on its outcome, although Beal and coauthors (1966) found that school districts most successful at winning approval of tax and bond elections were those that infrequently proposed such changes.

Demographic characteristics have also been linked to voter response in school tax referenda. For example, previous studies have been nearly unanimous in reporting that older voters are more inclined to

---

[1] Ed. note: See pp. 71, 72 for a more careful discussion of why the authors feel they can ignore the participation question.

oppose increased school expenditures and taxes than younger voters. Similarly, black voters are much more likely to support school tax increases than white voters, and some evidence indicates that inner city Catholics are more likely to oppose school referenda than Protestants. However, we wish to point out that these results are all consistent with another more general hypothesis about voter behavior—the hypothesis that voters in such elections are rational economic men and women who weigh the benefits and costs associated with passage and vote accordingly. It is to previous "tests" of the rational voter model that we now turn.

As we suggested above, rationality has been narrowly interpreted in these earlier studies. In general, voters were presumed to benefit from improved school quality if they had children in schools and not otherwise. (This implies that voters view more money as producing better schools, a view that has not gone unchallenged.) Similarly, homeowners who paid property taxes directly were viewed as bearing the brunt of school tax increases while renters were thought to be less burdened (Piele and Hall, 1973, pp. 99, 100). Accordingly, tests of the rational voter model sought to determine whether renters with children in schools were more inclined to support school tax increases than childless homeowners. In eight different studies it was established that voters with children in the public school system were more inclined to support school tax increases than childless couples. However, home ownership was found to be unrelated to opposition or support of school tax referenda. This led Piele and Hall to conclude that, "Although the benefit side of our cost/benefit model is well supported by the literature, the cost side is not" (Piele and Hall, 1973, p. 101). However, in several studies renters have been shown to be more inclined than homeowners to support school referenda (Smith and coauthors, 1964; McKelvey, 1966; and Banfield and Wilson, 1964).

Somewhat less narrow interpretations of the rational voter model have been tested, however. For example, McMahon (1966) explored the relationship between house value (a proxy for the size of the tax increase) and the direction of voting in school financial elections. He found the average value of owner-occupied housing in a precinct to be negatively related to support of tax and bond referenda. In a similar vein, Fish (1964) and Tebbutt (1968) found no significant relationship between the property tax rate and direction of support in bond issues; other studies have been unable to link assessed valuation per student and direction of outcome.

However, Alexander and Bass obtained somewhat different results in their more recent study of 975 school tax elections held in 496 different California districts between 1966 and 1972. Using data aggregated to the school district level, they considered 34 independent variables, including voters' income, education, occupation, age and family status, place of residence, and race. Also included were the characteristics of the election itself—the proposed new level of the property tax and the size of the change it represented—as well as assessed valuation per student, percent of owner occupancy, the amount of nonresidential property, and a measure of the average value of owner-occupied housing units in the school district.

Their results are relevant to our test of the super-rational voter hypothesis. Alexander and Bass (1974, p. v) conclude,

> School districts that pass and fail tax elections have very similar characteristics. Only a few variables were significantly different. Most important, the proposed tax, the existing tax, and tax change were all smaller in passing districts. . . . Multivariate regression analysis with a dichotomous pass-fail dependent variable showed that the variables related directly to the tax election itself (mentioned above) were the most important, with the proportion of families with incomes greater than $25,000 as the only other consistently significant and important variable.

In the school districts Alexander and Bass surveyed, then, voters might be said to conform to the narrow interpretation of the rational voter hypothesis, at least with respect to costs. That is, voters were consistent in opposing large increases in the property tax rate, especially when that rate was high to begin with. However, communities in which a high percentage of families had school-aged children did *not* pass school tax referenda with greater frequency than other communities; nor did communities with high percentages of elderly voters reject such referenda more often—in fact, "percent elderly" was positively, albeit insignificantly, related to referenda passage. Hence, the narrowly interpreted benefit side of voters' supposed benefit–cost calculation is unsupported by Alexander and Bass's careful econometric investigation.

One final aggregate study bears mention, that by Grubb and Osman (1976). They view the school tax election as an attempt to correct a disequilibrium between a district's actual level of educational spending and its desired level, which they estimated on the basis of each district's financial characteristics and those of its inhabitants. Using linear regression, they found that the percentage of yes votes in a district was positively related to the amount by which actual expenditures fell short of the district's "desired" spending; percent yes was also negatively but insignificantly related to the percentage of the population that was black and negatively and significantly related to the size of the proposed tax change.

We mention their findings because our model, like theirs, is one of disequilibrium. We differ from Grubb and Osman, however, in interpreting the nature of the disequilibrium to which voters react. We choose to view school tax elections as attempts to effect changes in school spending that will enhance the market values of voters' dwellings.

Before turning to our discussion and test of the super-rational voter hypothesis, we wish to mention Rubinfeld's study of school tax voting. His approach differs in a fundamental way from those studies we have referred to as aggregate. In analyzing the determinants of two school tax elections in a Michigan community in 1973, Rubinfeld used survey data on the reported voting decisions of specific individuals which he then linked to their individual demographic and socioeconomic characteristics. Thus, his conclusions about the effect of a voter's income, for example, on the likelihood of his or her voting yes are stronger than similar conclusions drawn from aggregate studies. This is so because the knowledge that wealthy communities support school tax increases more often than poor ones does not allow us to conclude that it is the wealthy individuals in these communities who are supporting the referenda. Rubinfeld's use of survey data neatly avoids this problem.

In the second of the two elections (necessitated by the failure of the bond issue in the first), Rubinfeld's analysis identifies a number of factors that significantly influenced the likelihood of a yes vote. These included the sex of the voter (females were more likely to support the tax increase), the presence of school-aged children in the voter's family, the number of years the voter had been a resident of the community, the voter's income, and a measure of the "average" price (tax cost) of school spending to the voter.

The careful specification of Rubinfeld's estimating equation and his access to data on individuals' votes and personal characteristics make his work the best of that done to date. Nevertheless, as he states (Rubinfeld, 1977, p. 31),

> Implicit in our model is the assumption . . . that the per pupil value of taxable property remains unchanged [regardless of the outcome of the local referendum]. . . . As a result . . . our model rules out the real possibility that individuals will vote for a millage

proposal solely on the grounds that it is likely to raise the value of
their own property. . . .

It is, of course, this real possibility that we wish to test. Hence, Rubinfeld's work provides a convenient pad from which to launch our discussion of voter behavior in school tax referenda.

II. THE SUPER-RATIONALITY HYPOTHESIS

The idea that those voting in school tax elections might be motivated at least in part by property-value effects should not be surprising.
Indeed, it would be somewhat surprising if they were not. As we
pointed out above, the effects of public services and property taxes on
property values are well established in the academic literature; moreover, this relationship does not go unnoticed by school superintendents
and real estate agents. Less clear are the conditions under which property value effects can be expected to play a major role in referenda
voting. Before describing an empirical test of our super-rational voter
hypothesis, therefore, we will discuss briefly the conditions under which
super-rationality is most likely to appear.

The idea behind super-rationality is quite simple. The house one
owns is an economic asset, the value of which partially depends upon
the tax-expenditure mix offered by the community in which it is located.
Of course, owners also consume the services of that asset. In that respect, a home is like a host of other assets which are both owned and
consumed by the same person. Assets of this type appear to present their
owners with contradictory roles. On the one hand, they ought to maximize the value of their assets. On the other hand, they ought to maximize the utility they receive from the services of those assets.

However, the existence of markets for the services of those assets
means that the conflict faced by their owners is less serious than it may
first appear. The best interest of an owner is served by the separation
of his investment and consumption roles. He must seek first to maximize the value of his assets and then make those consumption decisions
which maximize his utility. In reckoning the cost of various consumption bundles, the services of his own assets ought to be valued at their
market opportunity cost.

This separation theorem implies that once a household owns a
dwelling, the owners ought to vote in referenda to maximize the value
of their house. They can relocate in a metropolitan area if this house no

longer provides them with their most preferred combination of housing-cum-public services. Thus, in a school tax referendum, the rational homeowner ought to vote to maximize the value of his house. He can then move to the community that provides him with his preferred bundle of public services.

This, then, is the link to earlier tests of the rational voter model. Specifically, previous studies have considered only the consumption aspects of the decision to oppose or support school spending. But, because of the investment motive, aging homeowners or other childless couples might well decide to support increased school spending.

As previously mentioned, it is the existence of markets for the services of an asset that makes it rational for an owner to separate his consumption and investment decisions. If such markets do not exist, or if they are imperfect, that separation may no longer be rational. Briefly, there are three ways in which the housing market may fail to meet the requirements of the separation theorem.

First, there must be many communities in the metropolitan area and a wide range of expenditure packages from which to choose. In such a case, a childless homeowner, for example, could sell his dwelling if its market value increased sufficiently and move to another community offering considerably lower educational expenditures and a correspondingly lower gross rent. If, on the other hand, there are no other communities providing a mix of services at a gross rent that appeals to a household, there is little reason for that household to try to maximize the value of its property in anticipation of a possible move.

The ability of homeowners to act in such a manner—to "take the money and run," so to speak—depends on a second condition. That is, super-rationality will be facilitated by the absence of barriers to mobility. For, if it is prohibitively expensive to move or if real estate transactions costs are very high, households will be deterred from acting as property value maximizers—as super-rational voters, that is—even though there are alternative locations where they might be better off after reckoning in the gains from the sale of their old dwelling.

Not all the moving costs that act as obstacles to super-rationality are financial. The friendships, associations, and attachments that families make during their time of residence in a neighborhood are generally severed when they move. Moreover, these attachments are valued at next to nothing by the market—the warmth of the Smith family next door means little to a family who doesn't know the Smiths. Therefore, the stronger these attachments, the higher are the uncompensated psychic costs of moving and, hence, the less likely it is that any particular family will behave super-rationally in casting its votes in a school tax or other kind of referendum.

Finally, we can hardly expect people to behave super-rationally if they are unaware of the other residential opportunities that confront them in a metropolitan area. This holds true regardless of the range of residential possibilities open to the household and the relative ease with which it could take advantage of any particular opportunity. Note that super-rationality implies not only a knowledge of these other possibilities, it also requires that homeowners be able to calculate at least the *approximate* effect on the value of their home of an increase in school spending and property taxes. Homeowners probably have a fair idea of the annual increase in property taxes implied by a proposed tax rate increase. However, we realize we are asking a lot in expecting voters also to have an idea of the amount by which the gross rent of their dwellings will be enhanced if the tax-expenditure package is approved.

These three conditions, then—a wide range of residential alternatives, the absence of formidable barriers to mobility, and information about the alternatives and the effects of public services on property values—will help to determine the likelihood of super-rational behavior in school tax voting.

Because these three conditions are not likely to be fully met, we would expect voter decisions to reflect a mixture of consumption and investment motives. We turn now to an empirical test designed to determine the extent to which super-rational behavior plays a role in an actual referendum. Before proceeding, we should point out that we are concerned only with property value enhancement via referendum voting. We neglect the very real possibility that homeowners may support minimum lot size zoning or other land use restrictions for this same reason.

III. TESTING THE HYPOTHESIS

Description of the Referendum

In June 1970 the South San Francisco (California) Unified School District held a school tax referendum. If the referendum had passed (it did not, as we shall see), it would have raised the district property tax rate about 19¢ for each $100 of assessed valuation. This would have been sufficient to raise educational spending per pupil by slightly more than $83. Since the district was spending $646 per pupil prior to the election, approval would have increased school spending by 13 percent.

The South San Francisco Unified School District is comprised almost exclusively of the residents of the city of South San Francisco, a community of 46,650 located directly south of the city and county of San Francisco. Median family income in South San Francisco at the time of the election was $12,281, about $1,000 less than the median for San Mateo County, of which South San Francisco is a part. Two-thirds of the dwellings in the community were owner-occupied according to the 1970 census.

As we pointed out, the school tax referendum was rather soundly defeated. More than 5,500 of the 9,200 registered voters who voted in the election, or about 60 percent, opposed the tax increase and the added school spending it would have supported. There was, however, considerable variation among the individual precincts of the school district with respect to support for the proposal. The percentage supporting the tax increase ranged from a low of 10 percent in one precinct to a high of 56 percent in another. The purpose of the empirical work described in this section is to test our super-rational voter hypothesis by determining whether this variation in precinct returns was related to expected changes in residential property values.

Property Value Changes

These expected changes in property values did not fall like rain from on high, however. Rather, we generated them ourselves, making use of recent work we have done on the determinants of the annual costs of housing in San Mateo County. This work is described in considerable detail elsewhere (see Sonstelie and Portney, forthcoming). Briefly, it consists of hedonic estimates of how the annual gross rent of a dwelling is affected by its structural characteristics, those of the neighborhood surrounding it, and the quality of the public services provided by the community in which it is located. Included among these public services are educational expenditures per student for each school district. Thus, this function gives us an estimate of the increase in the annual gross rent of any dwelling that would result from an increase in the per-pupil educational spending of the school district to which it belongs. We coupled estimates of gross rent increases for every single-family dwelling in South San Francisco with the increased property tax liability each would incur if the referendum passed in order to obtain a measure of the expected effect of the tax-expenditure proposal on residential property values there.

It is important to keep in mind that these expected changes in property values will be linked to voting behavior only if homeowners expect the gross rent function to remain the same over time. The gross rent function will not be changed by changes in one community's menu of public services as long as that community is a small part of the metropolitan area. This is the case with South San Francisco and the Oakland–San Francisco SMSA of which it is a part.

Observations and Independent Variables

Because data on the votes of individuals were unavailable, our units of observation are the precincts in the South San Francisco school district. This has both desirable and undesirable features. On the positive side, the use of precincts allows us to observe revealed as opposed to reported electoral behavior. Thus, we eliminate the possibility that voters might knowingly or unknowingly err in reporting the direction of their vote in the election. On the other hand, we are unable to link expected changes in the value of individual dwellings to the votes of their owners. Rather, we must examine the average expected changes in property values in a precinct and link this to precinct-wide support for the proposal. However, the census tract and block data we use to construct the socioeconomic characteristics of the voters in the various precincts is much finer than data gathered at the community level. An optimistic view of our precinct observations, then, is that they are as disaggregated as they can be and still be based on revealed electoral behavior.

We have emphasized that the consumption benefits of increased school spending will be important if homeowners are not as mobile as our theory presupposes. In addition to a measure of average property value change in each precinct, therefore, we elected to include a measure of these possible consumption benefits—the percentage of total precinct school enrollment accounted for by the public school system. The smaller this percentage, the less likely it is that voters will support the referendum. Moreover, since other studies have all found family income to be a significant determinant of support for school spending, we also include that in our regressions. Finally, we included in some regressions the average increase in annual property tax liability that would have resulted from passage of the referendum. The inclusion of this term is consistent both with the findings of Bass and Alexander and with our belief that cash flow considerations might also play a role in voters' calculations.

One problem with the compilation of the precinct data is that the precincts are considerably smaller than census tracts. Therefore, where two precincts were located entirely within the same census tract, there was no variation between them with respect to median family income or public and private school attendance. However, many of the 54 precincts with which we began were comprised of parts of two or more of the 11 census tracts that make up South San Francisco. We also examined each precinct for the ratio of owner-occupied to total occupied housing units. Because our theory deals only with homeowners and the incentives they face, we excluded precincts with greater than 30 percent renter occupancy. This reduced the number of our observations to 33.

Estimation Procedure

Because the decision of any individual voter is binary (he could vote yes or no), we used a logit transformation of the dependent variable (Thiel, 1971, pp. 620–635). That is, our dependent variable is $\ln(Y/N)$ where Y is the proportion of total votes cast in support of the referendum and $N = 1 - Y$. Thus, our estimated coefficients should be interpreted as changes in the log of the odds of voting yes for given changes in the independent variables. Had we simply used "percent yes" as the dependent variable, this would not be true, of course, but this form would have presented other problems.

In actuality, a voter has another choice open to him beyond yes or no votes—we refer of course to abstention. In South San Francisco, precinct turnout varied between 23 and 59 percent on the referendum in question. We could assume that those who abstained did so because they were indifferent to passage or failure of the referendum—in other words, because the tax-expenditure package would make little difference to them regardless of the outcome. According to Amemiya's (1975) classification, behavior conditioned by such a reaction would be consistent with an "ordered response model."

On the other hand, abstention may be due to the recognition that the chance of one's vote affecting the outcome of the election is miniscule—in spite of the considerable difference that the final outcome might make to any voter. If all voters reason in that fashion, then vot-

TABLE 2.   Regression Results (dependent ln (Y/N))

Variable	Eq. (1)	Eq. (2)	Eq. (3)	Eq. (4)
Constant	−5.8226 (3.7)[a]	−4.6790 (3.5)	−5.4 (4.3)	−5.9061 (4.5)
PUBLIC	4.9571 (3.4)	4.54 (3.1)	4.86 (3.5)	4.8893 (3.5)
INCOME	0.00004 (0.5)			0.00007 (2.6)
ΔTAX	0.0075 (1.02)		0.01 (2.8)	
ΔPROP	−0.0001 (0.28)	0.0005 (2.1)		
R^2	0.43	0.37	0.43	0.41
Observations	33	33	33	33
F-ratio	5.3	8.8	11.1	10.4

[a] Figures in parentheses beneath coefficients are t-ratios.

ing becomes a random event triggered by other considerations unrelated to the possible outcomes of the referendum. The voters in this view constitute a random sample of all potential voters in the community. Thus, we can use the theory of binary choice to model the voting process. Our parameter estimates will be consistent, however, even if voting is not the random occurrence we hypothesize.

Results

Table 2 presents the results of our empirical estimates. Equation (1) is our basic regression and includes measures of public school enrollment as a fraction of total school enrollment (PUBLIC), median family income in the precinct (INCOME), average change in property tax liability for the single-family dwellings in the precinct (ΔTAX), and the average change in the value of the single-family dwellings in the precinct (ΔPROP). The results in (1) are somewhat disappointing. Only PUBLIC is significant and of the correct sign. Apparently, voters with children in the public schools are motivated to support increased spending by those schools. INCOME, while nominally positive as we would expect (if public education is a normal good), is insignificant. Both ΔTAX and ΔPROP are insignificant. We would expect higher tax liabilities to vary inversely with the dependent variable and property value increases to vary directly. This is not borne out by our results.

One reason for these somewhat puzzling results is clear, however. There is significant multicollinearity between certain of the independent variables. For example, INCOME is highly correlated with both ΔTAX and ΔPROP—the partial correlation coefficients are 0.86 and 0.84 respectively. Therefore, we ran the basic regression again omitting ΔTAX. Equation (2) demonstrates the effect of that change. While public school enrollment remains positive and significant, ΔPROP changes sign and becomes significant at the 5 percent level. That is, *the larger the average expected increase in property values in a precinct, the more likely it is that voters in that precinct will support the referendum.* In this pared-down regression, the super-rational voter hypothesis is not contradicted.

In equation (3) we tested to see if ΔTAX would have the expected negative sign if ΔPROP and INCOME were deleted from the estimating equation. It did not; and in fact it becomes significant with the absence of those variables. This may be due to its close association with income, however. That is, ΔTAX may in fact be measuring an income effect rather than the consumption "disbenefit" we intended it to measure. In equation (4) we omitted both ΔTAX and ΔPROP. As the results show, both PUBLIC and INCOME are positive and significant. Hence, in the absence of other variables, we observe a positive and significant income effect. In all the regressions, the independent variables explained about 40 percent of the variation in $\ln(Y/N)$.

IV. CONCLUDING REMARKS

The results presented above provide some support for our super-rationality hypothesis. That is, the average change in residential property values in a precinct is positively and significantly related to support for the referendum by the voters in that precinct in one of the equation specifications. These voters appear also to be influenced by their income, the expected change in property tax liability, and by the extent to which they rely on the public schools for the education of their children. In spite of our mild success, we do not feel that this is a particularly good test of our hypothesis. Our data are too riddled with multicollinearity to allow us to test accurately the effects we wish to explore. Clearly, a further test with better data would be desirable.

What if this super-rationality hypothesis is not falsified by other empirical tests? What would this imply about decision making at the level of local governments? There are several important implications of such a finding.

At the level of applied theory, confirmation of our super-rationality hypothesis would, in a fashion, complete the relationship described above between household mobility, the demand for local public goods, and the mechanism by which the *supply* decisions of local governments are made. House prices would not only reflect preferences expressed through mobility but would also guide citizens as they participated in the more common form of preference revelation at the local level—the referendum.

Completing this "circuit," if we may call it that, is important for another reason, however. Elsewhere (Sonstelie and Portney, 1976 and 1978), we have shown that super-rational behavior by homeowners could make possible the efficient provision of local public goods and services. This will be the case if, under certain conditions, each community provides that menu of public services that maximizes the value of the property within its boundaries.

Furthermore, it is conceivable in such a system that decisions on supplying public goods could be designed to attract the unanimous support of the residents of a community. This could be accomplished if the shares of the increased taxes necessary to finance more school spending, for example, were allocated to homeowners *not* on the basis of current property values as is now the practice, but rather in proportion to the property value increases that would be received by each if the policy in question were put into effect. If homeowners do vote in referenda to maximize the value of their property, everyone would favor a spending increase supported by such a taxation scheme. This follows from the fact that those benefiting not at all from the increased spending would bear none of the tax costs of the increased spending. On the other hand, those benefiting the most would bear the greatest proportional burden, yet they would always be better off as long as the proposed spending increase was "efficient"—that is, as long as it would increase the total value of the residential property in the community.

It is, we realize, a long way between the tentative support we have presented for our super-rational voter hypothesis and a world in which all local tax and expenditure decisions are unanimously supported or opposed. Nevertheless, we have attempted to indicate the direction in which such a journey should begin and we hope to have provided the first steps.

Daniel L. Rubinfeld

Comments

Paul Portney and Jon Sonstelie have written a stimulating paper in which voters in school millage elections are not only rational in considering the direct consumption benefits of education, but super-rational as well, in the sense that they respond to expected capital gains associated with changes in property values. The issues raised by the paper and my comments about them can best be divided into three parts. First, I argue that the authors suggest a number of interesting theoretical questions, which link the local public spending and voting literatures, and thereby point to some potentially fruitful areas of research. Second, I argue that the empirical evidence presented by the authors does not provide a good test of their super-rationality hypothesis, and finally, I present some independent data which help to shed some light on the subject and which in the process suggest just how difficult it might be to obtain a good test of super-rationality.

THEORETICAL ISSUES

The Portney–Sonstelie paper provides a link between two theoretical literatures in urban public finance, a link which ought to receive much greater attention from public choice social scientists. One literature is associated with the work of Charles Tiebout (1956). In this literature individuals are assumed to make locational choices within an urban area by choosing among bundles of public services. Under a set of rather restrictive assumptions concerning the distribution of tastes, and public service bundles, the resulting Tiebout equilibrium will be efficient in the Pareto sense. Within this context some authors attempt to measure the extent to which public services affect location decisions by empirically estimating hedonic housing price functions.[1] The estimation might involve regressing house value (or gross rent in the authors' case) on house attributes, one or more accessibility measures, and neighborhood attributes, including one or more public service measures.

A second theoretical literature examines the process of voting on local school millages, testing whether voting is rational, and attempting to measure the price and income elasticities of demand for public schooling (Rubinfeld, 1977). There are two facts that have received insufficient attention in this literature. One is that voting may have important effects on property values and migration. The other is that migration and the property value capitalization which results may have important impacts on voting, and thus public goods supply.

The possibilities for further research suggested by Portney and Sonstelie's paper are great, but it might be useful to mention a number of questions which come to my mind, some of which have been treated, and others which have not.

1. Voter Behavior. To what extent do the feasibility of relocating and the stage of the voter's life cycle affect voter turnout and the probability of voting for or against millages in the community in which a voter resides?

2. Bureaucratic Behavior. To what extent do supply conditions affect the decision to hold a millage election and the outcome when an election is held? Studies of the size and sequencing of millages,[2] and of the relationship between public employee unionism and millages (Courant, Gramlich, and Rubinfeld, forthcoming) are suggestive.

3. Intrametropolitan Location. In a metropolitan location model with fragmented jurisdictions and with majority-rule voting, will an equilibrium exist? If so, will it be stable?[3]

4. Property Value Capitalization. Under what assumption will capitalization of spending and taxes occur in equilibrium?[4]

5. Disequilibrium. How might we measure tax and spending capitalization if the housing market is in disequilibrium, an assumption which seems to be implicit in the authors' analysis?

---

[1] I have reviewed this literature in Rubinfeld (1978).

[2] T. Romer and H. Rosenthal of Carnegie-Mellon University have begun some promising work in this area.

[3] Some evidence to the contrary is available in Pauly (1976).

[4] Edel and Sclar (1974) argue that no capitalization is consistent with long-run Tiebout equilibrium, but I see no reason why capitalization could not occur. See M. Pauly (1976) for some discussion.

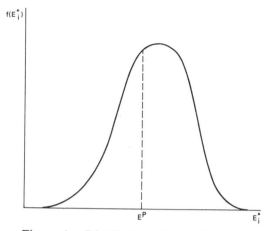

Figure 1. Distribution of desired per pupil expenditures. $E_i^* =$ desired spending level of voter i. $f =$ probability density function. $E^P =$ proposed spending level.

THE SUPER-RATIONALITY HYPOTHESIS

Deciding to vote for or against a millage based on one's expectations about capital gains seems to involve a lot of careful calculating (as the authors suggest), so any attempt to empirically test the hypothesis is likely to be a difficult one. Let me suggest in some detail why this is so. First, imagine that voters are otherwise rational, and decide whether to vote yes or no by initially calculating their desired level of school spending, based (among other things) on the number of children, household income, and the price of schooling.[5] If the level of desired spending is sufficiently greater than the proposed millage level, they vote yes. If the desired level is sufficiently less than the old millage level, they vote no. Otherwise they seem likely to abstain. Now take a given distribution of desired spending levels (E_i^*) in a community, as shown in figure 1. Then, those households likely to vote yes because of super-rationality (and no otherwise) are households just to the left of the proposed level of spending E^P. These households, however, will not necessarily be the households which stand to gain the largest increase in property

---

[5] The price of schooling is the cost to the family associated with the community provision of an additional dollar per pupil of public school expenditures. Within a community, house value and/or property tax payments provide a measure of the price of schooling. Across communities, the price varies with property tax base per pupil and with the state educational grant matching rate. See Rubinfeld (1977).

values (as suggested by the authors' paper).[6] The point is that whether super-rationality affects a vote depends upon the interaction between predicted increases in property values and the probability of a yes vote. Only when the predicted value increase is *large* and the probability of a yes vote is near 0.5 are we likely to be able to measure super-rational behavior. This puts substantial empirical demands on any serious attempt to test the hypothesis. It suggests that we need to isolate households just on the margin between a yes and no vote, and then see whether those households are likely to respond to the investment incentives associated with the millage outcome.

I can provide another view on the difficult nature of testing for super-rationality by arguing that such a phenomenon is not likely to be apparent unless the housing market is in *disequilibrium*. Consider a family without children living in a two-bedroom house. Other things being equal, the value of the house is likely to be relatively low because the *marginal buyer* of the house will be just like the current owner, with no children and a low demand for schooling. However, if the market is in disequilibrium, then it is possible that the marginal buyer is a family with children and a substantially higher demand for schooling that is unable to find the right size house in a community that spends at the household's desired level. In such a case, the marginal buyer may be willing to pay substantially for the house if and when the millage election is passed. As a result, super-rationality on the part of the original household is a reasonable possibility. The key point is that disequilibrium is necessary because in disequilibrium the marginal benefits from schooling may change sharply as the level of schooling increases. This is discouraging for any empirical testing that is done, because cross-section housing value equations usually presume housing market equilibrium, at least in the short run.

Having reviewed some of the empirical difficulties of testing the super-rationality hypothesis, let me briefly consider the authors' empirical work. The project was an extensive one, involving a large and interesting micro housing set, merged with precinct level voting data. The housing market data set, through the estimation of a gross rent function, yields predicted property value changes, which must (due to data limitations) be aggregated to the precinct level. This is unfortunate because aggregation is most reasonable with homogeneous precincts, whereas my earlier discussion suggests that heterogeneity may be important if one is to obtain a good test of the super-rationality hypothesis.

---

[6] The details are in the authors' earlier paper, Sonstelie and Portney (1976).

The outcome of the gross rent estimation and ensuing calculations is a variable measuring the average change in property values, which by construction is *highly correlated* with average house or property values in the precinct.[7] This poses a potentially serious problem because the level of property values seems likely to be highly correlated with income (more so in aggregated rather than micro studies) and also highly correlated with the price of schooling, which is measured in part by the authors' tax increase variable.[8] Not surprisingly, there is substantial multicollinearity, which makes it impossible to distinguish between the effects of the three variables under consideration. Only when the income and tax variables are dropped do the authors get their expected result. Let me stress, however, that the problem is not poor econometric work —the data set just doesn't seem sufficiently powerful for the test of such a refined hypothesis.

NEW EMPIRICAL EVIDENCE

My previous arguments suggest that the best way to test for super-rationality is with a micro data set. I have worked with such a data set, a survey-based sample of eligible voters in two elections. As a result, it was relatively easy to try to clarify things somewhat by attempting a super-rationality test with my data set (Rubinfeld, 1977). To do so, I have posed the authors' hypothesis in the following way: Why do families *without children in public school* vote for millage elections? Super-rationality would predict that those most likely to vote yes would be households with expensive houses (since, according to the authors' model, expensive houses suggest a higher increase in property values if the millage is passed), and those who are likely to leave the community in the near future. Data limitations force me to proxy the latter variable with a variable measuring the number of years of residence in the com-

---

[7] This might not have been as true had the authors chosen a different form for the specification of their gross-rent equation in their housing market power. In the form used by the authors, when expenditures rise, gross rents rise more than proportionately with property values. The tax rate increase to finance these expenditures rises proportionately with property values, however. The net result is that the change in property values is likely (within a community at least) to be positively (and highly) correlated with the value of property itself. See Sonstelie and Portney (1976) for details.

[8] The relationship between gross price and the price of schooling (as well as income) is of course an empirical one. Since the price of schooling within a precinct varies with house value, and millage rates are constant within each precinct, gross rents and property values are likely to be highly correlated. How high the correlation is when we move across precincts is more problematic.

TABLE 3. Voting Data—Mean Values of Variables

	All votes	Yes (with children)	No (with children)	Yes (without children)	No (without children)
% 18–34	23	24	26	27	21
% 35–49	23	64	63	22	24
% 50–64	35	12	11	40	33
% 65+	19	0	0	11	22
Income	17,389	23,585	19,400	24,267	14,650
Property taxes	905	1,091	1,021	918	900
% Teacher	4.4	16.5	2.3	15.6	0
% Female	60.8	56.6	52.9	60.0	61.1
Years of residence	16.1	7.7	11.6	12.7	17.5
% Married	87.3	99.5	98.8	95.6	84.1
% Private school		7.1	9.4	8.9	9.7
N	425	182	85	45	113

Source: Data set described in Rubinfeld (1977).

munity on the assumption that those long in residence are less likely to move than newer residents.

There are competing hypotheses, however. First, rationality suggests that the higher the price of schooling (as measured by house value or, within a community, by dollars of property taxes paid), the less likely a household is to vote yes. Second, young families (with few years of residence) are likely to vote yes because they expect to have children in schools. Third, families may vote yes because of concern for the social environment of the community as measured by certain personal characteristics of other community residents. Such a variable wasn't the focus of my micro survey, but one might argue that income provides at least a crude proxy—the higher one's income, the more likely that a family without children will vote yes.

A brief examination of the results summarized in tables 3, 4, and 5 suggests some evidence *consistent with* super-rationality. First, from table 3 notice that of those families without children in public school, yes voters were community residents fewer years than no voters. Of course, yes voters are also younger, so that the reason behind this empirical evidence is unclear. Second, yes voters pay slightly higher property taxes, and thus have more expensive homes, but the difference is statistically insignificant. In fact, if one were to compare house value with income, those voting yes have substantially lower value homes as a percent of income than do those voting no.

TABLE 4.   Voting by Years of Residence

No. of years	Entire sample	Without children No vote	Without children Yes vote
0–5	215	40 (35.4%)	23 (51.1%)
6–10	66	18 (16.0)	3 (6.7)
11–15	32	9 (8.0)	2 (4.4)
16–20	36	10 (8.9)	7 (15.6)
21+	75	36 (31.9)	10 (27.2)
N	425	113	45

TABLE 5.   Voting of Individuals Without Children (5 or fewer years of residence)

	Vote no	Vote yes
% 18–34	44	48
% 35–49	28	26
% 50–64	23	26
% 65+	5	0
Income	18,600	27,826
Property taxes	988	1,115
% Teacher	0	17.4
% Female	65	47.8
% Married	90.0	95.6
% Private school	13.0	10.0
N	40	23

A closer analysis of the mobility–residency issue can be made by examining tables 4 and 5. More than half of the families (without children) voting yes resided in the community five or fewer years, as opposed to 35 percent for those voting no. However, this result depends crucially on the arbitrary five-year cutoff, since a substantial number of no voters were in the six-to-ten-year group. It is interesting to note, however, that of those with five or fewer years of residence, those voting yes paid higher property taxes than those voting no, a result which is inconsistent with super-rationality.

Other than super-rationality, what helps to explain voting behavior? First, income, whether as a proxy for community environmental concerns or not, is much higher for yes than no voters. Second, a substantial minority of yes voters were educators, although I am unable to distinguish which school systems employed them. Finally, a surprisingly high percentage had children in private school—which suggests that preferences for public schooling are not single-peaked.

These results are not meant to be conclusive. The data set is specific to one community, the sample is limited, and I have said nothing here about voter turnout. They do suggest, however, just how difficult it is to test the super-rationality hypothesis. I should add that I find the hypothesis to be an intriguing one, and I hope that the authors' paper and these comments will spur others to pursue it and related issues in greater depth.

Edwin S. Mills

Comments

I suspect that economists who correlate property values and public school expenditures are in the right forest but barking up the wrong tree. My view of the situation is as follows.

Local government expenditures are a relatively minor determinant of the quality of public schools. Recent research on educational productivity emphasizes that increased expenditures have relatively little effect on educational attainment in public schools. Although communities that have high public school expenditures also tend to have high quality schools, the main causal link is not from expenditure to school quality.

Princeton's public schools are high quality not because we spend a great deal on them. In fact, we spend less per child than Newark or New York City. Instead, Princeton's schools are high quality because Princeton's land use controls exclude those whose children would make education expensive or of poor quality. Land use controls effectively exclude almost all poor and black people. Most Princeton residents have children who are relatively easy and inexpensive to educate.

Excluding the poor means excluding those whose presence would reduce the quality of the schools. It also means that the average income is high and high income people tend to vote for large educational expenditures. In part, the purpose is to improve the quality of the education, but in part it is because of the pure consumption aspect of education. High income people feel, with some justification, that it makes little sense to send their children from a fashionable home to a threadbare school. Hence, they vote public expenditures that carpet the floors, paint the walls, and so on.

Hence, I believe, the chief causal mechanism is that communities with exclusionary land use controls have high property values and, having excluded those who lower school quality, good schools.

REFERENCES

Alexander, Arthur, and Gail Bass. 1974. "Schools, Taxes, and Voter Behavior: An Analysis of School District Property Tax Elections." Rand Corporation Research Report No. R-1465-FF.

Amemiya, Takeshi. 1975. "Qualitative Response Models," *Annals of Economic and Social Measurement* vol. 4, pp. 363–372.

Banfield, Edward, and James Wilson. 1964. "Public Regardingness as a Value Premise in Voting Behavior," *American Political Science Review* vol. 58, pp. 876–887.

Barkume, Anthony. 1976. "Identification of Preferences for Election Outcomes from Aggregate Voting Data," *Public Choice* vol. 27 (Fall) pp. 41–58.

Beal, George, et al. 1966. *Iowa School Bond Issues Data Book* (Ames, Iowa, Iowa State University).

Courant, P. N., E. M. Gramlich, and D. L. Rubinfeld. (forthcoming). "Public Employee Market Power and Local Government Spending," *American Economic Review*.

Edel, M., and E. Sclar. 1974. "Taxes, Spending and Property Values: Supply Adjustments in a Tiebout-Oates Model," *Journal of Political Economy* vol. 82, pp. 941–954.

Ferejohn, John, and Morris Fiorina. 1974. "The Paradox of Not Voting: A Decision Theoretic Analysis," *American Political Science Review* vol. 28, no. 2 (September) pp. 525–536.

Fish, Lawrence. 1964. "An Analysis of Factors Associated with Voter Behavior in School Budget Elections." Unpublished doctoral dissertation, Washington State University, Pullman, Washington.

Grubb, Norton, and Jack Osman. 1976. "Adjustments from Disequilibrium in Local Finance: School Referenda in California." Unpublished manuscript.

Hamilton, Howard, and Sylvan Cohen. 1974. *Policy Making by Plebiscite: School Referenda* (Lexington, Mass., D. C. Heath).

McKelvey, Troy. 1966. "A Cooperative Study of Voting Behavior in Two Coterminous Systems of Local Government." Unpublished doctoral dissertation, University of California, Berkeley, California.

McMahon, Stephen. 1966. "Demographic Characteristics and Voting Behavior in a Junior College Election." Unpublished doctoral dissertation, University of Texas, Austin, Texas.

Oates, Wallace. 1969. "The Effects of Property Taxes and Local Public Spending on Property Values: An Empirical Study of Tax Capitalization and the Tiebout Hypothesis," *Journal of Political Economy* vol. 77, pp. 957–971.

Pauly, M. 1966. "A Model of Local Government Expenditures and Tax Capitalization," *Journal of Public Economics* vol. 6, pp. 231–242.

Piele, Philip, and John Hall. 1973. *Budgets, Bonds, and Ballots* (Lexington, Mass., D. C. Heath).

Riker, William, and Peter Ordeshook. 1968. "A Theory of the Calculus of Voting," *American Political Science Review* vol. 62, pp. 25–42.

Rubinfeld, D. L., 1977. "Voting in a Local School Election: A Micro Analysis," *Review of Economics and Statistics* vol. LIX, no. 1 (February) pp. 30–42.

———. 1978. "Market Approaches to the Measurement of the Benefits of Air Pollution Abatement," in A. Friedlaender, ed., *Air Pollution and Administrative Control* (Cambridge, Mass., M.I.T. Press).

Smith, Ralph, et al. 1964. *Community Organization and Support of the Schools,* Cooperative Research Project No. 1828, Field Services Division, Eastern Michigan University, Ypsilanti.

Sonstelie, Jon, and Paul Portney. 1976. "Property Value Maximization as a Decision Criterion for Local Governments," in Paul R. Portney, ed., *Economic Issues in Metropolitan Growth* (Baltimore, Johns Hopkins University Press for Resources for the Future).

——— and ———. 1978. "Profit Maximizing Communities and the Theory of Local Public Expenditure," *Journal of Urban Economics* vol. 5, pp. 263–277.

——— and ———. (forthcoming). "Gross Rents and Market Values: Testing the Implications of Tiebout's Hypothesis," *Journal of Urban Economics.*

Tebutt, Arthur. 1968. "Voting Behavior and Selected Communications in a Bond and Rate Referenda for a Suburban School District." Unpublished doctoral dissertation, Northwestern University, Evanston, Illinois.

Theil, Henri. 1971. *Principles of Econometrics* (New York, Wiley).

Tiebout, Charles. 1956. "A Pure Theory of Local Expenditure," *Journal of Political Economy* vol. 64, pp. 416–424.

Robert Cameron Mitchell

National Environmental Lobbies and the Apparent Illogic of Collective Action

Mancur Olson's *The Logic of Collective Action* was first published in 1965. In 1968 it appeared in paperback, and a revised edition of the book, both hard and softcover, was published in 1971. Though written by an economist, the work's conclusions are, as he points out, "as relevant to the sociologist and the political scientist as they are to the economist" (Olson, 1971, p. 3). If anything, this is an understatement, as the work directly challenges long-held paradigms in both of those fields by the simple expedient of applying to the study of groups and organizations the assumption that individuals are rational and act in a self-interested manner. Nevertheless, it has taken sociologists and political scientists more than a few years to come to realize its relevance. Now the news is out, however, and in the past several years an increasing number of scholars in those disciplines have been enthusiastically plowing the old fields of interest groups and social movements with the new plow of Olsonian rational choice analysis. Most find it too radical an innovation to adopt *en toto* and yet so provocative and suggestive that they are forced to rethink some fundamental questions about collective action. This activity has expressed itself in critical analyses of the model itself; in a reworking of the disciplines' existing paradigms in light of new insights gained from Olson; and, lately, in attempts to test the resulting theories empirically. Thus far the critique of Olson is well ad-

I am indebted to the two formal discussants of this paper for their valuable comments on the earlier version, which is now much revised. This revision has also benefited from the comments generously provided by Robert Birrell, James S. Coleman, R. Kenneth Godwin, Helen Ingram, John McCarthy, V. Kerry Smith, and, especially, Clifford S. Russell.

vanced, some very useful reconceptualizations of fields such as social movements have occurred, and the empirical testing is in its infancy.

Since the publication of Olson's book, and in apparent defiance of his logic, the numerous groups comprising the "public interest" movement have attracted sufficient public support to become viable and important lobbies for public goods of various kinds. Since Olson has cited the absence of such lobbies as an important confirmation of his theory, their obvious presence seems to require some explanation. Such empirical studies as have been conducted also suggest that the time has come to rework his theory. For example, four of these studies are of large economic interest groups such as the Canadian Teacher's Association (Manzer, 1969), the U.S. Conference of Mayors (Browne, 1976), the Confederation of British Industry (Marsh, 1976), and the Minnesota Farm Bureau (Moe, 1977). These organizations are precisely those most likely to conform to the Olson model (Moe, 1977, p. 36) and yet each of these studies finds Olson's theory to be a useful but less than fully adequate explanation for why members join these groups. Tillock and Morrison's Zero Population Growth Study (1979), the one empirical study of a public interest group in the literature, is even more emphatic about the theory's failings.

I agree with Brian Barry (1970) that more theoretical work is needed before useful empirical tests can be undertaken. I consider in this paper the applicability of Olson's model of collective action to a particular set of organizations that lobby for public goods—the national environmental public interest groups with general public membership. By systematizing and extending the work of a number of Olson's critics, most notably Denton Morrison and Terry Moe, I develop a revised rational choice theoretical paradigm of collective action to explain why individuals contribute to environmental lobbies. My current work on national environmental groups is not sufficiently advanced to provide an empirical test of the issues involved, so this discussion is limited to conceptual and qualitative analysis.

I. THE OLSON PARADOX

According to Olson's "theory of latent groups," rational individuals in "latent" groups[1] have no incentive to form or to contribute to

---

[1] Small (or "intermediate" in his terminology) groups are a special case in his theory and are considered at length in *The Logic of Collective Action*. He uses the term "latent" groups to refer to *large* numbers of people who would each benefit from the provision of a collective good if it were provided (Olson, 1971, p. 50). I adopt his use of this term in this paper although other writers use other terms for

organizations which seek to further their common interests by lobbying. This is so even when there "is unanimous agreement in a group about the common good and methods of achieving it" (Olson, 1971, p. 2). As he correctly points out, the then-prevailing sociological[2] paradigm tended to assume that holding common interests was sufficient in itself to motivate spontaneous collective action to obtain collective goods. This assumption led students of social movements, for example, to focus their analysis primarily on the grievances and social characteristics of movement participants.[3] Olson argues, persuasively I believe, that this approach ignores certain important properties of collective goods and large organizations which make collective action problematic.

Collective goods are nonexcludable (Peston, 1972) or nonexclusive (Olson, 1971). They are available to everybody in a group whether or not he or she has contributed to the attainment of these goods. The rational, utility-maximizing person, it is argued, will not be inclined to help achieve a group benefit which will then be enjoyed equally by those who do not contribute. He or she will be inclined to take a free ride, too. In addition to the free rider problem, Olson identifies two other properties of large groups which mitigate against the rationality of collective action for collective goods.[4] (1) Each individual's[5] con-

---

the same thing, e.g., Dahrendorf's "quasi-groups" (1959, p. 179) and Marx's "class-of-itself." As the environmental groups under consideration here represent the organizational embodiment of latent groups, I will consider his theory only as it applies to this class of groups.

[2] I will restrict my discussion here to my own discipline, but most of what I say is equally applicable to political science.

[3] It should be pointed out that a number of sociologists have developed a "resource mobilization approach" to social movements which directly challenges this earlier paradigm and draws upon Olson's insights in their reformulation of the field of social movements. See especially McCarthy and Zald (1977) and Oberschall (1973, pp. 113–145).

[4] If a collective good has the quality of "rivalness" (Peston, 1972) where one person's consumption of the good reduces the amount available to everybody else, a further incentive to not contribute would be introduced because the amount of the good that an individual contributor would get is likely to be negligible. With the exception of wilderness, virtually all of the goods sought by the environmental lobbies are ones in which consumption by one person does not decrease their availability to others. In a given wilderness area, however, increasing the number of simultaneous users beyond a certain point diminishes the wilderness experience for all users (and in fragile ecosystems may damage the ecosystem as well). The U.S. Forest Service has instituted a system of wilderness permits that limits the number of users of a particular wilderness area at a given time and the length of their stay. These are given out on a first-come, first-served basis. Persons who are unable to go to one part of a wilderness area are directed to other, less crowded areas. This rationing mechanism mitigates the effects of rivalness resulting from congestion. Increasing the amount of wilderness will decrease the queuing necessary to obtain that good.

[5] The sense in which "individual" is used here is the average individual. Obviously a big contributor, even in a large group, may rationally expect to "make a difference" by his or her contribution.

tribution will be such a small proportion of the group's resources that he will view it as inconsequential in affecting the outcomes of the group's action: the *inconsequentiality* problem. (2) The costs of organizing large groups are considerable, creating a hurdle that must be jumped before any of the collective goods can be obtained: the *organizing* problem (Olson, 1971, p. 129). This leads to the conclusion that

> ... however valuable the collective good might be to the group as a whole, it does not offer the individual any incentive to pay dues to any organization working in the latent group's interest, or to bear in any other way any of the costs of the necessary collective action (Olson, 1971, pp. 50–51).

In this situation "only a *separate and 'selective' incentive* will stimulate the rational individual in a latent group to act in a group-oriented way" (1971, p. 51, emphasis in the original). Coercion is one such incentive which is commonly employed by nations to collect income taxes as well as by labor unions who enjoy a closed shop. In the absence of coercion, it is necessary to supply positive incentives or private goods such as insurance policies, group travel discounts, and magazines.[6] These are individual, noncollective goods which the individual can acquire only through membership in the group which lobbies for the collective good. Therefore what distinguishes the unorganized consumers, white collar workers, and migrant agricultural workers[7] from the organized union laborers, farmers, and doctors[8] is that the latter

[6] Olson considers several other kinds of selective incentives besides services in his book. He discusses the role that social incentives such as social status and social acceptance play in small groups and in a footnote he raises the possibility that large-scale advertising campaigns might create a species of social incentives sufficient to motivate large latent groups, although he considers this highly improbable (Olson, 1971, p. 63). He also briefly considers moral incentives which have as their private good the reduction of guilt, but chooses not to use them in his analysis because: (1) they are difficult to measure, (2) his theory works without them, and (3) most organized pressure groups are explicitly working for gains for themselves, not for other groups, therefore "it is hardly plausible to ascribe group action to any moral code" (Olson, 1973, p. 61).

[7] Since Olson wrote those words, each of these groups has organized to some extent. For example, Nader's Public Citizen organization, which seeks public contributions, has a Tax Reform Research Group which studies tax questions, and lobbying and litigation arms which lobby for more equitable tax arrangements. The mere presence of these organizations does not necessarily invalidate the latent group theory, of course, because they may have developed ways to use coercion and/or selective incentives to accomplish their objectives. Whether or not this is the situation for these groups is worthy of analysis, but outside the purview of this paper.

[8] Industry lobbies are explained by factors outside the latent group theory (Olson, 1971, p. 134), which need not concern us in this analysis.

obtain their members by some combination of coercion and selective incentives (Olson, 1971, p. 135).

Olson's rational choice theory leaves virtually no room for collective goods or private moral goods such as self-esteem or guilt to act as a motivating force. In one place he writes that individuals will support the organization with a lobby working for collective goods *only* if the individual is coerced into it or has to support the group to get a noncollective benefit (1971, p. 134). On the next page he uses the word "mainly" to describe the effect of coercion and private goods on why individuals join labor unions, farm organizations, and professional associations (1971, p. 135). In another place he justifies his lack of attention to moral incentives on the grounds that there will be "sufficient explanations on other grounds [presumably referring to selective incentives] for all the group actions to be considered here" (1971, p. 61). In his conceptualization, members' support for the organizations' lobbying activities is merely an unintended "by-product" of the support which they give in order to obtain the private goods which the organizations control (1971, p. 13). Thus the provision of selective incentives is a necessary and (largely) sufficient condition for organizing individuals into lobbies.

At this point it is necessary to distinguish two polar types of collective goods. Some collective goods are limited to particular groups of people, such as wages to workers in an industry, a more equitable distribution of the tax burden to middle and lower income people, and price protection and benefits to farmers. Within the group everyone benefits, with the usual free rider problems. I will call these group goods. The second type involves goods which are available to everyone in the society, such as the benefits of clean air, which is almost a polar case of this type (Freeman, 1971, p. 10; Peston, 1972, p. 15). An appropriate label for these goods is public goods and I will use the term here in this narrow sense.[9]

Olson's analysis is restricted to group goods, for the most part. Furthermore, the collective goods with which he is concerned are economic goods, in the sense that higher prices for agricultural products, higher wages for union workers, and so on are directly stated in mone-

---

[9] I do not restrict public goods to those collective benefits provided by governments as does Olson (1971, p. 14) although often, and this is the case with environmental goods, governments do provide these goods. In my usage public goods are goods characterized by jointness of supply that are available to everyone in a society.

tary terms.[10] The national environmental groups, on the other hand, seek noneconomic public goods. They lobby for environmental amenities such as clean air, clean water, the preservation of endangered wildlife, open space, and wilderness. Put another way, they seek to diminish the impact on the environment of the externalities created by industrialization, urbanization, population growth, and the use of certain technologies, such as the internal combustion engine for small vehicles (snowmobiles and trail bikes). Is it appropriate to argue that Olson's theory should apply to the latent group of those who experience these externalities?

The answer to this question may seem to be clearly affirmative, since Olson announces boldly that "Logically, the theory can cover all types of lobbies. . . . It can be applied whenever there are rational individuals interested in a common goal." Neither does he limit it to just economic or material goods (Olson, 1971, p. 159). Nevertheless, in the brief section of the work which considers noneconomic lobbies, he goes on to qualify this statement; while the theory of latent groups sheds some light on certain noneconomic lobbies such as veterans organizations (which provide social goods at the local level), there are others for which it is not especially useful (Olson, 1971, pp. 159–160). He cites philanthropic lobbies and religious groups in this regard. Philanthropic lobbies are lobbies which seek goods for some group other than the group that supports them. Environmental groups would not fall into this category since their membership will share in the benefits achieved by their lobby, and they are not, of course, religious groups. He also cites the occasional band of committed people who work for causes which are admittedly "lost" and says that such "irrational" behavior can only be explained by recourse to psychology or social psychology, although the small size of such bands is consistent with his theory (Olson, 1971, p. 161). Environmental groups may be omitted from this exception too it would seem, as it would be difficult indeed to characterize their cause as hopeless.

It appears, then, that there is nothing inherent in Olson's theory that would preclude its application to environmental lobbies. Indeed, judging from his rather convoluted consideration of noneconomic lobbies (half the material in the six-page section on this topic is devoted to extended discussions in footnotes), such an exercise may help to

---

[10] Olson occasionally uses "public goods" as a synonym for collective goods (McFarland, 1976, p. 30). The group/public distinction is meant to clarify the confusion which results from this practice.

clarify the extent to which the theory of latent groups is a general theory of common action to achieve collective goods, or merely a special theory.

II. ENVIRONMENTAL LOBBIES

According to the historian Roderick Nash, there were only seven national and two regional conservation organizations in existence in 1908 when the Sierra Club led the fight to preserve the Hetch Hetchy valley from being inundated in order to provide San Francisco with a reservoir. Considering just the groups that have an action program (which may involve education) and including groups whose main focus is population and wildlife as well as those with wilderness and pollution interests, there are today some 75 national groups and hundreds more at the state and local level.[11]

The most visible and best known of the contemporary environmental organizations are the 15 large national membership groups which are listed in table 6. These include the National Wildlife Federation,[12] National Audubon Society, and the Sierra Club, to name the three largest. Several of the national groups also have local chapters—at the last count the Sierra Club had 250 local groups and National Audubon's chapters numbered 385. Reliable estimates of the number of Americans who were members of the groups in John Muir's time do not exist, but since the Sierra Club's membership in 1908 was only 1,000, the total cannot have been very large and surely amounted to far less than 1 percent of the adult population.

[11] This is exclusive of organizations that primarily promote the interests of hunters and fishermen or the consumption of natural resources.

[12] The total membership claimed by the National Wildlife Federation is 3,500,000. This membership consists of three parts: (1) associate members, who subscribe to *National Wildlife* and/or *International Wildlife* magazines, (2) affiliate members who belong to the many local groups, almost entirely sportsmen's clubs, which belong to the state affiliates of the federation, and (3) children who subscribe to the federation's *Ranger Rick* magazine. Only the 620,000 associate members can be counted as adult contributors to an environmental lobby, and further reference to the National Wildlife Federation's members will be limited to these members only. Virtually the entire budget of the federation is raised from associate member contributions and the sale of merchandise and wildlife stamps to the public. The national federation spends more on servicing the state affiliates than it receives from them. Furthermore, it appears that the major support for environmental goods such as controlling air and water pollution resides in the associate membership (Kimball, 1970, p. 121). Presumably the bulk of the affiliate membership who also place high priority on these goals are among the 20 percent of the affiliate membership who subscribe to the magazines and who are counted (also) as associate members.

TABLE 6.   Major U.S. National Environmental/Conservationist Membership Groups, Acronym, Date of Founding, and 1977 Membership

Primarily litigating
   1. Environmental Defense Fund (EDF), 1967 (45,000)[a]
   2. Natural Resources Defense Council (NRDC), 1970 (35,000)

Primarily Nonlitigating
General
   1. Environmental Action (EA), 1970 (16,000)
   2. Friends of the Earth (FOE), 1969 (19,000)
   3. Izaak Walton League (IWL), 1922 (60,000)
   4. National Audubon Society (NAS), 1905 (373,000)[b]
   5. National Parks and Conservation Association (NPCA), 1919 (42,000)
   6. National Wildlife Federation (NWF), 1936 (620,000 Associate Members)[c]
   7. Sierra Club, 1892 (178,000)[b]

Specialized[d]
   1. Cousteau Society, 1975 (150,000 in 1976)
   2. Defenders of Wildlife, 1959 (35,000)
   3. Nature Conservancy, 1951 (25,000)
   4. New Directions, 1976 (11,000)
   5. Union of Concerned Scientists (UCS), 1971 (45,000)
   6. The Wilderness Society (TWS), 1935 (68,000)

[a] Groups underlined are those which are participating in mail surveys of their membership as part of the Resources for the Future study of the environmental movement.
   [b] Membership figure is for "members" where family memberships, which cost more, are counted as two members.
   [c] NWF counts 3,500,000 members in all membership categories.
   [d] The specialized animal and population groups are outside the purview of this study. These include Friends of Animals (55,000 members), Fund for Animals (60,000), Negative Population Growth (1,000), and Zero Population Growth (10,000).

At the time of the founding of the Sierra Club and the Audubon movement at the end of the nineteenth century, the issues which concerned conservationists were largely restricted to the classic concerns of wilderness and wildlife. With the birth of the Izaak Walton League in 1922, water pollution was added to the list of environmental goods on the conservation agenda. By the 1950s, National Audubon had begun its long crusade against DDT, and the development of the extraordinarily wide array of issues which we now call "environmental" was well underway. Today these include not only wilderness and wildlife but also toxic substances, air and water pollution, energy, transportation, population, and recombinant DNA among others.

   The term "lobby" is used throughout this paper to refer to activities directed toward the end of securing a supply of a collective good.

For the environmental groups it encompasses a range of activities beyond classical legislative lobbying, such as the education of children and adults about the environment and wildlife. This is a traditional activity for most of the older groups, and the National Audubon Society and the National Wildlife Federation have especially extensive educational programs for all age levels. Such programs indirectly promote the supply of environmental goods by increasing the public's demand for them, thereby broadening the potential political base of support for their supply.

Although the development of Washington offices staffed by full-time professional lobbyists is relatively recent, legislative lobbying efforts by environmental groups is not. John Muir, Gifford Pinchot, and the other early conservationists were skilled politicians who knew how to marshal public opinion through the press, how to stimulate massive letter writing campaigns, and which arms to twist in Congress.

Their organizations did not have to satisfy Internal Revenue Service requirements for a tax-exempt status, however. When the IRS cracked down on the Sierra Club and removed its 501 (c) (3) tax status in 1966, many environmental groups established parallel tax-exempt foundations and joined other public interest groups in pushing for congressional action to loosen what they viewed as unfair restrictions on their legislative lobbying activity. This effort met with success in the passage of the Tax Reform Act of 1976. The act set new, specific ground rules by which groups can spend a portion of their funds on legislative lobbying while continuing to retain their (c) (3) tax-exempt status. As a result, several groups, such as the National Wildlife Federation (NWF) and the Environmental Defense Fund (EDF), have now hired their first full-time lobbyists, and those (c) (3) groups who already had active legislative programs are now breathing easier.

The Washington offices of the national groups also monitor the administrative branch of the government to ensure that environmental consequences of governmental actions are taken into account, as the National Environmental Policy Act requires, and that the vital but relatively low visibility processes of regulation, promulgation, and enforcement create the largest possible supply of environmental goods. This form of lobbying is becoming of ever-increasing importance to the groups now that the major body of environmental laws has been passed and the formidable task of implementing those laws drags on.

Late in the 1960s environmental law evolved as a potent instrument for environmental protection and a new institutional form evolved, the environmental law firm. The development of these firms was greatly facilitated by a crucial IRS ruling in 1970, which granted them tax-exempt status, and by timely and generous Ford Foundation funding. Another tactic, the direct purchase of ecologically significant land threatened by development, also reached fruition in the 1960s with the Nature Conservancy as its principal practitioner.

Until the 1960s, most of the national membership groups were quite small. Aggressive and increasingly sophisticated use of direct mail was coupled with an upgrading of many of the groups' periodicals so as to take advantage of the rising tide of interest in the environment, with the result that all through the 1960s and early 1970s the national groups' membership base expanded rapidly. For example, in 1908, the Sierra Club members were almost all on the West Coast. By 1960 this hearty band had increased to 15,000, with the vast majority still located on the Coast. The 1970 count was 107,000 and by 1977 it approached 180,000, with membership now spread across the country. Figure 2 shows the membership growth for ten of the national groups since 1960. For several of the groups, key foundation grants underwrote their membership recruitment efforts. In recent years, many of the groups have developed ways to involve their members more directly in environmental efforts through the use of field representatives, "hot lines," and through local chapters and groups.

The increase in activity and enlarged concerns of the environmental groups were greatly facilitated by the public awareness of environmental problems which culminated in the Earth Day extravaganza. Several new national membership groups were founded during this time: the two environmental law "firms," the Environmental Defense Fund (1967) and the Natural Resources Defense Council (1970); and three other organizations, Zero Population Growth (1968), Friends of the Earth (founded by David Brower, the former executive director of the Sierra Club, in 1969), and Environmental Action (1970), which was a direct outgrowth of the Earth Day movement. The most recent new group is New Directions, founded in 1976, with a partial emphasis on international environmental problems.

It is very difficult to present an accurate estimate of the number of Americans who support environmental lobbies today because complete data from the regional, state, and local levels are lacking. Taking just the organizations listed in table 6, a minimum figure of 1,000,000 adults may be estimated, once overlapping memberships have been taken into

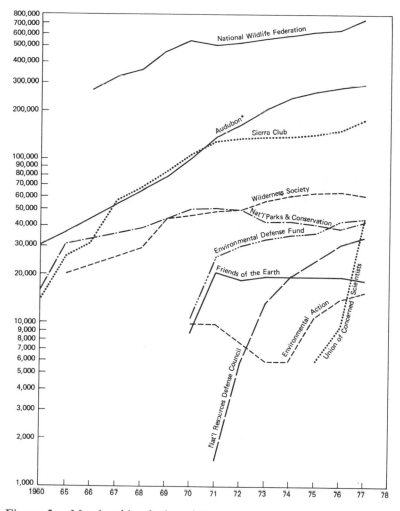

Figure 2.   Membership of selected U.S. national environmental groups, 1960–77 (on logarithmic scale). * Data are for memberships where family memberships count as one person.

account. Over a period of 22 months in 1974–75, the Federal Energy Administration commissioned a series of national telephone surveys of the general public. According to these surveys, which included a question asking the respondents whether they belonged to "environmental organizations such as the Sierra Club, Friends of the Earth and the National Audubon Society," 3.7 percent of adult Americans claimed to belong.[13] This gives an upper limit of 5 million *adult* Americans who contribute to environmental lobbies of one kind or another in the United States.

III. TOWARD A REVISED PARADIGM

The preceding section has shown that environmental organizations lobby to acquire diverse environmental public goods and that they have been successful in obtaining over a million contributors from the latent groups who stand to benefit from these goods. Somehow, despite the free rider and inconsequentiality problems, a substantial number of people whom Mancur Olson apparently relegated to the "forgotten groups" believe that the benefits of contributing outweigh the costs. In what follows I argue, contra Olson, both that public collective goods (or, especially, collective bads) are a major motivating force and that the contributors' actions are compatible with the public choice view of humans as egoistic, rational, utility maximizers. By modifying some of Olson's assumptions and by introducing some new variables into his model, I believe that the behavior of these individuals can be explained without recourse to private goods as the sole explanation, to a residual class of "irrational" behavior, or to a definition of selective incentives so general that the result is a tautology (see Barry's critique of Olson, 1970, pp. 33–37).

It is necessary to restrict the task at hand somewhat. First I will only attempt to explain why people have contributed to *existing* environmental lobbies during the past ten years. Olson is quite correct that there are considerable start-up costs in founding new groups. A number of the present lobbies were founded prior to the period under consideration and thus had the advantage of recruiting members into an existing organization. Several others were founded during this period,

---

[13] This figure comes from my analysis of the total data set. The various reports produced by the Opinion Research Corporation, the contractor for the surveys, did not report the results of this question because they merged the environmental group members with another group to create a hybrid category which they labeled "environmental activists." This misleading category was produced by pooling those who said that they belong to environmental organizations with those who said they had written to their congressman on an environmental issue during the past year, despite the fact that there was no assurance that those who wrote were taking an environmental stand on the issue. Some 10.9 percent of the sample said that they had sent such a letter or telegram. When combined with those environmental group members who had not written a letter, this yielded 13.7 percent of the total sample of over 22,000 who were then called "environmental activists."

however. The organizing problem was apparently overcome through a combination of factors, including several important foundation grants that provided crucial "front" money, the activities of entrepreneurs in the sense described by Frolich, Oppenheimer, and Young (1971), and the heightened utility for environmental goods which characterized the late 1960s and early 1970s. Second, I will consider only monetary contributions to the lobbies. Contributions of time or in kind are excluded.

Let us begin by making a conceptual distinction between public goods and public bads. Public goods are entities such as clean water and air, which have a positive value for individuals and which, once created, are available to all persons in a society. Public bads are entities such as polluted air and water, which have a negative value for individuals and which, once created, are potentially available to everyone in society. These are, of course, the opposite of each other. The avoidance of a bad is a good and vice versa. Likewise, a high utility for clean air implies a high disutility for polluted air. Nevertheless, someone considering an appeal from a lobby that is striving to work for cleaner air may be motivated to contribute by a desire for this amenity *or* a fear that if he or she does not contribute, the level of pollutants will get worse or stay the same. Furthermore, as I will argue later in this paper, the latter may be a more powerful motivating force than the former. This introduces a new dimension into the calculus of lobby contribution: the potential costs of not belonging.

The costs of not belonging are a special property of public goods, as another political economist, Albert O. Hirschman, has pointed out in a different context (1970, p. 101). Not only can public goods be consumed by everyone, but there is no escape from consuming them when they take the form of police protection or improved air quality, unless one were to leave the community in which they are provided. Likewise, public bads such as increased crime or poor air quality have a "no exit" quality about them.[14]

Table 7 summarizes the elements in my revised paradigm. Two of the three major factors, costs of contribution and benefits of contribution, are elaborations of Olson's paradigm. To these have been added the new factor, the costs of not contributing. Each item in the paradigm

[14] I am indebted to Denton Morrison (Tillock and Morrison, 1979, p. 23) and William Gamson (1975, p. 60), who independently recognized that Hirschman's insightful analysis of the factors determining loyalty to groups was relevant for the problem under consideration here.

TABLE 7. Factors Influencing Monetary Contributions to Lobbies Which Seek Public Goods

I. Costs of Contribution
   A. Money
   B. Time
   C. Loss of social status and reputation

II. Benefits of Contribution	III. Costs of Not Contributing

A. Possible increase in a public good
  1. Utility of the public good for the individual[a]
  2. Amount of the public good the individual expects to receive personally[a]
  3. Perceived effectiveness of collective action to achieve the public good[a]
	A. Possible continuance of or increase in a public bad
	  1. Disutility of the public bad for the individual
	  2. Amount of the public bad the individual has received or expects to receive personally
	  3. Perceived effectiveness of individual contributions in preventing the bad[a]

B. Receipt of private goods
  Types of goods:
  1. Goods and services[a]
  2. Sociability[a]
  3. Social status
  4. Self-esteem[a]
	B. Receipt of private bads
	  Types of bads:
	  1. Loss of goods and services
	  2. Reduced social status
	  3. Guilt[a]

[a] These variables were measured by Tillock and Morrison in their study of ZPG (1979).

is discussed below with reference to its importance in motivating contributions to environmental lobbies. Drawing on qualitative evidence, including the groups' carefully pretested mail appeals, I argue that under certain conditions a utility for environmental goods will motivate member contributions and that these contributions are compatible with behavior of the egoistic, rational, utility-maximizing kind because the cost is low, the potential cost of not contributing is high and the individual has imperfect information about the effectiveness of his or her contribution in obtaining the good or preventing the bad.

Cost of Contribution

I have identified three costs involved in monetary contributions here which seem to be potentially the most important, although others can no doubt be imagined. The *money* cost is the value of the contribution itself and the expense of transmitting it to the recipient. *Time* in this context refers to the amount of effort which an individual might have to make in order to hand his or her money over to the group. This is not an inconsiderable addition to the marginal cost; consider the situation of a person who may be inclined to contribute to the Natural Resources Defense Council but who does not know its address. The cost of the loss of social status or reputation refers to the stigma which an individual might possibly suffer if it became known that he was a contributor or member of a lobby which was despised by people of importance to him.

While these costs are definitely a hurdle in the way of a potential contributor, there are several important techniques the environmental groups have at their disposal to reduce them. First, the organizations ask for relatively small amounts of money as a minimum contribution to qualify the person as a *bona fide* contributor to the group. The annual cost of membership in the groups under consideration here varies from the National Wildlife Federation's $7.50 to Friends of the Earth's and New Directions' 1978 dues of $25.00. The costs of these or more generous gifts are further reduced by the tax-exempt status enjoyed by all of these groups except the Sierra Club, Environmental Action, Friends of the Earth, and New Directions. A majority of the groups offer lower membership dues for less well off categories of potential members such as students, senior citizens, and "low income" people.

Second, the lobbies greatly reduce the potential costs of time and loss of status through their recourse to the social invention of direct mail. Direct mail involves a package, consisting most commonly of an appeal letter, a descriptive brochure, and a return mail envelope, that is sent directly to an individual prospect at his home address. The return mail envelope is already addressed to the group and is postage paid. The recipient's name and address label is usually affixed to this envelope. Accordingly, all the individual has to do to make a contribution is to write out a check, enclose the check in the envelope, and place the envelope in the mail. When renewal time comes around, the group will send a series of reminders requesting a renewal which also include the return envelope. With the exception of the Izaak Walton League, the Nature Conservancy, and the Sierra Club, each of the national environmental lobbies relies almost exclusively on direct mail to recruit and sustain their membership. The other groups have chapter structures through which they recruit the majority of their members, but it is interesting to note that each of these groups was actively developing major direct mail projects in 1977 to supplement their existing membership procedures.

The effect of direct mail in reducing the potential cost of time for the giver should be apparent. In situations where social status or reputation might be in jeopardy, direct mail also minimizes this cost. The privacy of one's mail, especially if directed to one's home, is considerable. The individual makes a truly private declaration of intent toward the group. Whether or not the individual chooses to publicly identify with the group becomes entirely optional.

Direct mail has its drawbacks, to be sure. Its use restricts the reach of the groups considerably, as only a small portion of the latent group are among the people who are on the direct mail prospect lists because they subscribe to certain types of magazines, purchase certain types of goods by mail or, most commonly, contribute to other public interest groups. People with lower income and educational levels are much less likely to be on such lists. Direct mail is also expensive. These days, most environmental groups will send more than a million pieces of direct mail to "cold" prospects. For mailings of this kind, a return rate of 2–3 percent is considered to be excellent. A rate much below 1 percent is usually uneconomical. Even with a good return rate, a mailing may not pay for itself in the first year, however. Often, it is only as the new members renew that a "profit" is achieved. Finally, there is evidence which suggests that direct mail has reached a saturation point in recent years. Some groups report that direct mail costs more and returns less these days than it used to.

Nevertheless, the fact is that direct mail works. Thus far it has converted enough free riders into easy riders to ensure substantial financial support for the national environmental lobbies over the past decade. The degree to which it works, however, depends upon its success in promoting the benefits of contributing and the costs of not contributing, to which I now turn.

Benefits of Contribution

Possible Increase in Public Good.   Small as the cost may be of contributing to an environmental lobby, the individual who elects to do so presumably expects to receive benefits that are worth more than the money forgone. One benefit of contributing to an environmental lobby would be an increase in one or more of the environmental public goods which the lobby seeks to obtain. The effectiveness of public goods as a motivating factor in this respect depends upon three independent but related aspects of the public goods for the individual.

UTILITY OF THE PUBLIC GOOD FOR THE INDIVIDUAL.   How much does the individual value the environmental goods that the lobby seeks to provide? Presumably the greater the utility of an environmental good for an individual, the more likely it is that that individual will contribute to ensure its provision, other things being equal.

In his analysis of latent groups, Olson seems to assume an invariance across individuals in this utility, but this is surely not the case. Across individuals the utility is likely to vary as a result of the individual's socialization and experience of the good (among other factors). The individual who was brought up to revere nature, who was taught by an imaginative nature-loving biology teacher, and who has traveled in wild areas, is more likely to have a high utility for wilderness than someone who has not. The utility for environmental goods also varies over time. Until recently, many people in the United States regarded tidal marshes as waste land. Today this view is held by a smaller proportion of the population than before, as a result of the educational efforts of ecologists and environmentalists who have portrayed tidal marshes as exceedingly productive and important ecosystems. Something of the same shift in perspective seems to have taken place at the turn of the century with respect to song birds and in the 1960s and 1970s regarding wild areas suitable for hiking and camping. Much of the educational activity of the environmental groups is directed toward increasing the utility which environmental goods have for individuals.

With the important exceptions of wilderness and wildlife, the environmental lobbies' carefully pretested direct mail appeals emphasize environmental bads far more than environmental goods, however. This suggests that only environmental goods with certain characteristics are sufficiently powerful as a motivating force to elicit contributions from potential supporters. Through the use of photography in the appeal brochures, the grandeur, wholeness, and peace of wilderness can be instantly conveyed to someone for whom it already has some value. The strong appeal of "furry animals" to recipients of direct mail is legendary among its practitioners. On the other hand, solar energy, clean air, and the marginal cost pricing of electricity are apparently less evocative than corporate stupidity and greed, the dangers of nuclear energy, and air pollution.

AMOUNT OF THE PUBLIC GOOD THE INDIVIDUAL EXPECTS TO RECEIVE PERSONALLY. Although public goods are available to everyone, in practice their consumption varies. Presumably individuals who expect to backpack in a wilderness area some time in the next few years will be more inclined, other things being equal, to contribute to the Wilderness

Society than people who do not have this expectation. Probably the only truly public aspect of wilderness preservation is the knowledge that it has occurred, although for many nonbackpackers, the existence of wilderness sites for hiking and camping will have an option value because even if they are not presently inclined toward those pursuits, they or their children may be so inclined in the future. This variable is independent of the preceding one. The Wilderness Society prides itself in having some members whose only experience of wilderness is vicarious, through pictures, who have no expectation of ever visiting a wilderness area, and yet who value the thought of the good so highly that they support the society's efforts to obtain more of it. Other people, such as loggers, may live near wilderness and thus "use" it while not valuing it as wilderness.

PERCEIVED EFFECTIVENESS OF COLLECTIVE ACTION TO ACHIEVE THE PUBLIC GOOD. If a cause has no apparent prospect of success, it is likely to be surrounded by an atmosphere more conducive to irrationality than rational choice. This would not appear to be the case with environmentalism. The development and success of environmental litigation as a weapon in the hands of environmentalists has made an especially important contribution to the environmental movement's perceived efficacy. In the past decade the environmental lobbies have achieved some substantial, highly visible victories in the courts,[15] in congress, and in the legislatures of many states. Furthermore, environmental goods are so varied and the arenas so numerous that each group has little trouble developing a repertoire of claimed successes to display in its literature. Finally, most of the groups have celebrities and experts who are willing to lend their

---

[15] Rabin (1976), in a general article on public interest law, maintains that environmental litigation groups "invariably" suffer from low visibility. While it is certainly true, as he argues, that major victories may require years of complex litigation, much important work behind the scenes, and may even appear to the unknowledgeable layperson as a defeat, sufficient well-publicized victories have in fact occurred to validate my generalization. Representative cases in which the Environmental Defense Fund has obtained at least a temporary favorable action either in court or by a governmental agency and which were well publicized include the various DDT cases, the tuna-porpoise issue, the banning of the use of Tris in infant's sleepwear, and the fights against Mirex. Similar representative cases for the Natural Resources Defense Council include: a series of suits concerning implementation of the Clean Air Act, the effort to get the breeder reactor program included under the National Environmental Policy Act, the Monongahela clear-cutting case, and suits against EPA to get it to implement a program to clean up toxic water pollutants and to list lead as a pollutant under the Clean Air Act. These litigation groups take great care to publicize these victories to their membership. The success enjoyed by NRDC and EDF thus far in building a membership suggests that Rabin is too pessimistic when he declares that "the prospect of generating membership support for reform activity based on the law office model is problematic at best" (1976, p. 258).

name to the group to help it establish the legitimacy of its claimed successes. Here again, however, overcoming environmental bads rather than obtaining environmental goods tends to dominate the appeal letters.

Receipt of Private Goods.   Olson's by-product theory holds that selective or private goods are a necessary and may be a sufficient reason for individual contributions to groups. It will be argued here that although environmental lobbies do offer their members private goods of one kind or another, overall these private goods account for a relatively minor part of people's motivation to contribute. Their main role seems to be one of reinforcing or supplementing the public goods incentive.

Four types of private goods are listed in table 7. Two of them are goods conveyed by the group directly to the individual: goods and services and sociability. Sociability[16] is a good which is potentially available to the ordinary member only in those groups which have local chapters: the Sierra Club, the Izaak Walton League, the National Audubon Society, and the Nature Conservancy. The precise extent to which sociability acts as an incentive in these groups for the ordinary members is an empirical question for which data are currently unavailable. We do know that: (a) a large number of the environmental lobbies have no chapters and therefore provide very little or no opportunity for the ordinary member to meet his fellow members and (b) a sizable proportion (c. 40 percent) of the membership of two of those groups that do have chapters (Sierra Club and Audubon) never partake in chapter activities, but relate to the group solely through the mail.

Goods and services, on the other hand, are commonly offered by environmental lobbies as private goods to their members. As their prominence appears to lend important support to Olson's basic argument, their role requires analysis. Table 8 summarizes the major[17] private goods

[16] Sociability is an especially relevant private good for the voluntary workers and leaders of these groups as Olson, among others, has pointed out. A profile of David Foreman, the Wilderness Society's southeastern representative in the *Wilderness Report,* reports on his basic theories of organization, one of which "is to make the wilderness movement not just a cause but a gathering of friends who enjoy doing things together. 'You can't meet a finer bunch of people than wilderness activists, which is a real high point of this job' Dave says" (Wilderness Society, 1977, p. 4).

[17] Various minor benefits are offered to their members by the groups. These include free decals (Audubon, Cousteau, NPCA, NWF), membership cards (Audubon, Cousteau, Environmental Action, NPCA, NWF, the Sierra Club), the opportunity to buy special merchandise (Audubon, NWF) and discounts on books (Audubon, Cousteau, FOE, NWF, the Sierra Club). All of these minor benefits are directly related to either the public environmental goods which the group seeks to obtain or to the individual's identification with the group. In 1977, however, NWF offered prospective members the chance to participate in a "World of Nature Sweep-

TABLE 8. Cost and Major Private Goods Incentives for Joining National Environmental Lobbies

| | Dues-1978[a] | Magazine | | Outings |
		Pictorial and/or editorial quality	Frequency per year	
National Wildlife Federation	$7.50	Very attractive	Bimonthly	Few
National Audubon Society	$15.00	Very attractive and very informative	Monthly	None
Sierra Club	$20.00	Attractive, informative	Ten times a year	Many
Cousteau Society	$15.00	Somewhat informative	Quarterly	None
The Wilderness Society	$15.00	Attractive, informative (magazine) Informative (newsletter)	Quarterly Ten times a year	None
Izaak Walton League	$15.00	Attractive (magazine) Informative (newsletter)	Bimonthly Bimonthly	None
Environmental Defense Fund	$15.00	Somewhat informative	Bimonthly	None
Union of Concerned Scientists	$15.00	Somewhat informative	Unspecified	None
National Parks & Conservation Association	$15.00	Attractive, informative	Monthly	None
Defenders of Wildlife	$15.00	Attractive, informative	Bimonthly	None
Natural Resources Defense Council	$15.00	Informative	Bimonthly	None
Friends of the Earth	$25.00	Informative	Bimonthly	Few
Environmental Action	$15.00	Informative	Biweekly	None

[a] For regular individual membership.

supplied to members of 14 national environmental organizations. Each has a periodical (which I will call a magazine for convenience here,

stakes" complete with 1,226 prizes and featuring a Himalaya Nature Tour as the grand prize. More recently (June 1978), the National Audubon Society offered its members the opportunity to join a group insurance plan as a new membership service. These rather strictly personal benefits may or may not be the forerunners of a new trend. According to the Audubon Society's letter, "the Society and the wildlife it protects will also benefit from the modest service charge included in the plan," so an attempt is made to link even this benefit with environmental public goods. Nevertheless, Fischer (1976), citing Titmuss (1971) and Notz (1975) in her discussion of rationality and altruistic behavior, suggests that the provision of extrinsic rewards may well reduce psychic payoffs by reducing intrinsic motivation. If true, the gains made by the groups who employ these benefits may be at the expense of reducing their members' commitment to the group and the cause they promote.

though the Friends of the Earth publish a tabloid and the EDF newsletter is just that) and some of them also provide opportunities for members to join guided outings of one kind or another. These outings are limited in size and usually involve backpacking to scenic areas.

Granted that private goods are provided to members, the real question is the degree of importance they play in motivating people to contribute to the environmental lobbies. A variety of considerations strongly suggests that while they may be the major motivating factor for some contributors and certainly play a secondary role for many others, their role is not compatible with Olson's by-product theory, which holds that private goods are the primary if not the sole reason for individuals to contribute to the organization. Among these considerations are the following:

Outings

- The Wilderness Society recently (1977) dropped its outings program. The original purpose of the program was to provide an opportunity for members to experience wilderness firsthand and thus to increase their use of wilderness. In recent years, they have had problems with some outfitters who did not show a proper regard for the areas they were using, they found that the program took up a lot of staff time that could be better applied to their education and lobbying programs, and the supply of private outfitters has increased sufficiently to meet the need for this type of program. The discontinuance of this private good has not affected member contributions in any significant way.
- The Sierra Club outings program was founded for the same purpose as the Wilderness Society's. Although the program is extensive, only 15 percent of a sample of the 1978 membership reported ever going on a club outing.

Magazines

- Some groups, such as the Environmental Defense Fund and the Cousteau Society, provide only a short, relatively uninformative newsletter as a private benefit. Obviously, such minimal private goods are a poor bargain if they are the only incentive motivating an individual's gift.
- If private goods were the primary motivation for membership contributions, the groups would feature these goods in their direct mail appeals. My analysis of the direct mail appeals for twelve of the national environmental groups shows that only one, the National Wildlife Federation, presents private goods as the primary membership

benefit.[18] Two others, Audubon and the National Parks and Conservation Association, place a great deal of emphasis upon their magazines in the color brochure which accompanies the appeal letter, but the primary emphasis of the appeal is on the public goods which the groups seek to protect and obtain. For the rest of the groups there is even less emphasis on the magazine (and other private benefits) in their appeals. Indeed, the direct mail packages of EDF, NRDC, FOE, and the Sierra Club (in a 1976 appeal) barely mention the magazine or other private goods at all.

- Despite the emphasis that the National Wildlife Federation places upon private goods in its mail solicitations and the relatively low price of those goods (the magazine is a good buy at the membership rate of $7.50 a year), only 26 percent of the NWF associate members in a 1973 survey spontaneously mentioned the magazine and/or other private goods when asked why they belong to the federation. On the other hand, 69 percent of the members cited one or the other aspect of the fight for environmental public goods as the reason for their membership.[19]

- As shown in table 9, between 17 and 49 percent of the members of five representative groups make extra contributions above the ordinary membership fee. With the exception of Friends of the Earth, no additional private benefit is offered to these donors although very large donors ($100 or more) may receive special treatment in the form of special letters of thanks, invitations to special events, and the like. Only a small proportion of the people who give extra contributions reach that level of generosity, however.

[18] The six-page color brochure which the federation used in 1977 and 1978 prominently displays the caption: "For just $7.50 a year, you will receive all 8 of these great benefits available only to NWF members." Among the eight are the membership card and decal, membership discounts on books and records, nature-oriented vacations, decorator wildlife art prints in the magazine, the wildlife camp for youngsters, the action ballot which gives an opportunity to speak one's mind on conservation issues, an advisory service on conservation and natural history, and *National Wildlife* magazine. Although the brochure does mention the environmental crisis and the support which membership in the federation provides for their lobbying efforts, the overall emphasis of this brochure is on the private goods.

[19] In 1973 NWF commissioned a telephone sample survey of its associate members (those who are recruited by direct mail and who receive the magazine) that included the question: "What are your reasons for belonging to the National Wildlife Federation?" I have coded the 481 responses (some of them multiple) given by the 434 respondents. Thirty-eight percent of the responses involved the respondents' utility for wildlife, wildlife protection, and the environment. A further 31 percent of the responses specifically mentioned the respondents' identification with the lobbying goals of the organization, or their desire to help with the goals, or their desire to belong so the organization would be a more effective lobbying force.

TABLE 9. Percent of Membership Making Higher than Basic Membership Contributions for Selected National Environmental Organizations, 1977

	%
Environmental Defense Fund	32
Friends of the Earth	15[a]
National Parks and Conservation Association	21
Natural Resources Defense Council	49
Sierra Club	2.4[b]
Wilderness Society	17

Note: These data were gathered by personal interviews with the membership directors of each of the groups.

Most environmental groups offer prospective members the opportunity to join at a certain minimum rate. They also offer the opportunity to voluntarily pay a greater amount of money at the time of joining. Usually this behavior is encouraged by labeling other membership categories such as "family," "supporter," "sustaining member," and specifying a higher rate for these categories. These data are the percent of the total membership who voluntarily pay more than the minimum membership fee. Record-keeping practices vary by group so these data are approximate.

[a] Unlike the other groups, FOE does offer special benefits in the form of free books to donors who give at the higher levels. The retail value of books is less than the additional gift.

[b] This figure is the percent of Sierra Club members who donated $50 or more to the club in addition to paying their membership dues. Data for lesser amounts were unavailable at the time of compiling this table.

• Each group has a proportion of its membership who actually reject the private goods. For example in 1977 about 1,000 members of Friends of the Earth and 4,500 Sierra Club members specifically requested that the magazine not be sent to them.

The role that private goods incentives play for environmental lobbies simply does not fit Olson's by-product theory. Indeed, we can turn Olson on his head and argue that the provision of private goods by the groups is a by-product of their lobbying function. All of the groups were originally and explicitly founded as lobbies, not as magazine publishers or wilderness outfitters. Moreover, their private goods are inextricably linked to their collective public goods. The magazines and outings serve to reinforce or to increase the members' utility for the environmental goods which the groups seek to obtain and to impress the member with the groups' accomplishments. The magazines convey information and keep the members up to date on environmental developments. Yet they do not offer the kind of strictly consumer information about products and places to go which commercial magazines such as *Backpacker* and *Wilderness Camping* provide. In many instances they also serve the organization's lobbying purposes by exhorting the members to write to decision makers about specific environmental issues. Such environmental information has a distinctly public quality to it, as Harriet Tillock and Denton Morrison argue on the basis of their suggestive pilot study of the membership of a related organization, Zero Population Growth. ZPG members greatly valued the information contained in the *ZPG National Reporter*. According to Tillock and Morrison:

> it is clear that (1) the information is *about* the public good, not separate from it, and (2) members often value the information because they are involved in the dissemination of population information as a meaningful, necessary, intermediate step toward the creating of zero population growth. . . . Thus, the information they receive is intrinsically valued as a private good and instrumentally valued as a means for creating the public good. ZPG members would be happy if all knew what they know, i.e., information is not *designed* as separate good, nor as a selective good (1979, p. 21, emphasis in the original).

The two remaining potential private goods, social status and self-esteem, may be acquired as an indirect consequence of association with a particular group. An individual may enhance his social status through association with a group whose reputation is high among those whom the individual wishes to impress. For those groups that have local chapters, an individual might gain the opportunity to associate with people whose social standing is high and thereby increase his own social status. The available evidence suggests that this type of private good is not an important motivating factor for the environmental lobbies' contributions. No doubt there are some circles where the display of a Sierra Club emblem on one's car window may confer some status and others where membership in the local Audubon Society may offer the chance to rub elbows with some of the "right" people. But none of the environmental groups are exclusive—*anybody* can join and participate in the local chapters if the group has them. My analysis of the direct mail appeals sent out by thirteen of the groups over the past three years found only one reference to this type of good. A National Audubon Society brochure mentioned that in the local chapter the member will "find outstanding citizens who share your interests and concerns."

The last of the private goods to be considered and one which raises the crucial issue of measurement is self-esteem. The individual, by contributing toward a good which he regards as "good" in the moral sense, may derive a personal sense of satisfaction and an enhanced sense of self-esteem from the act, quite apart from whether he expects to receive any of the public good. Denton Morrison calls this "reform utility." It involves the desire for goods that have the character of being legitimately expected for everyone, according to widely held societal values. They are deserved, not just wanted. Reform utility presses toward a change in society in a way that is right by some criterion of worth or value that lies outside the individual and his particular desires. Terry Moe makes a similar point when he discusses "purposive incentives" as private goods (Moe, 1977, pp. 19–20). He observes that "collective goods can actually generate their own selective incentives" (p. 20). By contributing toward efforts to protect wildlife or to increase mass transportation, the individual may feel better about himself because these goods are linked to certain values which he holds strongly. This heightened self-esteem is related to but distinct from the reduction of guilt which I will consider below in my discussion of environmental private bads.

Although my analysis of the work of the environmental lobbies and their membership recruitment efforts through direct mail leads me to hypothesize that self-esteem is much less a motivating factor than the desire to avoid environmental bads, the role of self-esteem must be taken into account empirically in any test of the model since it is a highly plausible alternative explanation for member contributions. This raises the issue of whether moral incentives such as this one can be measured. Olson explicitly denies this possibility and it is precisely on this ground that he eschews the application of his theory to philanthropic lobbies. He apparently believes that only economic and some social incentives (such as social status) are amenable to measurement and therefore capable of producing theoretical propositions which can be refuted (1971, p. 160). His grounds for this view are unnecessarily skeptical.

These grounds are briefly mentioned in another one of those important footnotes with which his book abounds: "it is not possible to get empirical proof of the motivation behind any person's action; it is not possible definitely to say whether a given individual acted for moral reasons or for other reasons in some particular case. A reliance on moral explanations could thus make the theory untestable" (1971, p. 61).

While definitely determining moral motivations is undeniably beyond the capability of contemporary social science, sufficient progress has been made in attitude measurement and survey research to suggest that Olson's skepticism is overdrawn. Without denying the difficulties involved—few people would directly admit to joining the Wilderness Society because it happened to enhance their social status, even if that was, in fact, their primary motivation and they were aware of it—there are approaches to the problem of measuring moral incentives which are reasonably valid and reliable, yet subtle enough to tap motivations which people might not admit to under direct questioning. Indeed, Denton Morrison and Harriet Tillock, among others, have produced some highly suggestive empirical evidence about why people contribute to lobbies, evidence which, in their case, involved the measurement of moral incentives.[20]

IV. COSTS OF NOT CONTRIBUTING

The individual who values environmental goods, but who fails to contribute to environmental lobbies, incurs a cost if the group fails to obtain these goods for lack of sufficient contributions. Olson nowhere considers the costs of not contributing in his calculations, yet they are vital because the available evidence suggests that they are the primary motivating force for many contributors to environmental lobbies and that their role as a motivating force is compatible with behavior of a rational, self-interested kind.

The primary cost of not contributing is the continued existence of environmental bads and, more important, the possible increase in environmental bads in the future. If one assumes a concave utility function, as shown in figure 3, the incremental disutility for an individual positioned at the status quo at point A is greater per lost unit of environmental quality than the incremental utility per unit of gained quality. This function is based on the assumption that individuals are more sensitive to imagined losses from presently experienced conditions than to imagined gains.

Possible Continuance of or Increase in a Public Bad

Disutility of the Public Bad for the Individual. In considering the disutility of a public bad,[21] we are dealing with the individual's fear or

[20] Denton Morrison has suggested one possible measure of a moral incentive in the form of an attitude which I paraphrase here: "Do you feel that you would have abandoned a good cause if you dropped your membership in organization X?" Another similar question was asked of his ZPG sample, "I would get a lot out of being a ZPG member even if ZPG doesn't accomplish its goals" (evaluated by the respondents in terms of whether it was the most or least important reason for joining ZPG and whether the individual in general agreed with the statement or not). No one chose it as the most or least important reason. Forty-nine percent agreed that it was an incentive for them which ranked it eleventh out of fifteen possible incentives in importance (Tillock and Morrison, 1979, Table II). See also Moe (1977, pp. 29–31).

[21] One alternative to the use of the word "bad" is "evil." This is Hirschman's choice. I prefer "bad" because it is a more precise opposite of the sense in which "good" is used here. Neither good nor bad is meant here to have a moral connotation. The opposites good and evil necessarily have precisely that connotation.

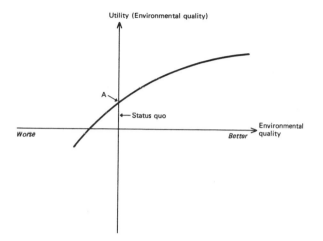

Figure 3. A hypothetical utility function for "environmental quality."

distaste about litter, polluted air, the extinction of endangered species, the flooding of a valued river valley, the clear-cutting of a scenic wild area, the potential for a nuclear catastrophe, and the like. This rehearsal of some of the available environmental bads should suggest the emotive power they hold for some individuals. Insofar as the individual finds these bads abhorrent, they have a disutility for him. The greater the disutility the more likely it is, other things being equal, the individual will contribute to lobbies which seek to decrease these bads or to prevent their increase.

Judging from the content of the environmental lobbies' direct mail appeals, the threat of the continuance of environmental bads or their possible increase appears to be more powerful as an incentive to contribute than the possibility of an increase in environmental goods (with the exception of wilderness). According to the National Parks and Conservation Association, *"our National Parks are in danger"* (emphasis in the original); Jacques Cousteau evokes the dread possibility that the oceans might "die"; the National Audubon Society warns against "sacrificing" our land, water, and air to appease the "furies of inflation"; the Environmental Defense Fund raises the "threat from poisoned air, water and food"; the Natural Resources Defense Council offers itself as an "inspired and effective approach to preserve a liveable world"; the Friends of the Earth remind us that "continue to pollute the air in our major cities and there will soon be no such thing as fresh air for us to breathe"; and the National Wildlife Federation seeks to meet "the crisis [of] the continued survival of man and wildlife on this fragile planet." The clear message of these appeals is that we are in serious danger and that if we don't do something about it soon things will get worse. Human "survival" is said to be at stake.

The impact of the environmental lobbies' appeals is heightened by the fact that environmental bads possess certain characteristics which give them an especially high disutility for some individuals. Among these characteristics are visibility, irreversibility, potential catastrophic consequences, and immorality.[22] Clear-cutting and smog are highly visible, especially when environmentalists take aerial pictures of them. The loss of the Grand Canyon as a river bed and the reduction of the ozone layer would be, for all intents and purposes, irreversible. Much of the disutility of atomic power for its opponents comes from the irreversibility of the waste management problem and a fear of the potential catastrophic consequence of a melt-down. One characteristic of many environmental bads is that they appear to involve a public good (clean air, natural forests, wetlands) which is threatened by degradation for private purposes. According to an Environmental Action appeal letter: "When the government told U.S. Steel to stop fouling the water in Ohio, the company in effect said, 'Try to stop us'." It is in this sense that many environmental bads may be viewed as immoral.

Perhaps the most important factor which makes the disutility of environmental bads such an important motivating force for contributions to environmental lobbies is the fact that the bads have a very strong no-exit quality to them. Because of the pervasiveness of many environmental problems, the interlinkages between the components of ecosystems, and the global effects of many pollutants such as CO_2, it is hard to escape their effects and likely to become increasingly difficult to do so. If this is the case, then an important consequence of not contributing to the environmental lobbies would be the possibility of having these bads continue at their present rate or even higher levels. Not surprisingly, this consequence figures importantly in a number of the groups' appeals. Jacques Cousteau is especially explicit about the importance of the no-exit factor in a 1978 fund-raising letter: "I beg you not to dismiss this possibility [of the death of the oceans] as science fiction. The ocean can die, these horrors could happen. *And there would be no place to hide*" (emphasis added). More typically, the appeal letters touch on the no-exit

---

[22] For a similar list of traits, although for an opposite condition, see Jeremy Bentham's dimensions of pleasure in his *Principals of Morals and Legislation* (1789).

factor indirectly by emphasizing the seriousness, pervasiveness, and inter-connectedness of present environmental problems. For example, Environmental Action reminded potential contributors that "almost half of all our nation's streams and rivers are officially polluted." The implication is that if things are still this bad, they are likely to continue to be as bad or worse in the future in the absence of effective lobbying by Environmental Action.

The Amount of the Public Bad the Individual Expects to Receive Personally. If one assumes a connection between present experience and the expectation of future experience, it seems reasonable to suppose that the greater the experience of environmental bads for a given level of disutility for these bads, the greater the likelihood an individual will make a contribution to a lobby. Certainly at the local level, where specific environmental bads are being fought, such as a dam which would flood a free-flowing river or a highway which would destroy a neighborhood, impressionistic evidence suggests that those who are most affected are especially likely to become active in a protest group. A "save the river" group will be likely to have a high percentage of its membership from the group of people who actually use the river or who live alongside it. In this case the environmental good has *both* public and private aspects to it (White, 1976, p. 262). At the national level, however, where groups are working on a variety of issues, most of which are more generic in character, the fit between direct experience of the bad and contributing to its alleviation is looser. It is probably for this reason that only two of the twenty-five different direct mail appeals I have analyzed try to personalize the impact of environmental bads. A Wilderness Society brochure, under the subheading "The Loss Hurts!" speculates that "a huge clearcut obliterates your favorite hiking trail . . ." and an Environmental Defense Fund letter opens by pointing out that "you are being robbed of a precious inheritance." Otherwise the bads are portrayed as general threats to society, our land, our cities, the environment, our wildlife, and so on.

Perceived Effectiveness of Individual Contributions in Preventing the Bad. For a contribution to an environmental lobby to be consistent with an individual's rational self-interest, the lobby must be perceived as effective or potentially effective in obtaining the good or mitigating the bad, *and* the individual has to have reason to believe that his contribution makes a sufficient difference to be worth the cost. In a somewhat arbitrary manner I opted to consider the issue of the effectiveness of the lobbies in my discussion of the possible increase in public goods and to treat the related issue of the significance of individual contributions here. Obviously *both* are important to either obtaining public goods or mitigating public bads. The argument that I made earlier about why environmental lobbies may be viewed as effective is especially applicable here since, as I noted at the time, in their direct mail appeals the lobbies themselves emphasize their achievements in preventing bads far more than they do in obtaining goods.

The question of whether individual contributions may be reasonably viewed as making a difference, the inconsequentiality problem, is the other major property of large groups which Olson identifies as making individual contributions toward public goods irrational in the absence of private benefits. Wouldn't any but the largest contributions have an "imperceptible" effect in helping a lobby achieve its goal? A contribution of $15, $50, or even $1,000 is obviously but a small fraction of the Environmental Defense Fund's two million dollar budget. Even if he had a high disutility for environmental bads, why would someone contribute $15 to this lobby when the contribution would hardly make a difference and its absence would go unnoticed?

Viewed strictly in terms of a model such as Olson's, which considers only the costs and benefits of contributing, it is hard to see how a rational individual would feel that his contribution would be worthwhile under these conditions. However, the perception that he may experience a public bad that he cannot escape from if he doesn't contribute may well lead to a decision to act on the basis of the minimax regret strategy under conditions of uncertainty which Ferejohn and Fiorina (1974) have shown to be a rational explanation of why people choose to vote. To paraphrase Ferejohn and Fiorina: If asked why he contributed to an environmental lobby, an individual might reply: "My God, what if I didn't contribute and for lack of my contribution the group was unable to prevent the emasculation of the Clean Air Act, get the Alaska Bill passed in Congress, or prevent the occurrence of another PBB disaster like the one that occurred in Michigan?" In short, he might feel that it is worth the gamble that his contribution will make a difference.

Something very close to the above logic was recently articulated by a member of the Environmental Defense Fund. Apparently the questionnaire which I had sent him as part of my study of the environmental movement had caused him to reflect on just why he, as a low-income person who is skeptical that his efforts will make any difference, bothered to contribute to EDF. In an unsolicited comment scrawled on the back of the questionnaire he wrote:

> I support participation efforts because, though the probability of real or lasting success seems small to me, (a) I may be wrong, and (b) it's about the best thing that can be done under the present circumstances . . . and of course unforeseen dramatic changes *might* make participatory programs much more likely of success, especially those programs, like yours, (EDF's) that are already operative and effective to some degree (emphasis in the original).

Interestingly, my direct mail letters yielded no examples of a direct, unabashed, minimax regret appeal, although they provide plenty of raw material for such a decision in their description of environmental bads. What they do do, however, is to emphasize the fact that large numbers of people *have* contributed. Although this strategy may encourage some potential contributors to take a free ride, the emphasis on size has two positive features which presumably outweigh this effect.[23] (1) It demonstrates that the group is no fly-by-night operation but already possesses such authority as being able to speak for x number of members can provide and (2) it may indirectly encourage minimax regret decisions by showing the prospective contributor that many other people have made the same decision. This appears to be the point which the Environmental Defense Fund is trying to make in the penultimate paragraph of a five-page direct mail appeal letter:

> The support you can give to EDF through your membership is invaluable. Without people like you willing to lend a hand, there would be no EDF. If you share the goals EDF is working to achieve, I urge you to take your rightful place, along with 40,000 other concerned Americans, as a member. Please join today.

Receipt of Private Bads

In the same way that private goods may motivate contributors to environmental lobbies, so may private bads. Of the three that I discuss here only one, guilt, is a likely candidate for explaining a significant proportion of the motives behind the contributions to environmental lobbies.

Loss of Goods and Services. The mitigation of some environmental public bads, such as a proposed superhighway that would increase

---

[23] Ed. note: For a discussion of the "matching" motivation, see Guttman (1978).

the air pollution in a crowded residential area, may also involve the mitigation of a private bad for some people, as in the case of an individual whose house will be condemned by the state to make way for the highway. Insofar as such an individual protests the highway because his house will be torn down, his motivation is obviously based on the fear that if he does not protest he will suffer a private bad. White (1976, p. 262) argues that these kinds of private benefits are powerful motivating forces, and indeed they are. At the national level for the environmental lobbies, however, the probability of a direct connection between their activities and private bads of this kind is very remote. The situation may be quite different at the local level where this factor may or may not be of considerable importance.

Reduced Social Status.   As noted earlier, joining a group may enhance an individual's status. Not joining a group naturally means forgoing that possibility, but it may involve more than this. Conceivably one might be thought less of by one's friends who were ardent members of a particular group if one failed to join their group. This would obtain most commonly in small group situations, of course, and I have not seen any evidence that this private bad motivates contributions to the large national environmental lobbies. Nevertheless, it bears mention here because it may be applicable to other lobbies that seek public goods.

Guilt.   Prior to reading an appeal from an environmental lobby, an individual may already have felt a responsibility to contribute to increasing environmental goods and experienced remorse that he had not yet done so. Alternatively, the individual may have this feeling of remorse aroused by the stimulus presented by the lobby in its appeal. In either case, the individual experiences guilt which, because it is punishing to some people, constitutes a private bad for them. By making a contribution to an environmental group, the individual's guilt may be reduced (to a greater or lesser extent). One of the costs of not contributing to an environmental lobby for such individuals would be to continue to suffer from this private bad. Guilt is analytically distinct from the private good of self-esteem. To be sure, the individual who enjoys a reduction in guilt may also enjoy an enhanced self-esteem, but not necessarily. He may simply feel less remorseful without feeling particularly good about himself. Likewise, someone who enhances his self-esteem by contributing may very well have felt that he had already fulfilled his responsibility by other acts or contributions when confronted by mail from a particular group.

Protecting the environment and preserving wildlife and wilderness involve widely held values; participation in organizations to achieve societal values is highly regarded by society. As such, guilt is a plausible explanation for contributions that otherwise fly in the face of reason. It will be recalled that Olson relegates subjective private goods such as self-esteem to the trash heap of untestable and unneeded variables. My working assumption is that guilt, like self-esteem, can be measured, although with difficulty. I also hypothesize that guilt, like self-esteem, is much less a motivating factor than the desire to avoid environmental bads[24] and am currently engaged in research to see whether or not I am right about it.

Imperfect Information

Terry Moe has shown that small member contributions toward public goods become more understandable if Olson's implicit assumption of perfect knowledge on the part of the potential contributor is weakened (1977, p. 14).[25] He argues that it is unrealistically restrictive to assume that individuals have full knowledge of the marginal costs, marginal benefits, and the prevailing level of supply of the relevant public good (or bad) when they contemplate a contribution. If potential members underestimate the marginal cost and/or overestimate the benefits, they "may find it quite rational to make a contribution" (1977, p. 14).

[24] The national environmental lobbies do not attempt to arouse guilt in their direct mail. The one exception is a 1977 appeal letter from David Brower, the president of Friends of the Earth, which opens with a discussion of responsibility. After noting that there are those who are eager to shirk their responsibilities for the quality of their lives and environment, he then writes that "this letter is being sent to you in the hope that you are someone who faces your responsibilities. . . ." The relative lack of guilt-inducing material in the lobbies' direct mail appeals does not necessarily prove or disprove the absence of guilt as a motivating factor, of course. Guilt is a painful feeling which people try to avoid and the direct elicitation of it might well lead to an emotional rejection of the lobby's request for a contribution. Moreover, a more subtle approach may suffice to raise guilt feelings since the potential givers have already been identified through the process of list selection as concerned and involved citizens who value environmental goods.

[25] Moe (1977) has developed a revised theory of interest groups that modifies Olson's original model through relaxing certain of his original assumptions. Moe's work covers a much broader range of topics than the present discussion, which is restricted to group maintenance and within that to the subtopic of inducing potential and present individual small members to make contributions. In his analysis of the factors that promote group maintenance, he argues that the continuing "provision of an appropriate *mix* of political and nonpolitical incentives" is necessary. His use of "political" here refers to the group's lobbying goals of obtaining more of a collective good and is equivalent to what I call the incentive of a possible increase in a public good. He does not consider the costs of not contributing in his theory.

To say that misperceptions of this kind may lead to contributions is to say something that is almost true by definition. Since individuals differ in their perceptions of reality, we could simply account for the actions of contributors by claiming that they overestimated the benefits that would ensue or that they underestimated their costs. To avoid this trap, we have to show that the misperceptions are not arbitrary or random, but are the result of structural conditions in society or factors that are subject to control by the environmental lobbies.

It is difficult to see how imperfect information about the costs of contributing to an environmental lobby might affect individuals' decisions about whether or not to contribute. Conceivably the after-tax cost of a gift might be underestimated if an individual miscalculated his tax rate, but from my knowledge of environmental groups, this occurrence is not likely to be widespread nor of any real overall consequence. The benefits of membership are another matter.

The groups' portrayal in their direct mail appeals of the seriousness of environmental problems and of their effectiveness in helping to solve these problems comprises a major informational source for most prospective members. Insofar as the environmental lobbies are viewed as credible sources of information, and public opinion surveys suggest that they enjoy a high level of credibility in this regard (*U.S. News and World Report,* 1978; Ebasco Services, 1976), their information has a reasonable chance of being taken seriously. Insofar as their claims are unchallenged in the media and in other sources of information available to the prospective member, the credibility of the lobbies' information is further enhanced. As implied by the "motherhood" label that was applied to environmental issues around 1970, there was virtually no public challenge to those who argued that environmental problems were very serious and would require immediate remedial action. In recent years, as more and more government programs for environmental protection have become implemented and as the economy has faltered, these matters increasingly have become the subject of debate. Nevertheless, the nature of environmental issues is such that the lobbies have thus far been able to maintain their credibility. Most environmental questions involve matters which are sufficiently complex and for which definitive data are unavailable so that there is no scientific consensus on the correct answer. Typically, the actors on *both* sides of the debate are scientists or experts with respectable credentials and what is at issue are matters of judgment, such as the degree of probability that a disaster will occur, the relative magnitude of a particular environmental hazard's effect on human health, or the extent to which the regulation of pollutants will fuel inflation or lead to a loss of jobs.

Under circumstances such as these, the environmental lobbies have an incentive to highlight (if not to exaggerate) the threat posed by environmental bads and/or the desirability of the collective goods they seek to obtain and their organizational effectiveness in preventing the bads or obtaining the goods. Given the lobbies' important role in providing information and the inherent uncertainty about the facts and consequences of many environmental issues, an assumption such as Olson's that prospective contributors have perfect information is highly unrealistic. The information available to most contributors will be biased toward a high estimate of the potential benefits of contributing and the potential costs of not contributing.

Conclusion

In the preceding analysis I have wrestled with what has come to be known as the Olson paradox or problem—that individual contributions to the production of collective goods are problematic. I have argued that the free rider and inconsequentiality problems may be overcome by public goods lobbies without recourse to private goods as the prime or only motivating factor. I do not mean to suggest that private goods are without any motivating force at all, however. It is certainly no accident that the four largest environmental lobbies have attractive magazines nor that almost all of the lobbies provide their members with a publication of some kind. But these private goods supplement the public goods and bads incentives that have a powerful motivating force of their own. My conclusion is that Olson's denial of the motivating role of these goods and bads in his by-product theory is incorrect. In a situation where individuals have a high disutility for public bads that they are unable to escape, where they have imperfect information, and where the cost of contributing to a lobby is low, the act of contributing is consonant with a rational strategy of seeking to minimize the maximum regret.

Russell Hardin

Comments

The remarkable quality of Olson's (1971) logic of collective action is that, if the logic is right, there is often little need to gather data on individual members of an interest group to determine whether they will contribute to organizing the group and providing it with its collective good. In the case of groups whose members wish to be provided with very costly goods, it is unlikely that many members can expect net positive returns on their own contributions. Environmental groups are generally interested in such goods as the preservation of multimillion dollar stands of redwood and billion dollar programs of pollution control. By Olson's logic their plight seems hopeless. They can act collectively only if extremely large numbers of people each contribute a collectively significant but individually negligible sum to the cause.

Environmentalists nevertheless have formed vital political groups. Robert Mitchell therefore wishes to explain the interest group activity he details by expanding the economists' rational calculus to include various "noneconomic" but self-interested concerns such as guilt and self-esteem. The usual explanation for why some latent groups achieve political success does not resolve the problem that Mitchell addresses. It is generally agreed that political entrepreneurs (such as Muskie, Jackson, Nixon, and Carter in environmental politics) seize upon an issue that clearly has popular support, so that a large latent group of voters may be provided its collective good without organizing. Mitchell is concerned to explain why people in the vast, supposedly latent group of environmentalists contribute, against Olson's logic, to the political activity of a number of environmental organizations.

This paper benefited from comments by John Chamberlain, Stephen Elkin, Andrew McFarland, Denton Morrison, Mancur Olson, and Clifford Russell. The research that went into it was supported by Resources for the Future, the National Fellows Program of Stanford University's Hoover Institution, and the University of Maryland General Research Board.

As Mitchell notes, Olson discussed economic interest groups, that is, groups seeking wage increases, higher tariffs, exclusion of the "unqualified" from professional practice, and so on. Much of the beauty, and in this context the irony, of Olson's theory is that he hardly needed to glance at data to explain the successes and failures of these groups, whereas Olson's critics, such as Mitchell, must fairly wallow in data to prove their points. Olson of course is an economist; his critics are generally political scientists, sociologists, and psychologists. Fortunately, the latter all find it comfortable to wallow. Mitchell's present paper, however, is a preliminary effort, largely speculative and uncluttered with data. In what follows I will first compare contemporary environmental group activity with Olson's analysis of collective action—this discussion will be based on readily available data. Then I will review most of the items in Mitchell's expanded version of Olson's theory, suggesting varied interpretations of many of the data Mitchell proposes to collect and analyze. Finally, I will conclude with comments on what is to be explained.

OLSON'S LOGIC OF COLLECTIVE ACTION AND ENVIRONMENTAL POLITICS

According to Mitchell's analysis of the membership rolls, there are 1,000,000 people who belong to the groups listed in his table 6, each person belonging on average to two of the groups. Multiplying the membership figures of table 6 by the dues of the organizations in table 8 yields a total of about $15 million for the six organizations in table 8. How much did all the organizations spend on political activity? In fiscal 1977, the Sierra Club spent $1.9 million of the $4.5 million it received in dues and contributions (it received an additional $2.6 million in return for services and products [*Sierra,* May 1978, pp. 22–25]). It is plausible that at least 20 percent of all political expenditures by national environmental groups is from the Sierra Club. If so, these groups spend less than $10 million annually. This is an embarrassingly small figure. Mobil spends $1 million on its weekly op-ed page advertising campaign in seven newspapers (*New York Times,* 1978). The nation spent $15 billion on pollution abatement in 1976 (CEQ 1977, p. 328) plus additional sums on conservation and related causes. An environmental optimist might happily conclude that one dollar of politics buys $1,500 of abatement. A pessimist might ask why, with odds like that, the tens of millions of professed environmentalists don't contribute many more tens of millions of dollars to the cause. Olson could give the pessimist a compelling answer.

Counting only cash outlays, it is clear that environmentalists contribute very little to their cause except what they, as consumers, are coerced to spend for price increases mandated by government regulation and what they, as taxpayers, are coerced to contribute to the government transactions costs of this regulation and to the direct costs of conservation. One might unfairly and somewhat provocatively note that almost every theory that fits 1,499 out of 1,500 parts of a given reality can be found probably in physics or another natural science. Introducing several additional terms into Olson's "special" theory in order to make it general enough to explain a fraction of the remaining part of the environmental protection Americans receive is a modest enough enterprise, but even an economist could conscientiously give that one part in 1,500 over to extrarational motives such as ethical concerns (one ought not destroy millennial redwoods), outrage (Mobil has no right to dump its poisons into my sinuses), fair play (others are contributing—so should I), fundamental misunderstanding of Olson's logic (if I don't contribute, nobody will).

Presumably, such motivations as ethics, outrage, and fair play are clear enough, although it may be difficult to assess their importance. I will note below how they may fit the data which Mitchell proposes to collect. The problem of misunderstanding, however, merits a digression. At an inarticulate level most people may well comprehend Olson's logic (even though they might be struck by clear articulation of it). But there may be a part of the population who, when the logic is made explicit in a particular instance, do not comprehend it at a conscious level. For example, when I discussed Olson's theory in an undergraduate class at the University of Maryland, a clear majority of the students thought I was crazy. Speaking of labor union organizing, they insisted against logic that if you don't join, the union will fail. What I thought was merely a Kantian ethic they seemed to think was a causal relation. After half an hour they were not persuaded of Olson's logic, but in a sense I began to be persuaded of theirs. Perhaps these people nevertheless understood Olson's logic at a subconscious level and therefore can be trusted not to contribute heavily to environmental and other public interest groups except in those unlucky moments when they are directly asked to contribute "in their own interest" to good causes. Under such pressure, the illogic of their conscious reasoning might then lead them, as in class they forcefully argued, to contribute. Such people taken together may meet enough unlucky moments to contribute a considerable part of the woefully slight environmentalists' political budget.

MITCHELL'S MODIFIED THEORY OF COLLECTIVE ACTION

Mitchell's modified theory of collective action is a rational calculus which leads to predictions or, at least, explanations of behavior by those concerned with the environment. One million people belong to his long list of organizations. Several million other environmentalists do not. Suppose there are many million who would be willing to vote a tax to pay for a substantial degree of environmental protection. The cost of the tax they would be willing to vote would be a crude measure of the value they placed on environmental protection. Why do they not simply contribute some amount less than this tax to environmental group politics? Because, Olson argues, the benefit from the collective good to any of them from his or her own contribution must be negligible—even a lavish contributor is unlikely to notice the effect on environmental quality from his or her contribution. Of course, all these people must benefit from the publicness of any successful political action by other environmentalists.

How then can we conclude that environmental activism is rational in the narrowly self-interested sense? Mitchell's table of "benefits of contribution" and "costs of not contributing" includes five measures of the utility of the collective good to the individual and one measure of the individual's effect on providing the good. Though the first five must be substantial for many American environmentalists, the last must be negligible (except in small cases such as when one person works successfully to protect a butterfly habitat or to expand a park area). Hence, the first five items should have no effect on a strictly rational calculus of whether to contribute except insofar as they correlate with receipt of private goods from joining an environmental group.

Suppose Mitchell collected data on all these items and found that they had an effect on propensity to give to environmental causes independently of private goods and bads associated with membership and nonmembership (as presumably he expects to find). Such a result might only be a spurious correlation, that is, might only imply that the calculus is missing *principles of private concern*. For example, a Kantian acting under the categorical imperative would contribute to the cause only if he rated the "perceived effectiveness of collective action to achieve the public good" as positive. A contractarian, one who plays fair, would contribute only if he rated the "utility of the public good for the individual" as positive and expected others to be playing fair as well. One is likely to be outraged only if one rates the "disutility of the public bad for the individual" as high. Because of slow-wittedness or strong socialization, some people might overrate the "perceived importance of individual contributions in preventing the bad" or in providing the good. This item may therefore be a good surrogate for measuring the extent of failure to understand Olson's logic. In sum, the items Mitchell lists as "public good" benefits of contributing and "public bad" costs of not contributing have no role to play in the typical environmentalist's rational calculus of whether to contribute, but they may well be spuriously correlated with extrarational motives for contributing.

Let us turn to Mitchell's "private goods" and "private bads" incentives for contributing to environmental group efforts. Consider one of the most important of Mitchell's groups: the Sierra Club. Sierra Club political activity is probably *not* a by-product of other club functions, except in the important sense that without the other functions the club might not exist and thereby be available as a political force. One cannot easily separate the costs of Sierra Club political activity from other expenses as reported in annual financial reports. But it appears that if there were no voluntary contributions above membership dues, there would be little or no money available for direct political activity such as lobbying and legal actions (*Sierra,* May 1978, pp. 22–25, and *Sierra Club Bulletin* for earlier years). This is despite the fact that a large percentage of the members (40 percent in a 1971 survey [Coombs 1972]) report that they joined solely to "show general support of club's conservation activities" and not to participate in club activities. Hence, it seems likely that the Sierra Club receives all its funds for political activity from contributions motivated by political convictions, while active club members' dues at most barely cover the costs of their private benefits, with no residual for the collective good of political action. Among the half dozen private goods and bads in Mitchell's table 7 that might motivate contributions to the Sierra Club, "goods and services" therefore do not create a surplus for collective action.

Mitchell's three sociability and status items also may have little effect on the collective good since they come already from active membership and may not be enhanced greatly by voluntary contributions beyond dues. (Also, there is not likely to be much status or sociability given to those who contribute dues but who do not wish to be active in the organization.) These sociability items may nevertheless correlate with propensity to contribute sums beyond dues. But it will be difficult to infer causal direction. Those who enjoy the social and status effects of club membership may expose themselves to moral exhortation or consciousness-raising which changes their values enough for them to want to volunteer more support to the club. This may be because pressures and contributions are a matter of public record among the members (as some churches and temples post the amounts contributed by their members), so that the extra contributions are indeed buying status and sociability. But it may be strictly voluntary action unrewarded by enhanced or maintained status. In this case, contributions to the group's collective good may be a by-product of club activities, but the by-product is not rational action in the narrowly self-interested sense of Olson and Mitchell. Hence, again the sociability and status items may in large part be surrogate measures for extrarational motives for action.

We are left with "self-esteem" and "guilt," which may be the self-interest correlates, in psychological well-being, of morally motivated action. Perhaps it is partly a matter of taste whether one ascribes moral action to an ethical code or to self-interest due to a sense of self-esteem from adhering or guilt from violating that code. But I think there is much more to ethical behavior than merely the avoidance of embarrassment or feelings of guilt. The past decade's fiction is littered with countless characters who feel guilt for having been born or having survived, but graced with few who are pushed by guilt into doing good as perhaps Lord Jim was. In fairness, some of us who live outside fiction bear heavy burdens of guilt for not paying our share to environmental interest groups, public television, and the Metropolitan Opera. (Some of us, including, I presume, almost all economists, bear no such burdens.) I have a colleague who suffers a great lot of guilt, both generalized and specific, who claims that whenever he receives a request for contributions from certain kinds of organizations, he simply writes a check for the requested standard amount and sends it off. No doubt he would be grateful if his name were added to several dozen more mailing lists. Until everyone of his ilk makes every relevant mailing list, however, I would bet that more contributions to environmental interest groups are motivated by unencumbered moral choice and fair play than by guilt—but I am willing to stand corrected by relevant sociological surveys.

Of course, to say that many people may be motivated by extrarational concerns does not mean they are utterly irrational. An ethical concern for the environment would not lead one to burn money in a clean manner, but rather to contribute it to an effective organization such as one of those in Mitchell's table 6. The devices for reducing the costs of contributing which Mitchell discusses may therefore have substantial effects on extrarationally motivated contributions.

CONCLUSION

Where does this pessimistic account leave us? It says that Olson's logic of collective action fits the behavior of the vast (latent) group of environmentalists very well. One might object that environmentalists have had enormous impact on American public policy—again, upwards of $15 billion is spent annually on pollution abatement alone. But this objection does not mean that Olson's logic is wrong or that his theory leaves out significant items of self-interested group action. It means only that a narrowly conceived group theory of politics is wrong. A mere $10 million in environmental politics accomplishes very much, both because it serves notice to political entrepreneurs that there is an interest to be represented and because a couple of million dollars well placed can buy reasonably effective regulatory agency oversight and a remarkable lot of precedent-setting litigation. In a narrowly conceived group theory in which group political success depended on the balance of group and countergroup resources, the contemporary environmental groups would be almost as marginal in effect as they are in Olson's analysis of rational action by self-interested actors.

If, as seems to be true of the Sierra Club, the bulk of environmental group politics is based on extrarational, perhaps especially ethical, motivations, one might be discouraged to note nevertheless that ethics plays such a small role in public life. Adam Smith and his descendants might be less discouraged since an ethics in power could be a disagreeable ethics, and they might sooner have their government represent contrary interests than contrary ethics. As one's answer to Stone's (1974) double entendre, "Should trees have standing?," may be ethical rather than self-interested, so may one's answer to the question, "Should convicted felons be executed?" For the latter question, however, widely held ethical positions cut both ways. If a narrowly conceived group theory of politics, in which groups' members acted from ethical *as well as* rational positions, governed outcomes, American redwoods and felons might fall together. But the lumber industry is free to cut fewer redwoods than it would like, and the apparent majority of Americans are granted fewer executions than they would like for the simple reason that government policy is not the vector sum of group pressures.

Sociological studies, such as that which Mitchell proposes to do, as opposed to efforts by economists sitting comfortably at their desks inventing half their data, are probably the best way to assess the distribution of ethical (and other extrarational) motivations in a population, and are a good way to assess the impact of such motivations on behavior. The results of such studies are likely to be far murkier and less conclusive than Olson's analysis, with numerous attitudinal items to be correlated with behavior beyond even those of Mitchell's table 7. The result would of course be a more general explanation of group behavior than Olson offers in that it would take a larger range of motivations into account. But it would be far less general in the compelling sense that it could not so readily be applied to new situations by someone sitting at his desk exercising his mind to comprehend scattered, naturally occurring data. The kinds of questions one would be inclined to raise with the sociological class of explanations would commonly be historical: Why do people increasingly favor capital punishment? Why is abortion an issue now? Why do so many of our contemporaries care about whales and so few about the snail darter? These would relate as much to the generation of preferences as to actions based on preferences. The questions which appliers of Olson's theory are inclined to ask are surprisingly ahistorical. The generation of preferences is taken for granted and what is left is the sifting of data to weigh relative interests. The data set for a sociological study must be enormous and specific, while that for the Olsonian analyst may be modest and include largely common sense, even conjectural data about how much various goods may be worth to a typical individual. For the Olsonian, the appearance of a billionaire interested in funding environmental politics would be a random event not to be analyzed extensively. For the sociologist, it might be an interesting historical phenomenon to be considered at length. For either, the understanding of group activity or inactivity on an issue would be only a small part of the analysis of politics over that issue.

Denton E. Morrison

Uphill and Downhill Battles and Contributions to Collective Action

I do not have any very serious criticisms to make of Robert Mitchell's paper. I think the general direction he is going is the right one. I have gone in basically the same direction in some of my own research (Tillock and Morrison, 1979) and I think Mitchell adds nicely to a growing body of work that critically addresses Mancur Olson's theory and that attempts to develop an alternative to it. Because of the excellent data that Mitchell will eventually be able to bring to bear on the Olson theory and the alternatives to it, his work promises to be an exciting contribution. I can only urge him on!

One of the theoretical notions in the Mitchell paper strikes me as worth some further thinking, development, and subsequent empirical examination. This is the notion that goods and bads should probably not be considered as theoretical opposites, that is, they are not symmetrical. Hirschman (1970), of course, pointed this out some time ago, but it has never been adequately appreciated, developed, or examined.

It seems to me that Mitchell's work and other research in the social movements area might profit from a classification of public goods something like the following:

1. Public goods we have and which we do not want to lose, but which are perceived by some as threatened, that is, *threatened goods,* goods which may become bads. Many, if not most, environmental goods fall into this category, for example, wilderness, many bodies of air and water, the ozone layer.

2. Public goods which we have lost and which we want to recover, that is, *lost goods,* goods that have become bads. Many environmental goods are of this type, and it seems logical that the loss of these goods

lends credence and urgency to the threats to other goods, for example, some bodies of air and water, some wilderness, some land.

3. Public goods which we never have had, but which some now want, that is, *new goods*. Perhaps goods such as highway and mine safety qualify as examples in the environmental area; for many other social movements these goods are central, for example, equal opportunity, publicly financed abortions.

Collective actions for new goods and for lost goods represent "uphill" battles, and I submit that generating contributions for such battles, especially for new goods, is probably more difficult and uncertain than for "downhill" battles, that is, collective action to protect threatened goods. The goods we have we know *are,* in fact, good, that is, have utility. Besides, they have a much richer and more complex utility structure than can be the case for new goods. Our land, water, air, and wilderness are not just commodities or idle wishes. Their value is firmly tied to family, economic, religious, and community institutions in very complex, culturally integrated ways. New goods are inherently more uncertain. How do we know that we will like equal opportunity or abortion on demand? A logical and/or moral case can be made, but concrete experience is lacking.

I would also submit, as implied above, that most environmental goods are threatened goods while relatively few are new goods. This may help account for the fact that, among the social movements we have around us, the environmental movement has been, at least in my opinion, relatively more effective and relatively more viable than the others. As Mitchell points out, environmental losses that are threatened are often of an irreversible character. You save the redwoods or the Grand Canyon now or never.[1] Put this way, it is clear that the efficacy of contributions for many environmental collective actions is intrinsically higher now than it ever will be in the future, and probably higher compared with contributions to other causes for lost or new goods. And, as Hirschman

---

[1] Ed. note: This problem of irreversibility has been at the core of the recent research on natural areas done by John Krutilla and his colleagues. See Krutilla and Fisher (1975). In Morrison's context, an important and depressing irony is that it will always be "now" in the battle to save the Grand Canyon, a stand of redwoods, or part of Alaska. That is the other side (or the asymmetry) of the postponement decision: i.e., if we don't flood the Grand Canyon today we can always do it tomorrow if our needs and preferences change. Though there are various institutional barriers that can be raised to make future development harder (e.g., wilderness designation), there is no absolute barrier analogous to the irreversible development itself.

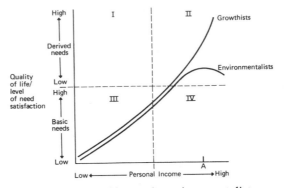

Figure 4. Growthist and environmentalist perspectives on the relationship of income and quality of life.

has pointed out, the losses that are threatened are inescapable ("no exit"); you cannot escape a society without the Grand Canyon and therefore you and your progeny *will* suffer this loss. This is different than with new goods, since, in fact, many people can and do by individual effort and talent achieve much of what equal opportunity would bring, even in the absence of equal opportunity. Consequently, incentives to contribute to collective action to create equal opportunity should logically be less than for many environmental goods, given (hypothetical) equal utility for both.

This, I would hypothesize, is one reason why contributions to collective action for environmental goods have been rather easily generated and sustained. I would also hypothesize that another important reason is that those who perceive threats to environmental goods are precisely those who (1) can easily afford contributions and (2) are less adversely affected than others by the concrete economic costs of preserving environmental goods. To explain this it is necessary to use a figure that somewhat oversimplifies things, but that describes the broad, fundamental difference in the viewpoint of environmentalists and their adversaries, the growthists. Figure 4, then, shows the differing perceptions of environmentalists and growthists on the relationship of income and quality of life. Environmentalists generally see marginal and then negative returns to quality of life beyond some point of economic growth. Empirically it is unequivocal that most environmentalists are found to the right of point A on figure 4. The main ways they differ demographically from growthists are (1) they have a higher level of education (providing the cognitive basis for their perception of environmental threats) and

(2) they are in situations where their economic security is not directly or immediately influenced by the costs of environmental reform (they are in the professions or training for them, especially in education, and in government). When we note that most of those who logically would give higher utility to new goods such as equal educational and job opportunity and higher wages are in quadrant III, it follows that (1) the environmental organizations will have an easier time generating contributions and (2) the environmentalists will tend to be in conflict with underdog movements while growthists will form coalitions with underdogs.

This, of course, helps give the environmentalists an "elitist" label both because of their composition and their ideology. It does *not* mean that they are wrong in their perception of threats to environmental goods. It does raise the question of whether there are inherent conflicts between the public goods and the group goods Mitchell distinguishes. Seemingly, the incentives for contributions to group goods would be inherently higher (at least according to Olson's logic). But, of course, many public environmental goods are, *de facto,* group goods, since they are used and/or appreciated almost exclusively by the environmentalists, for example, wild rivers. Thus, Mitchell's distinction, although theoretically important, must be interpreted in research in terms of what it means in practice, not just in terms of what is logically involved.

I hope this discussion has some implications that will help Mitchell improve his already excellent study and perhaps influence other research on social movements. Probably the more general implication is that research on social movements must be *comparative* between types of movements to be most fruitful.

REFERENCES

Barry, Brian M. 1970. *Sociologists, Economists and Democracy* (London, Collier-MacMillan).

Browne, William P. 1976. "Benefits and Membership: A Reappraisal of Interest Group Activity," *Western Political Quarterly* vol. 29, no. 2, pp. 258–273.

Coombs, Don. 1972. "The Club Looks at Itself," *Sierra Club Bulletin* (July/August) pp. 35–39.

Council on Environmental Quality. 1977. *Environmental Quality: The Eighth Annual Report of the Council on Environmental Quality* (Washington, D.C., GPO).

Dahrendorf, Ralf. 1959. *Class and Class Conflict in Industrial Society* (Stanford, Calif., Stanford University Press).

Ebasco Services. 1976. *A Second Survey of Public and Leadership Attitudes Toward Nuclear Power Development in the United States* (New York).

Erskine, Hazel. 1972. "The Polls: Pollution and Its Costs," *The Public Opinion Quarterly* vol. 36 (Spring) pp. 120–135.

Ferejohn, John A., and Morris P. Fiorina. 1974. "The Paradox of Not Voting: A Decision Theoretic Analysis," *American Political Science Review* vol. 68, no. 2, pp. 525–546.

Fireman, Bruce, and William Gamson. 1977. "Utilitarian Logic in the Resource Mobilization Perspective." Unpublished working paper number 153 of the Center for Research on Social Organization (Ann Arbor, University of Michigan).

Fischer, Elizabeth M. 1976. "Altruism and Rationality: A Conceptual Scheme with Implications for Social Change." Paper prepared for the Social Science Research Council Advisory and Planning Committee on Social Indicators (New York).

Freeman, A. Myrick III. 1971. *The Economics of Pollution Control and Environmental Quality* (New York, General Learning Press).

Frolich, Norman, Joe Oppenheimer, and Oran Young. 1971. *Political Leadership and Collective Goods* (Princeton, N.J., Princeton University Press).

Gamson, William A. 1975. *The Strategy of Social Protest* (Homewood, Ill., Dorsey Press).

Guttman, Joel. 1978. "Understanding Collective Action: Matching Behavior," *American Economic Review, Papers and Proceedings* vol. 68, no. 2 (May) pp. 251–255.

Hirschman, Albert O. 1970. *Exit, Voice, and Loyalty: Response to Decline in Firms, Organizations, and States* (Cambridge, Mass., Harvard University Press).

Kimball, Thomas. 1970. Speech to the Annual Meeting of the National Wildlife Federation, March.

Krutilla, John V., and Anthony C. Fisher. 1975. *The Economics of Natural Environments* (Baltimore, Johns Hopkins University Press for Resources for the Future).

McCarthy, John D., and Mayer N. Zald. 1977. "Resource Mobilization and Social Movements: A Partial Theory," *American Journal of Sociology* vol. 82, no. 26, pp. 1212–1241.

McFarland, Andrew S. 1976. *Public Interest Lobbies: Decision Making on Energy* (Washington, D.C., American Enterprise Institute).

Manzer, R. 1969. "Selective Inducements and the Development of Pressure Groups," *Canadian Journal of Political Science* vol. 2, pp. 103–117.

Marsh, D. 1976. "On Joining Interest Groups," *British Journal of Political Science* vol. 6, pp. 49–57.

Mitchell, Robert Cameron. 1978. "Environment: An Enduring Concern," *Resources* vol. 57 (January/March) pp. 2, 20–21.

Moe, Terry M. 1977. "Rational Action and Pluralist Behavior: A Revised Theory of Interest Groups." Unpublished paper presented at the Annual Meeting of the American Political Science Association, September, Washington, D.C.

New York Times. 1978. January 15, sec. 3, p. 14.

Notz, W. M. 1975. "Work Motivation and the Negative Effects of Extrinsic Rewards: A Review with Implications for Theory and Practice," *American Psychologist* vol. 30, pp. 884–891.

Oberschall, Anthony. 1973. *Social Conflict and Social Movements* (Englewood Cliffs, N.J., Prentice-Hall).

Olson, Mancur. 1971. *The Logic of Collective Action: Public Goods and the Theory of Groups* (Rev. ed., New York, Schocken Books).

Peston, Maurice. 1972. *Public Goods and the Public Sector* (London, Macmillan).

Rabin, Robert L. 1976. "Lawyers for Social Change: Perspectives on Public Interest Law," *Stanford Law Review* vol. 28, no. 2, pp. 207–261.

Samuelson, Paul. 1955. "Diagrammatic Exposition of a Theory of Public Expenditure," *Review of Economics and Statistics* vol. 28, no. 2, pp. 207–261.

Sierra. 1978. May, pp. 22–25.

Stone, Christopher D. 1974. *Should Trees Have Standing?* (Los Altos, Calif., William Kaufman).

Tillock, Harriet, and Denton E. Morrison. 1979, forthcoming. "Group Size and Contributions to Collective Action: An Examination of Mancur Olson's Theory Using Data from Zero Population Growth, Inc.," in Louis Kreisberg, ed., *Research on Social Movements, Conflicts, and Change* (New York, JAI Press).

Titmuss, R. M. 1971. *The Gift Relationship: From Human Blood to Social Policy* (New York, Vintage Books).

U.S. News & World Report. 1978. *The Study of American Opinion: Public Attitudes Toward Emerging Issues, Business, Government, Labor, Professions, Institutions* vols. 1 and 2 (Washington, D.C.).

Utrup, Kathryn. 1977. "Public Opinion and the Environment, 1969–1977." Unpublished paper.

White, Louise. 1976. "Rational Theories of Participation," *Journal of Conflict Resolution* vol. 20, no. 2, pp. 255–277.

Wilderness Society. 1977. "Profile: Dave Foreman," *Wilderness Report* vol. 14, no. 5, p. 4.

Charles R. Plott

The Application of Laboratory Experimental Methods to Public Choice

Many claim that laboratory experimentation is impossible in economics and political science. Given the academic questions currently central to these disciplines, such claims, while debatable, are certainly understandable. The major focus of the field of public choice, however, is somewhat different from the traditional fields, and as a result laboratory methodology seems to be particularly appropriate.

Two widely held beliefs are partially responsible for the development of public choice theory and account for some of its nonconformity with academic traditions. The first belief is that a major ingredient of social policy analysis is, by necessity, a choice between alternative modes of social organization and institutions. According to this thesis, social policies are determined by particular organizational features of the public sector. Public officials are cynically viewed as following a self-interest postulate, responding to the incentives of their organizational environment and failing to act on philosophical principles and arguments about public needs, unless such actions are consistent with their own self-interest, broadly defined. It follows that the nature of public policy is substantively shaped by the incentives of those involved in policy formulation and implementation, and that social organization and institutions must be "correct," in order for the "proper" behavior to automatically flow from the public sector. Consequently, the research focus for those interested in social policies should be upon alternative modes of organization and their performance characteristics.

The financial support supplied by the National Science Foundation is gratefully acknowledged.

This first belief holds, for example, that it is not enough to demonstrate that market organization leads to inefficient results where public goods or externalities are involved. One must ask additional questions about the performance properties of the alternative modes of organization which would replace those which exist. While a monopoly, for example, may lead to distasteful results, public utility commissioners responding to a variety of political influences may induce worse results (even when the commissioners have ample funds to hire economists to apply cost-benefit techniques to the problem). Even if one could identify the optimum level of various economic activities, there is no assurance that the optimum would be attained unless the mode of social organization resolves conflicts among citizens, politicians, and bureaucrats in a way which assures that the "optimum" is the outcome. Ideal policy analysis in this view consists of surveying various modes of organization and finding the one best suited to deal with the problem at hand. The scientific problem is to find tools functional for this task.

The second belief is that principles of economics (and game theory) are central to the behavior of social organizations. This carries a much deeper implication than the mere self-interest postulate. It means that the individual is viewed as strategically applying powers and information afforded by the institutional structure in accord with his own independent preferences rather than as having his preferences follow endogenously from the social position, organizational structure, or role in which he finds himself. Of course the dynamics of preference formation (as differentiated from simple learning theory) receive a nod here and there, but the preferences definitely tend to be viewed as the *independent* and not the *dependent* variable. Thus equation (1), the "fundamental equation" (where $\oplus$ signifies nothing more than some unspecified abstract operation),

(1)   Preferences $\oplus$ institutions $\oplus$ physical possibilities
        = outcomes

so characteristic of economic models, has become a distinguishing feature of the theory even though the institutions with which the theorist deals may bear no resemblance to those found in markets.

Both the scientific questions and the approach to policy analysis that result from this view of the world differ somewhat from academic tradition. The scientific questions following the "fundamental equation" involve identifying the general (in that they are not tied to market modes of organization) behavioral principles that dictate the supposed relationships between preferences, institutions, feasible outcomes, and actual outcomes. While existing and historical situations and modes of organization play an important role, they are not necessarily studied for their own sake as they are in the mainstream of the academic disciplines. Rather, they are viewed as an important source of data against which hypothesized principles can be tested. Policy analysis is similarly removed from preoccupation with existing institutions. It becomes a type of "institutional engineering" whereby the basic principles are used to construct "new" or "synthetic" institutions which have prespecified performance characteristics. These resulting institutions may or may not resemble any existing institutions; consequently the basic principles sought should not be specifically tied to markets or any other historical mode of organization.

One obvious problem with this public choice approach is the lack of data. It is very difficult, expensive, and sometimes impossible to uncover the historical situations against which the relative accuracy of competing models can be gauged. Old ideas tend to die because of time, if they die at all, and not because they can be discredited by the evidence. As a result, it is difficult to identify a noncontroversial set of principles which unify a set of successful models. Furthermore, it is very difficult and extremely expensive to gain experience with the behavioral characteristics of new or "synthetic" modes of organization. One cannot turn to history for experience since by definition the mode of organization has never existed before. Social experiments are an exciting possibility but they are expensive, difficult to control, and can easily exceed the limits of practicality or even legality.

I. LABORATORY METHODS

Laboratory experimental methods appear to be a natural supplement to other modes of public choice research. One does not have to look far to find claims that laboratory methods are inherently irrelevant and "artificial." Such a belief may be justified in the case of the traditional academic disciplines, but a theoretical argument can be applied to disarm such a priori claims in the case of public choice research.

The argument rests on two axioms, both of which are inherited from economics and both of which follow loosely from the fundamental equation.[1] Axiom one is that the behavior of various modes of organiza-

[1] For a different argument see Smith (1979b).

tion is independent of the *sources* of preference as long as the preferences themselves remain unchanged. This is not to say that the sources are uninteresting or unimportant variables. It simply means that once preferences are fixed, behavior follows regardless of the underlying explanation or motivation of the preference. In economics, for example, it makes no difference whether I would pay $10 maximum for a shirt because (a) I think it is pretty; (b) my wife thinks it is pretty; or (c) I want to eat it. In all cases my contribution to the market demand for shirts is the same and *ceteris paribus,* so is the market price. So, without inquiring into the ultimate motivations of individuals, one can study the possible consequences of organization (e.g., monopoly, competition) which result from a fixed pattern of preferences.

Axiom two is that the relationship between outcomes, preferences, and institutions is (supposed to be) independent of the nature of the social alternatives. For example, a competitive market for capital for a given configuration of demand and supply should behave the same as a competitive market for wheat or health services, given the same conditions. A committee operating under majority rule with a given pattern of preferences is supposed to behave the same regardless of whether the options are potential college presidents or alternative regulations regarding pollution abatement.

The next step of the argument involves the theory of induced preferences (see Smith, 1976). By applying this theory to a laboratory setting, any desired configuration of preferences for a fixed set of individuals can be induced over abstract commodity spaces. Let X be any set of objects toward which individuals have no initial attitudes (e.g., letters of the alphabet, points on the blackboard, or hypothesized units of widgets). Each individual i is assigned a function $Q^i(x)$ indicating the amount of money he will receive if x is the outcome of the social decision process. As long as the individual prefers more money to less, and as long as there are no side payments, a preference ordering is induced over X by the operation $xR_iy \Leftrightarrow Q^i(x) \geq Q^i(y)$ for all $x,y \in X$.

Armed with this simple procedure and a belief in the two axioms above, it follows that the relationship between preferences, institutions, and outcomes can be studied in the laboratory. We have a set of social alternatives, X, which specify and define the limitations of the system. The fact that they may be abstract, hypothetical, or uncomplicated makes no difference to the theory (by the second axiom above). We also have a pattern of preferences, R_i, over these options. The fact that the preferences were induced through a monetary incentive is irrelevant (by the first axiom). We need only impose an organization or set of institutions through which the conflicting opinions about what "society" should choose from X are resolved. We can now study the resulting social choices.

Admittedly, the current technology for creating well-defined institutions and organization in laboratory settings leaves something to be desired. But, the basic applicability of the laboratory does not seem controversial. Indeed, if one accepts the axioms, then the laboratory society we have created is in fact a real society (perhaps a very simple one) characterized by individual preferences and institutions, and the behavior of this society should follow the same principles as any other society.

Once the laboratory society has been created, what can one do with it? To date three types of uses have been explored: (1) the resolution of competition between closely related but competing general principles, (2) the exposure of ideas about social behavior that are simply nonsense, and (3) obtaining experience with the operation of modes of organization that have never existed before and are not well understood theoretically. Examples of each of these uses will be outlined below.

II. COMPETING PRINCIPLES

Once preferences and institutions are known, can one really predict the outcome? For certain selected situations the answer is "yes." Surprisingly enough, the "tool box" of mathematical models frequently contains several models which are amazingly accurate at predicting the behavior of simple processes. However, the *exact* reasons for almost all of the successes are unknown. The word "exact" should be emphasized since many theories are consistent with all observations to date. Nevertheless, the theories are different. This multiplicity of explanations naturally invites attempts to resolve the competition among several ideas.

The differences among theories fall into two categories—aside from the fact that for at least some imaginable parameter values they predict differently. First, there is an existence problem. Some models, for example, the core of a majority rule game, only make predictions for a very restricted class of parameter values. Second, there is a "relevance" problem. In certain types of situations one would expect one theory (model) to be applicable and another not applicable. For example, one expects that the behavior of markets characterized by a large number of traders who are unable to collude would be modeled better by a competitive

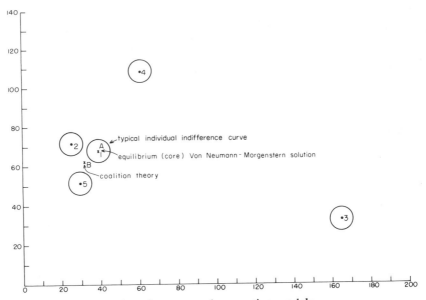

Figure 5.   Individual preferences and competing models.

than by a cartel model. Of course the problem here is that the words "large" and "collude" are not defined (unless one wishes to eliminate the fundamental equation by defining the institutional variables "large" and "coalition" circularly in terms of the outcome resulting from the process).

Thus in order to test one theory against another, it is necessary to find situations where both theories are "applicable," both make predictions, and the predictions differ. The laboratory method is ideally suited for this task.

In order to demonstrate how this methodology works, we will study the behavior of a five-man committee that operated under majority rule and followed a simplified version of *Robert's Rules of Order*. The committee's task was to choose a point on the blackboard. A predetermined point was designated as the motion on the floor. Amendments (movement of the point) were offered, discussed, and voted upon one at a time. Anyone was free to propose amendments. The committee meeting lasted until someone called the question or there were no more amendments and a majority accepted the motion on the floor.

Three competing models will be considered as candidates for explaining the results. The first is the voting equilibrium or core (of a majority-rule game without side payments). It is point A on figures 5

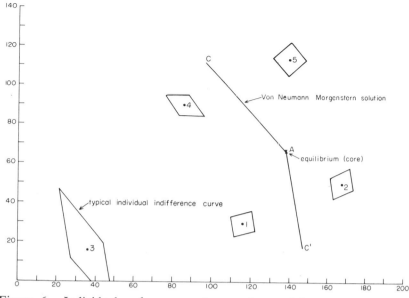

Figure 6.. Individual preferences and competing models.

and 6. The second is the Von Neumann–Morgenstern solution. It is point A in figure 5 and the line CAC' on figure 6. The third is the Caplow–Gamson–Kormarita coalition theory. Our interpretation of this model predicts point B on figure 5.

It is well known that if the committee meets for the first time without premeeting deliberations and if all individuals are highly motivated, then the equilibrium-core[2] model tends to predict the outcome (Fiorina and Plott, 1978; Berl and coauthors, 1976). The coalition-based models are simply not as accurate. One concludes either that the coalition models are (relatively) false or that they are not applicable because of, say, the single meeting environment. The question is then raised about the case of committees that do not have a single meeting but are instead involved in a series of meetings. Do the coalition theoretic ideas apply there?

In order to answer this question, five individuals were asked to participate in a four-evening experiment. On each evening they were to meet three times. Thus the group participated in a sequence of twelve meetings. In each meeting the task was the same. They were to pick a

---

[2] To some it might seem to be unnecessary to differentiate between the voting theoretic notion of an "equilibrium" and a game theoretic notion of a core since the concepts are mathematically equivalent. The distinction is made here only to preserve the different lines of background theory.

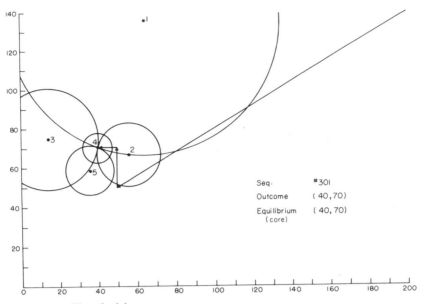

Figure 7.   First decision.

point on the blackboard. However, the preference of each differed from meeting to meeting.

The results of the meetings are contained in figures 7 through 18 and in table 10. The points on the figures represent individual maximums. The numbers beside the point are an individual index and the arrows represent the path of the motion on the floor. The termination of the

TABLE 10.   A Single Committee Involved in a Sequence of Decisions

Session	Experiment index	Equilibrium core	Outcome	Distance from equilibrium
	301	40, 70	40, 70	(0, 0)
1	302	56, 67	60, 75	(4, 8)
	303	138, 66	138, 66	(0, 0)
	304	39, 68	39, 68	(0, 0)
2	305	61, 69	61, 69	(0, 0)
	306	56, 67	56, 67	(0, 0)
	307	None exists	140, 75	
3	308	40, 70	40, 70	(0, 0)
	309	None exists	39, 70	
	310	None exists	69, 55	
4	311	39, 68	39, 68	(0, 0)
	312	138, 66	134, 68	(4, 2)

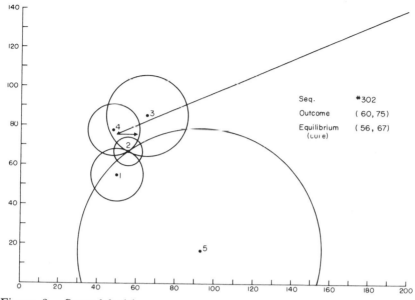

Figure 8. Second decision.

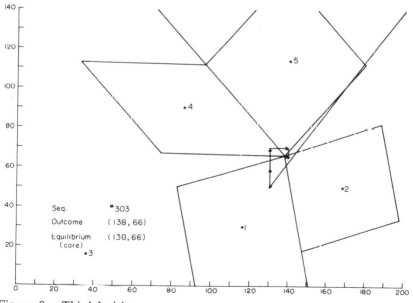

Figure 9. Third decision.

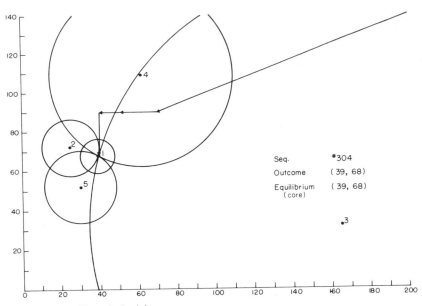

Figure 10.   Fourth decision.

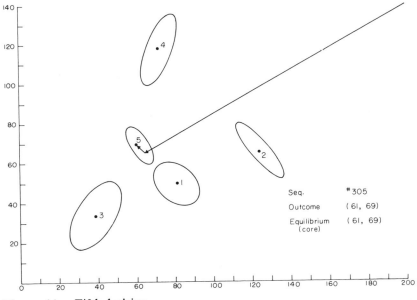

Figure 11.   Fifth decision.

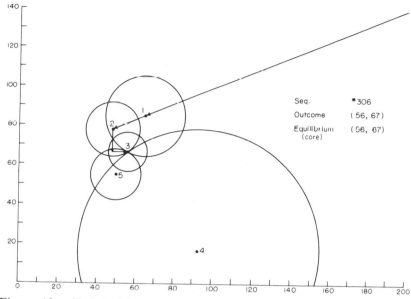

Figure 12. Sixth decision.

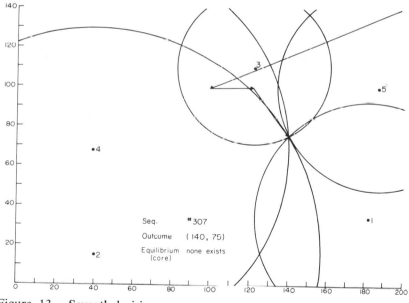

Figure 13. Seventh decision.

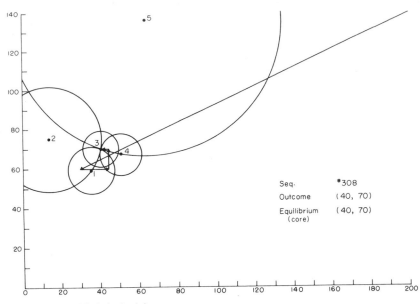

Figure 14.   Eighth decision.

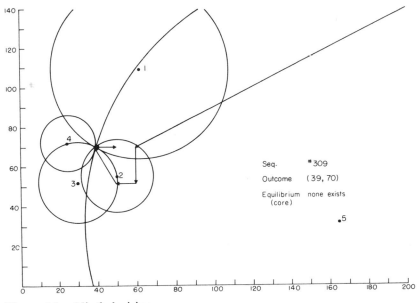

Figure 15.   Ninth decision.

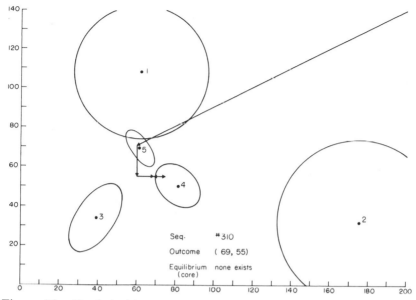

Figure 16. Tenth decision.

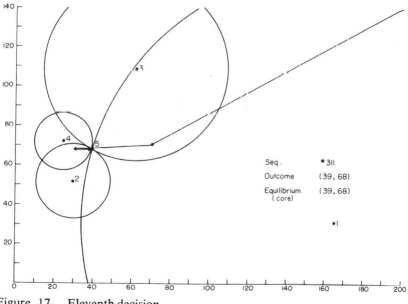

Figure 17. Eleventh decision.

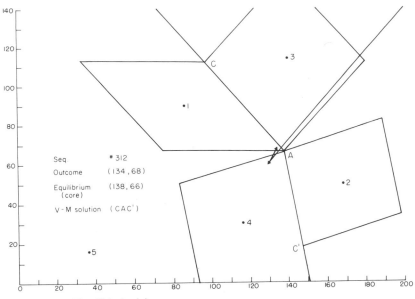

Figure 18.   Twelfth decision.

arrow is the point chosen by the committee. A representative indifference curve is drawn for each individual. These are graduate students and employed adults. The monetary incentives through the relevant ranges tended to be high—about $.75 to $1.00 per unit. On average the earnings amounted to about $8.00 per meeting.

As shown on table 10 the equilibrium (core), when it exists, is a very accurate model. Deviations from it were always slight. The interesting experiments are shown in figures 17 and 18. For these final two experiments the preference configurations are those represented in figures 5 and 6, which separate the equilibrium (core) from the coalition-based theories. The equilibrium (core) is the outcome for figure 17 and the outcome is near the equilibrium (core) for figure 18.

From the results we can draw two important conclusions. First, it is not true that one must *necessarily* apply the equilibrium (core) theory to the supergame which results from considering the sequence of meetings as a single game. One simply cannot dismiss the core or equilibrium as applied to each separate meeting in favor of the core or equilibrium of a dynamic model. This is a most important result because in many theoretical circles the model which has worked so successfully here would have simply been dismissed out of hand in favor of some dynamic version. The second conclusion is that the coalition theories receive no support. There may indeed exist situations for which the theories are applicable, but the mere fact that sequences of decisions and continued association between committee members are present does not constitute a sufficient condition for the introduction of the coalition-related theories.

The major point now needs reiteration. If one accepts the "fundamental equation," then the laboratory provides a tool for separating very closely related theories. Naturally one would want to observe the behavior of many more groups before coalition theories are generally rejected or before "myopic" models are accepted. This reservation, however, is not a criticism of laboratory methods; it is a call for even more experimentation. The example does seem to establish the power of the methods. When one can observe situations in which competing theories give separate predictions, there is a possibility of rejecting some theories in favor of others and thereby giving the "fundamental equation" a rather explicit functional form.

III. IDEA REJECTION

From time to time it is possible to have very reasonable ideas that are nonsense. They have an internal logic but they lead to predictions that are so wildly inaccurate they are worse than no prediction at all. Some theories can simply be "obviously wrong." The problem is that they can be designated as "obviously wrong" only after some confrontations with the proper data and, when one must rely on field data, the proper data may never be available. Perhaps this is the reason one can see across the social sciences substantially different theories and methods that purport to deal with the same phenomena. Ideas can become ideologies in essence, because the simple situations necessary to reveal their ridiculousness cannot be uncovered in field settings.

The laboratory can be used to provide some wholesale rejections of ideas. Two examples will be covered. The first is a successful rejection of an idea about principles of committee behavior. The second, which is not successful, is an attempt to reject an idea about market behavior in the presence of an externality.

From the data reported in section II, one is tempted to elevate the equilibrium (core) and the related game-theoretic structure to the level of a behavioral law. The postulate would become "if the institution is majority rule, then the committee decision will be the core of the associated cooperative game." It would be nice if this were true but it isn't.

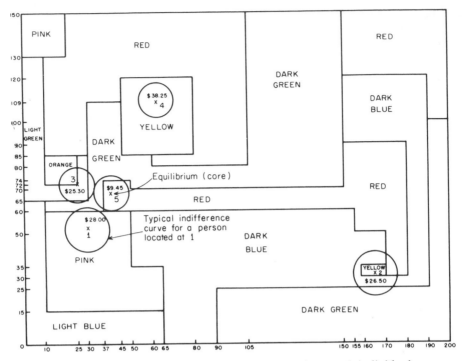

Figure 19. Issue space, individual maximum points, and individual maximum amounts.

In order to see the problem, consider figure 19. The configuration of preferences is exactly like figure 5. Five individuals were to pick a point from the blackboard using simple majority rule. This time, however, *Robert's Rules of Order* were not used. Instead, a prespecified agenda of nonamendable motions was followed.

The blackboard was partitioned into colored areas (the subjects actually saw charts with colors). The agenda had five items. The first item was a choice between the dark-colored points and the light-colored points. The second item was a choice between the blue-based colors and the non-blue-based colors, etc. The agenda is elaborated in detail in figure 20.

The experiment was conducted six times. The outcomes are listed in figure 20. As can be seen, only one of the six resulted at the equilibrium (core) of (39, 68) and in this particular session the agenda was effectively disregarded. The remainder are systematically distributed to the left of the equilibrium (core). While these outcomes may seem "close" to the equilibrium (core), further experimentation and theory leave no doubt that this difference with the experiments reported in the

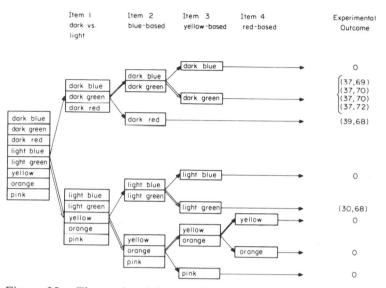

Figure 20.   The results of six experimental sessions with an imposed agenda.

previous section is due to the subtle change in procedures (see Levine and Plott, 1977 and Plott and Levine, 1978 for a developed theory of agenda influence). The agenda can be used to systematically remove the outcomes from the equilibrium (core).

Our conclusion is clear. It is simply incorrect to apply the equilibrium (core) model without close attention to procedural details. Furthermore, the fact that these particular procedural details are so overwhelmingly influential leads us to suspect that the cooperative game-theoretic way of modeling the process is itself quite wrong. Before this latter speculation is justified, however, a great deal more research is necessary.

The second example deals with an idea about how markets react when externalities are present. The standard model asserts that when private costs diverge from social cost, price will be determined by the demand and private cost supply curve. That is, the theory claims that markets with externalities will behave the same way as markets without externalities (efficiency considerations aside, of course).

Now suppose we construct a laboratory market under circumstances that are known to be favorable for the accuracy of the market model. This "biased" setting in favor of the theory is of course the key to successful rejection of an idea. If the market model repeatedly fails to work after the introduction of an externality, then we would be forced to think

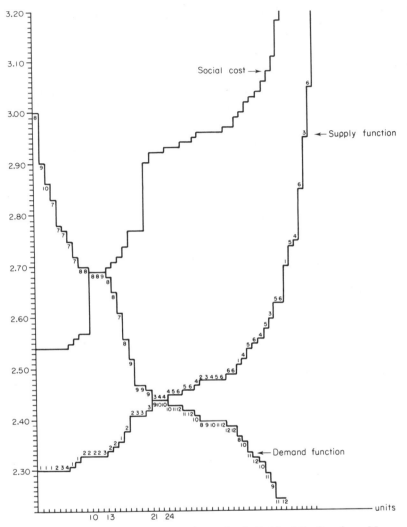

Figure 21.   Market demand and supply, individual limit prices. Numbers below (above) the curve represent the individual demander (supplier) who has the indicated limit price.

along new dimensions (psychology?). That is, if the traditional model does not work under circumstances which are thought to be most favorable for its applicability, then we are forced to rethink the whole approach.

As is usual with market experiments, subjects are partitioned into "demanders" and "suppliers." Subject demanders make money by purchasing from sellers and reselling to the experimenter according to a predetermined formula. Subject sellers make money by buying from the experimenter according to a predetermined schedule and selling to buyers. Since the contracts with the experimenter are unique for each buyer and seller, any demand or supply structure desired can be induced. For an elaboration on the theory of induced preference, the reader is again referred to Smith (1976).

Externalities are introduced by imposing a tax $T^i(X)$ on individual i, where X is the total volume traded in the market during a given market period. This function, which induces "damages" as a reduction in profits, is completely understood by i. Whenever a trade is made by any other subject, i is aware of his own resulting damage. The market is organized as an oral auction market so individuals are much closer to the sources of discomfort than in most naturally occurring externality situations. As a result, individuals can become aware of the social consequences of their actions and have an opportunity to deviate from the actions predicted by the competitive model.

The market demand, supply, and social cost functions are shown in figure 21. The results of the sequence of market periods are shown in figure 22. As is obvious from the figure, the market behaved as if there were no externalities at all. The prices and quantities converge exactly to the competitive equilibrium. The attempt to summarily reject the model simply failed. Whether or not markets with externalities behave no differently from markets without externalities remains to be seen. However, in the laboratory markets studied to date, the fact that people know that their trades hurt others does not seem to inhibit their trading activities (Plott, 1978). We are certainly not free to conclude, as we hoped, that the demand and supply model is "nonsense" when externalities are present.

IV. THE BEHAVIOR OF NEW MODES OF ORGANIZATION

The third purpose of laboratory methods has been to provide experience with new modes of organization. The laboratory can provide an opportunity for studying the behavior of collective choice processes which have no "natural" origin. Such "synthetic" processes cannot be studied by reference to history, and "field" experiments are generally very expensive. For the study of these processes, the laboratory provides an inexpensive research tool.

The motivation for the research covered in this section seems to be the reverse of the motivation of the examples covered in the text above.

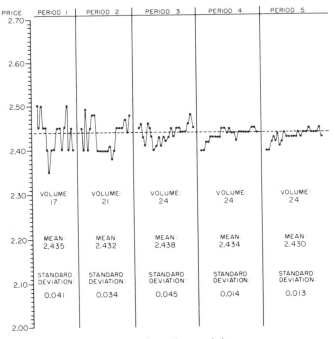

Figure 22.   Time series of trading activity.

In the earlier discussions, some ongoing process (or a simple example of an ongoing process) was chosen and the research objective was to understand how and why it functions the way it does. The objective was to find a model (or mechanism) which reflects the essence of the process. In this section the research is primarily motivated by a mechanism (a mathematical model or theory) which is devoid of operational detail. The objective is to find a system of institutions—the rules for individual expression, information transmittal, and social choice—or a process as Smith (1978) calls it, which mirrors the behavioral features of the mechanism. The theory suggests the possible existence of processes with certain performance qualities. The problem is to find them. This is institutional engineering in its purest form.

A few examples of applications of this methodology exist. By using an abstract committee mechanism as a guide, Plott and Levine (1978) designed committee procedures that could be used to influence if not determine the behavior of voting committees. The procedures involve the strategic categorization of options into a series of "agenda items" which are sequentially discussed and voted upon by majority rule. By application of experimental methods they were able to refine the procedures and analyze the results of a field experiment (Levine and Plott,

1977). The agenda on figure 20 used to demonstrate the lack of generality of the equilibrium concept is an example.

A series of studies by Ferejohn, Forsythe, and Noll (1977; 1979a,b) focus on the design of a process for the selection of Public Broadcasting Service programs and the distribution of program costs among member stations. The voting process currently used by the stations and the behavior of several variations of the process have been examined with laboratory methods.[3]

Vernon Smith (1977a,b; 1978, 1979a) has designed a process based upon the Groves–Ledyard mechanism for providing a collective good. (See *Public Choice* vol. 29, Special Supplement to Spring 1977, for a series of papers which deal with such mechanisms.) The laboratory results to date are encouraging in that the optimum quantities tend to emerge. Smith has also examined the behavior of several other processes. Of these, his "auction process" is perhaps the most interesting because it highlights the potentials afforded by laboratory experimental methods.

The experiment begins in the usual way by inducing preferences over a commodity space. In this case the subject i is paid an amount $Q_i(x)$, depending upon the quantity x of a public good the group collectively purchases. Again, there are no side payments or interactions outside the prescribed process. The cost of the public good is q dollars per unit. If x_0 is chosen by the group, and if individual i pays B_i per unit, then $\sum_{i=1}^{n} B_i x_0 = q x_0$ where q is the cost per unit of the public good. All costs are covered and the individual receives a reward of $Q_i(x_0) - B_i x_0$.

The process itself involves a sequence of trials before the final choice is made. Smith describes the process as follows:[4]

1. Let each agent i submit a bid and a proposed quantity (b_i, x_i) with the understanding that his share of unit cost is $(q - B_i)$, and his share of total cost is

$$(q - B_i)x_i \text{ (where } B_i = \sum_{j \neq i} b_j)$$

The quantity, q, is the constant marginal cost of the public good.

---

[3] Ed. note: See the paper in this volume by Ferejohn, Forsythe, and Noll.

[4] The specific details are as follows:

(i) *Starting rule.* On trial t, each subject independently and privately selects two integers $[b_i(t), x_i(t)]$, each confined to specified intervals, and records these choices on a prescribed record sheet.

(ii) *Transition rules.*

(ii.a) The experimenter records each $[b_i(t), x_i(t)]$, computes, then posts $B(t)$,

2. Give each agent the right to veto or agree to the unit cost, $q - B_i$, allocated to him by all other agents. He signals agreement by choosing $b_i = q - B_i$ and a veto by choosing $b_i \neq q - B_i$. Also give each agent i the right to veto or signal agreement by choosing

$$x_i = \bar{x} = \sum_{k=1}^{n} x_k/n \text{ (agree), or } x_i \neq \bar{x} \text{ (veto)}$$

3. Group agreement prevails if and only if agreement is signaled by every agent $i = 1,2,...,n$, in which case $\bar{x}$ units of the public good are purchased, with each agent paying the unit cost share $q - B_i$.

The induced marginal valuation functions $[V_i(x) = Q_i(x) - Q_i(x - 1)]$ for each of the five participants in one of his experiments are reproduced on figure 23.[5] The cost of the public good is \$45 per unit and the optimal quantity is six units. The Lindahl prices at six units are indicated for each individual, as are the bids for all trials in one of his experimental sessions. As can be seen from the time series, the bids tend to converge to the Lindahl prices. The group choice also tends to be the optimal quantity. These results are striking. The optimal quantity with Lindahl prices is indeed a Nash equilibrium *but so is every other* quantity price vector that yields a positive return for every individual.[6] Why

---

and $\bar{x}(t)$ on a blackboard, the posting to remain until the end of the process, where $B(t) = \Sigma_i b_i(t)$ and $\bar{x}(t) = (1/n \, \Sigma_i x_i(t))$.

(ii.b) Each subject records $B(t)$, and $\bar{x}(t)$, then computes, and records $B_i(t) = B(t) - b_i(t)$ and $q - B_i(t)$.

(ii.c) Each subject determines his private net valuation of $[q - B_i(t), x_i(t)]$ from a precomputed table of the values $v_i = Q_i(x_i) - (q - B_i)x_i$. The resulting $v_i(t)$ is recorded on his record sheet. This completes trial t.

(ii.d) Each subject then proceeds to trial $t + 1$ and chooses $[b_i(t + 1), x_i(t + 1)]$ as in (i).

(iii) *Stopping rule.*

(iii.a) The process stops on trial t^* if $b_i(t^* - 1) = q - B_i(t^* - 1) = q - B_i(t^*)$, $x_i(t^*) = \bar{x}(t^*)$, for all i, and $t^* \leq T$;

(iii.b) Otherwise the process stops on trial $t = T$.

(iv) *Outcome rule.* If the process stops by (iii.a) the group has reached *equilibrium* (agreement), and each subject is paid $v_i(t^*)$ in cash. Otherwise he receives a modest wage. In some experimental sessions this outcome was modified so that each i received $v_i(t^*) + \$2$ if (iii.a) occurs, otherwise \$2 (Smith, 1978a).

[5] These data are taken from Smith (1979a).

[6] In order to see this, simply consider the stopping rule. Suppose the group has reached any quantity and cost distribution that yields each individual a positive return. At the termination of the experiment, each individual, given the behavior of others, is faced with either a positive return by replaying his acceptance strategy or getting zero return. Thus the point is a Nash equilibrium.

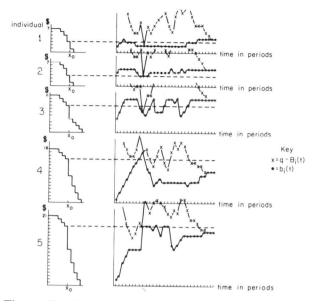

Figure 23.   Individual public good demand curves and contribution decisions.

should the process terminate at the particular (optimal) Nash equilibrium? Smith explores the phenomenon, but it remains a mystery. It also is a tribute to engineering, intuition, and laboratory skill that a process that "works" could have been created from intuition and loose analogy with other processes while on paper the process perhaps should not work at all.

V.   CONCLUSIONS

The thesis of this paper has been that given the general framework and research directions found in public choice theory, laboratory experimental methods provide a new and useful tool. The body of the paper has been devoted to providing some generalizations (with examples) about the laboratory work undertaken so far. However, having advocated the development and uses of laboratory methods, one must necessarily face tough critical questions, two of which loom immediately.

First, to what extent can laboratory methods be used to attack the complicated policy questions which motivate much public choice theory? At this time it seems much too early in the development of the subject to estimate its ultimate usefulness. There have been direct applications. The Public Broadcasting Service experiments provide an excellent example of an application. The agenda experiments include a real application. One hopes that policies can be designed in light of experiences in simple, inexpensive laboratory situations and thereby eliminate some of the enormous cost to society at large which is incurred when experience is gained through the actual implementation of new policies. More applications are needed.

The direct applications and "simulations" of specific processes may not be as important as the knowledge one can gain about the relative reliability of general models. Our current nonlaboratory means of eliminating theories is not particularly effective. New theories appear but other theories do not seem to die—they just get old. At least the laboratory provides a context in which some ideas can be rejected. Whether or not some ideas will become generally *accepted* because of their success in laboratory environments is a different and more problematic issue. It is probably safe to say that there are none currently accepted because of laboratory experiments.

The second question is even more difficult. How seriously should one take the "fundamental equation"? It provides a useful, maintained hypothesis but it will probably experience a great deal of evolution. For example, it currently makes no real provision for the evolution of institutions themselves. Economics and public choice are full of theories about institutional and organizational evolution (e.g., firm entry, new political party development). Could it be, for example, that preferences and opportunities *alone* determine the structure of institutions (including the constitution)? These questions might be addressed without changing the "fundamental equation" but before that can be done, a lot of work must be done on determining exactly what goes under the title of an "institution." Are customs and ethics to be regarded as institutions? What about organizations such as coalitions? These are embarrassing questions which suggest that the "fundamental equation" is perhaps not as fundamental as we would like. The extent to which laboratory methods can cope with them simply remains to be seen.

John R. Chamberlin

Comments

Professor Plott presents a strong case for the usefulness of laboratory experiments in studying public choice problems, and in his closing comments suggests that these methods hold considerable promise as aids to political designers in evaluating new ideas concerning the structure of public institutions. I share his enthusiasm for experimental work, and consider the work done by him and his colleagues to be some of the most exciting to have taken place in the field of public choice in recent years. I also share his hope that laboratory experiments may be useful as a proving ground for innovations in institutional design arising from public choice theory. Over the years, the field of public choice has generated a wide variety of insights into nonmarket decision making, but these insights have seldom had the impact they might have because they have often been sufficiently different from business-as-usual that they have been difficult for practitioners to evaluate. Experimental methods may well prove to be a medium by which the insights of public choice theorists can be communicated to designers in an effective way. To be fully effective, however, experiments must be designed with careful eye to the context with which the designer is concerned.

The main advantage of laboratory experiments is that through the application of the theory of induced preferences and a suitable experimental design, one can achieve an *internally valid* result; that is, one can be reasonably sure that differences in behavior are due to variation in experimental conditions. Another important advantage of laboratory experiments, as Plott points out, is that they can be used to carry out "critical" experiments—those which resolve competing claims of different models concerning the same behavior. This seems to me to be an arena in which experimental methods can make unique contributions, although they are used all too infrequently in this manner. The use of critical experiments to demonstrate the superiority of new methods of decision making is extremely important, for if a political designer can be shown that a new method performs better than the method currently being used, and this demonstration can be carried out in a controlled environment in which differences in outcomes must be due to differences in the decision making processes involved, then there will be much less resistance to the adoption of innovative ideas. It is crucial to this effort, however, that the experimental conditions be sufficiently like the conditions in the naturally occurring environment with which the designer is concerned that he/she is convinced that the experimental results are not only internally valid but *externally valid* as well; that is, the results must remain valid when transferred from the laboratory to the institutional context in which they are to be used.

If laboratory experiments are to be useful to political designers, it is necessary that the results be both internally and externally valid. This raises some difficult issues for the study of nonmarket decision making, because the steps usually taken to ensure internal validity may lead either to doubts about the external validity of the results or to important restrictions on the types of decisions which can be studied experimentally. Several of these issues are raised by three important assumptions which underlie Plott's "fundamental equation":

$$\text{Preferences} \oplus \text{Institutions} \oplus \text{Set of alternatives} = \text{Outcomes}$$

These three assumptions, which are not completely independent of each other, are that (1) individuals are motivated by self-interest, (2) there are no (important) interactions among preferences, institutions, and the set of alternatives, and (3) the independent variables are truly independent of outcomes. The remainder of my discussion focuses on these assumptions and the implications they have for the usefulness of laboratory experiments as a guide to institutional design. Since these assumptions are not peculiar to experimental work, but characteristic of much of public choice theory, my comments are also intended to express some broader concerns I have for the directions in which the field is going.

Nonmarket decision making is concerned, almost by definition, with situations in which private interests differ from "the public interest." Indeed, much of the public choice literature consists of demonstrations that pursuit of self-interest by politicians, bureaucrats, or voters results in inefficient allocations of resources in a democratic society, and attempts to design institutions which can channel the pursuit of self-interest to produce less inefficient allocations (or perhaps even efficient allocations, as the recent work on demand-revealing processes has argued).

In economics, which has supplied the theoretical foundation of public choice theory, the self-interest postulate has proved to be adequate to both the positive and normative demands of the discipline. Predictions based on the postulate correspond reasonably well with reality, particularly where aggregate behavior is concerned; and the theorems of welfare economics provide a justification for self-interested behavior by demonstrating that in many cases such behavior is not socially harmful. The fact that the "invisible hand" guides self-interested behavior to an efficient allocation of resources, and the fact that markets result in fair allocations if the original endowments are fair, provide a strong ethical argument in favor of egoistic behavior (or at least provide strong counterarguments against attacks on self-interested behavior in this context). Support, both positive and normative, for self-interested behavior on the part of voters, politicians, or bureaucrats is much weaker. We are faced with individuals who vote when it appears to be irrational and who participate in other forms of political activity to a much greater extent than models based on self-interest can adequately account for.[1] On the normative side, we lack theories of political and bureaucratic behavior which can provide the same ethical support for self-interested behavior upon the part of public servants that the invisible hand provides for participants in the private sector. The ambiguous norms for political behavior do not go unrecognized by participants in the political process, and the ability of a political designer to affect the degree to which political behavior is selfish or public-spirited is an important aspect of designing institutions. In addition to the importance of the self-interest postulate in neoclassical economics and liberal political theory, a fact which helps explain why it very naturally became a part of public choice theory, there is another reason why the postulate is useful in laboratory experiments. The self-interest postulate is convenient in these studies because it greatly simplifies the process of inducing preferences. This is usually carried out by (1) giving each subject a payoff function (with considerable money at stake) defined on the possible outcomes, (2) restricting each subject's knowledge of the payoff functions of others, and (3) defining the issues to be decided in a sufficiently abstract or nonsensical way that subjects will not have strong feelings about outcomes separate from those generated by their payoff functions. The experiments discussed by Plott were largely carried out in this fashion, and as a result the threats to internal validity from subjects acting inconsistently with their payoff functions are extremely

---

[1] Ed. note: See the paper by Mitchell in this volume for a discussion of one such phenomenon.

weak. The threats to external validity may be correspondingly increased, however, and the care given to ensuring self-interested behavior may greatly lessen the usefulness of the results to a political designer. The extreme care given to the latter two points above suggests that unless the experimenter is very careful, subjects' behavior may be affected by the knowledge of others' utility functions or by the political context in which the decision is made. But this in turn suggests that the experiment has then been designed to exclude important parts of "political reality" in order to achieve internal validity.

The fact that self-interested behavior is more easily induced in experimental work if subjects are unaware of the induced preferences of others and if the issues under discussion are free of important political content, attests to the important nature of the assumption that there are no significant interactions among the independent variables in Plott's fundamental equation. Again, such assumptions seem plausible in experimental studies in economics where self-interested behavior is the norm and where, as Plott mentions, it makes no difference whether we talk about competitive markets for capital, wheat, or health services because the nature of the alternatives can be treated as independent of preferences. But in noneconomic circumstances, particularly those in which the ethical support for self-interested behavior is not strong, the nature of the alternatives and the institutional structure in which decisions are made affect preferences, and the interactions among these variables are central to understanding the situation and to designing institutions. In his oral comments on his paper, Plott mentioned the problems (i.e., threats to internal validity) which occur if one attaches "real" labels to issues (such as, to use his example, aid to the blind). In such cases, subjects may not act in accordance with the payoff schedule they are assigned, but impose value judgments of their own on outcomes. The fact that one must be very careful (and very restrictive) in designing experiments if one is to avoid such behavior is a strong testament to the willingness and ability of individuals to act unselfishly if the context seems to call for it.

Given these concerns, experimentalists must choose either to retain the self-interest postulate, and thereby restrict the advice that can be offered to political designers to those contexts in which such behavior is ethically appropriate and empirically validated, or to attempt to go beyond the postulate to model unselfish behavior in ways that are sensitive to the contextual influences that the designer must consider in selecting an institutional structure. Choosing the first of these alternatives may be appropriate for the field of public choice. It plays to the comparative advantage of the field, and the set of nonmarket decisions that can profitably be studied using the self-interest postulate is certainly substantial. In addition, attempts at abstract models of unselfish behavior have been notoriously unsuccessful, perhaps primarily because such behavior is so sensitive to the context in which it occurs. Nevertheless, I am reluctant to see public choice theory stick with the self-interest postulate because it means conceding that the field cannot address many of the questions that lie at the core of political life. Nor can I escape the feeling that in restricting itself to applications of the self-interest postulate, the field decreases its chances of influencing political designers.

The final aspect of the "fundamental equation" that is of concern is the assumption that the influence between preferences and outcomes is unidirectional. While necessary for specific modeling purposes, and no doubt true in the experiments themselves, the assumption that outcomes do not affect subsequent preferences denies much of what sociology and political theory consider to be at the heart of the issue. It is undeniable that institutions transform the preferences of the individuals who come in contact with them, and for public choice theorists and experimentalists to not take account of this process when suggesting innovations cannot help but delay the acceptance of their ideas. This is particularly relevant to the earlier discussion of the role of the self-interest postulate in public choice theory. It is possible to design institutions that "teach" citizens to be selfish, and a number of important social problems with which our society has difficulty coping seem to me to be partially due to the fact that we have been "taught" by our social institutions that selfish behavior is acceptable. I personally am not buoyed by the prospect of future institutions reinforcing the selfishness of political behavior, so that I consider inattention to the dynamic relationship between preferences and outcomes a major obstacle to the successful implementation of innovations from public choice theory.

The preceding remarks may give the mistaken impression that I believe that the prospects of political designers benefiting from experimental work in public choice are sufficiently bleak that designers should turn their attentions elsewhere. Transplanting an idea from the theorists' written page to the reality of a naturally occurring political environment is always a risky undertaking, and any help that can be obtained along the way is useful. There is no doubt that laboratory experiments, by demonstrating that new methods of decision making can yield superior outcomes in carefully controlled environments, may decrease the hesitancy with which designers approach new ideas. Nor is it necessary that laboratory experiments carry the entire burden. Laboratory experiments may be used to provide preliminary evidence concerning the promise of an idea, and can be followed up by social experiments. Compared with laboratory experiments, social experiments are weak on internal validity and strong on external validity, a fact which means that these two types of experiments complement each other quite well. An idea that meets the "internal" test of a laboratory experiment and the "external" test of a social experiment will have met fairly high standards, and will have much to recommend it to political designers. I am hopeful that such combinations of experiments may help to bring about the acceptance of new institutional structures that will be superior to those we now rely on. For such efforts to be fully successful, however, those designing laboratory experiments must view their efforts not in isolation, but in relation to the needs of designers and to the capabilities of other methods, such as social experiments, to build on and complement the results of laboratory experiments.

Charles R. Plott and Vernon L. Smith

Further Comments

Professor Chamberlin's comments raise several deep issues which we feel should receive more attention.[1] His argument, starkly put, is: (1) political norms play an important part in most political (as opposed to economic) processes; (2) such norms are based on motivations other than self-interest; (3) self-interest is a basic assumption of the experimental methodology outlined by Plott; therefore, (4) there can be only limited external validity involved with such experimental methods.

Clearly the truth of the hypotheses (1) and (2) depends upon what is meant by the term "political norms." Likewise the ability to incorporate such norms into the experimental environments outlined by Plott depends upon the nature of such norms. If norms play the role of an institution—a rule which can be articulated and is followed by some or all—certainly they can be added to the experimental settings. If the norms are like attitudes which induce special shapes to preferences over outcomes (which of course could depend upon the preferences of others), then their manifestations, the special shaped preferences, can be incorporated even though the norms themselves may be absent. Those two classes of theories of norms are easy to deal with. Others may be more complicated.

The assertion (3) is incorrect. Self-interest is not a basic postulate which underlies the *methodology* and it was not listed by Plott as one of the basic axioms. The self-interest postulate is an integral aspect of many of the theories that have been examined, but experimentalists, having faced the data from experimental committee behavior, are very sensitive to alternative theories. In fact, a few experiments have been designed explicitly to capture aspects of the "normative" phenomena to which

---

[1] Ed. Note: Professor Smith was not at the conference but acted as an outside reviewer of the proceedings manuscript. His review comments on this subject prompted this joint response.

Chamberlin alludes (Fiorina and Plott, 1978; Isaac and Plott, 1978; Cohen, Levine, and Plott, 19 / 8). While one might claim that the experimentalists have devoted most of their effort to developing and testing "self-interest"-based theories, it would be wrong to presuppose that ethical and related behavior is not present or is in some sense precluded in principle by experimental methods.

Criticism of experimental methods based on the problems of maintaining both external and internal validity often seem to arise from the assumption that what is important about an experiment is that it be "real worldlike" in some subjective sense, informally conjectured by the investigator. Critics frequently have in mind some sort of "simulation" of a complicated naturally occurring situation and look to the experiment to provide forecasts about how events will unfold in the future (perhaps under various scenarios). Laboratory methods may be ultimately useful in such contexts but that has not been the primary purpose so far.

The primary purpose of most laboratory experiments in the area discussed by Plott has been to explore the accuracy of general theories and models within very simple settings. Such general theories typically abstract from "political norms" except to the extent that they might influence the shape of an individual's preference over outcomes. Therefore it would be quite wrong in testing such theories for the experimentalist to muddy the results by not carefully controlling the preference parameters. Experimental care as dictated by particular theories should not be construed as fundamental limitations of the methods.

Aside from the particular experimental methodology developed in the Plott paper, there are some broader methodological problems raised by the Chamberlin view. It is misleading to discuss the concept of internal and external validity within the context of a simple dichotomy between the laboratory and "political reality." Empirical tests of a model using different sets of cross-sectional observations on economic or political agents may show high consistency, or "internal" validity, but the results need not be "externally" valid with respect to time series observations or to cross-section studies in another country. Studies of the incentive effects of food stamp vouchers may be "internally" consistent, but not be "externally" valid with respect to the incentive effects of education vouchers. Obviously parallelism, or the question of the generalizability of a particular empirical result to allegedly different environments, should always be an open issue. The experimentalist, just because he may get sharper, less ambiguous results, should not be required to carry any more of a generalizability burden than investigators using other methodologies.

We would like to suggest that the statement (p. 162) requiring "that the experimental conditions be sufficiently like the conditions in the naturally occurring environment with which the designer is concerned that he/she is convinced that the experimental results . . . [are] externally valid," is unsatisfactory as a general criterion for judging the appropriateness of or relevancy of an experimental design. There will always be some aspect of reality that a designer might suspect is important, and which is missing from an experiment, that might cause him or her to remain less than convinced that the results are externally valid. *Even* if he/she is so convinced, that will not make it true, that is, "externally" valid.

The bottom line is that the robustness of empirical results on behavior across different environments can only be determined empirically. Whenever replicable laboratory behavior has been demonstrated, then it is entirely fitting to seek field tests of the hypothesis that the behavior is manifest in more complex environments. Some such work has already been reported by Smith (1979b), Levine and Plott (1977), and Ferejohn, Forsythe, and Noll (1979a). So far, the results are reassuring in the sense that there are many laboratory findings that seem also to characterize very "rich" field situations. But more such hard comparisons are welcome.

REFERENCES

Berl, J. E., R. D. McKelvey, P. C. Ordeshook, and M. D. Winer. 1976. "An Experimental Test of the Core in a Simple N-Person Cooperative, Non-sidepayment Game," *Journal of Conflict Resolution* vol. 20, no. 3 (September) pp. 543–579.

Cohen, Linda, M. E. Levine, and C. R. Plott. 1978. "Communication and Agenda Influence: The Chocolate Pizza Design," in Heinz Sauermann, ed., *Coalition Forming Behavior*, vol. 8 in Contributions to Experimental Economics [Tübingen, Germany, Mohr (Paul Siebeck)].

Ferejohn, J. A., R. Forsythe, and R. G. Noll. 1977. "Implementing Planning Procedures for the Provision of Discrete Public Goods," Social Science Working Paper 154, California Institute of Technology.

————. 1979a. "An Experimental Analysis of Decision-Making Procedures for Discrete Public Goods: A Case Study of a Problem in Institutional Design," in Vernon L. Smith, ed., *Research in Experimental Economics* vol. 1 (Greenwich, Conn., JAI Press).

————. 1979b. "Practical Aspects of the Construction of Decentralized Decisionmaking Systems for Public Goods" (this volume).

Fiorina, M. P., and C. R. Plott. 1978. "Committee Decisions Under Majority Rule: An Experimental Study," *American Political Science Review* (June) pp. 575–598.

Isaac, R. M., and C. R. Plott. 1978. "Cooperative Game Models of the Influence of the Closed Rule in Three Person, Majority Rule Committees: Theory and Experiment," in Peter Ordeshook, ed., *Game Theory and Political Science* (New York, NYU Press).

Levine, M. E., and C. R. Plott. 1977. "Agenda Influence and Its Implications," *Virginia Law Review* vol. 63, no. 4 (May) pp. 561–604.

Plott, C. R. 1978. "Externalities and Corrective Policies in Experimental Markets," Social Science Working Paper 180, California Institute of Technology.

———— and M. E. Levine. 1978. "A Model of Agenda Influence on Committee Decisions," *American Economic Review* vol. 68, no. 1 (March) pp. 146–160.

Smith, V. L. 1976. "Experimental Economics: Induced Value Theory," *American Economic Review* vol. 66, no. 2 (May) pp. 274–279.

————. 1977a. "The Principle of Unanimity and Voluntary Consent in Social Choice," *Journal of Political Economy* vol. 85, no. 6 (December) pp. 1125–1140.

————. 1977b. "Mechanisms for the Optimal Provision of Public Goods," in R. Auster and B. Sears, eds., *American Re-Evolution/Papers and Proceedings* (Tucson, Arizona, University of Arizona).

————. 1978. "Experimental Mechanisms for Public Choice," in P. C. Ordeshook, ed., *Game Theory and Political Science* (New York, New York University Press).

————. 1979a. "Incentive Compatible Experimental Processes for the Provision of Public Goods," in Vernon L. Smith, ed., *Research in Experimental Economics*, vol. 1 (Greenwich, Conn., JAI Press).

————. 1979b. "Relevance of Laboratory Experiments to Testing Resource Allocation Theory," in J. Kmenta and J. Ramsey, eds., *Evaluation of Econometric Models* (New York, Academic Press).

John A. Ferejohn, Robert Forsythe, and Roger G. Noll

Practical Aspects of the Construction of Decentralized Decision-making Systems for Public Goods

Recent developments in computer and communications technology have made feasible the use of genuine decentralized decision-making systems by large groups. For example, many cable television systems have the technical capability to allow two-way communications between subscribers and the cable headend. These technical developments have made it possible to have instant referenda on a variety of public issues, and as this possibility has become more real, the implications of direct, nonrepresentative democratic procedures for our system of government have received more and more attention.

Usually the assumption is made that the best way for the general public to express its opinion is through some kind of majority-rule voting institution. While voting institutions possess certain advantages, they have serious shortcomings as well. The most important are the lack of incentives to acquire information about alternative actions, and the inability to account directly for intensities of preferences.

In large electorates, the probability of the individual vote being pivotal on any particular issue is so small that individual voters have little incentive to acquire much information about the impact of any particular decision. Moreover, without opportunities for vote trading, logrolling, or some other form of side payments, voting systems make no distinction among voters according to the magnitudes of gain or loss that are associated with the alternatives. Established legislative bodies have

Financial support for this research was provided by the National Science Foundation, grant number APR76-01920.

complex institutional arrangements that give incentives to members to develop expertise in particular narrow areas, to defer to the judgment of other legislators in other areas, and to engage in bargains over votes. Thus, while one legislator's vote is usually inconsequential, each individual has the chance to develop substantial power in some areas through the development of expertise, and to trade this power to achieve objectives on other issues. The institutions by which this is accomplished— committees, seniority, and so on—seem unlikely to develop in a direct democracy. Consequently, many observers are concerned about the quality of decisions that would emerge out of a referendum system.

This paper explores the possibility that perhaps the voting model of decision making may not be the appropriate one to apply in this area. Instead, it explores a class of decentralized decision-making institutions that is similar to the market economy. For our purposes, the defining characteristic of such systems is this: Individual agents are endowed with resources that they may dispose of at will in trade, production, or consumption. Allocations in such systems have the equilibrium property— that is, agents cannot unilaterally improve themselves, given their resources and their set of feasible actions. (This is usually defined on the assumption that agents are price-takers.)

Neoclassical economic theory furnishes evidence that such systems work efficiently in circumstances in which all goods are private and widely traded. In this case, all the information that society needs in finding efficient allocations is expressed in the decentralized market behavior of the agents. Until recently, the prevailing belief among economists has been that the potential applicability of market systems is not much wider than for allocating private goods. With externalities in consumption or production, standard market activities will generally fail to reveal information that is relevant for social choice and, for this reason, allocations which are in some sense better than the ones produced in the market are likely to exist.

Recent work by Groves and Ledyard (1977), Green and Laffont (1977), and others suggests that even in the presence of external effects, decentralized systems can be designed that permit society to allocate public goods efficiently. The construction of such mechanisms appears, upon reading the original papers, to be a delicate matter, and one might wonder about the extent of potential applications for the new decentralized systems. Not surprisingly, there is little research on this question; after all, these proposals are quite new. However, the evolution of axiomatic methods of analysis and the development of experimental methods in economics have permitted Vernon Smith (1978) and ourselves (1978) to launch early investigations into these questions.

In this paper, we report on the applicability of decentralized decision-making procedures for public goods. We introduce first a set of allocation problems that we would like to be able to solve. The solutions to such problems suggest a natural set of design constraints—that is, a list of constraints that any proposed system must satisfy. We investigate the class of institutions that has these properties. Finally, we discuss some experiments using proposed institutions in environments typical of (though simpler than) those that seem to arise in the real world.

I.   SOME ALLOCATION PROBLEMS

This section suggests some allocation problems that are natural candidates for the use of decentralized decision-making procedures. In each of these problems the design constraints—the required characteristics of alternative systems—seem to be evident from the verbal description of the problem.

Problem 1:   The network of public television stations is interested in acquiring programming. Each station has a programming budget and preferences over various bundles of programs. The total amount available for programs is the sum of the budgets. Which programs should they buy?

Problem 2:   A group of small school districts is interested in cooperating in the acquisition of textbooks in order to take advantage of the lower prices available on large orders. Each school has a textbook budget and the total amount of funds available for textbook acquisition is the sum of these budgets. Each school has preferences among the available bundles of textbooks and the choice of books is supposed to depend on school preferences. Which books, and in what amounts, should the consortium acquire?

Problem 3:   A community is interested in purchasing equipment for public safety—ambulances, fire engines, rescue vehicles. Each citizen has a budget and has preferences among various possible packages of safety equipment. The total community resources equal the sum of the individual budgets. How much equipment should be purchased?

Problem 4:   The residents of a condominium development are considering the purchase of playground equipment for the common use of their children, or the conversion of an adjacent vacant lot into a park and playground. Each family, based upon the income, age, and tastes of its members, is willing to pay up to some maximum amount for various alternative recreational development plans. What recreational plan should be adopted?

Problem 5:   A private foundation is undertaking a major financial commitment to support research in some important interdisciplinary field. Several program officers from different parts of the foundation have been asked to allocate part of their budgets to this new venture, and to serve together on a committee to evaluate and select some proposals for financial support. The foundation wants the group to evaluate the proposals together in order to assure that each of several disciplines relevant to the field are adequately covered in the proposals that are eventually supported. Which projects should be supported?

Problem 6:   A diversified corporation has decentralized its investment planning among its divisions. Each division wants access to econometric forecasts about the national economy—growth in demand, inflation, interest rates, and so on—to use in selecting its investment strategy. Each has a budget for acquiring such information, and, in order to avoid the unnecessary costs of obtaining the same information several times, wants to cooperate with the other divisions in obtaining a common econometric forecast. The problem is complicated by the fact that each division has somewhat different desires with respect to the details of the forecast that will be acquired. What kind of forecast should they buy?

Each of these problems shares certain features. The bundles of commodities are available only in discrete units—a set of proposals from which some will be selected. The set of such bundles would typically be expected to be large but finite, and each commodity has public good characteristics. Additionally, these problems generate certain design features that a reasonable allocational institution ought to satisfy. Among these are: (1) nonbankruptcy: individual agents cannot be made to pay more than their budgets; (2) nondeficit: together the group cannot spend more than it collects from its members; (3) efficiency: the final allocation must not be Pareto dominated by another feasible alternative.

Additional constraints may also arise. For example in problem 2, a school should not have to pay more of its textbook budget for the finally chosen package than it would spend if it did not join the consortium. It does not seem natural to require this property for problem 3 because the goods in question may not be marketed outside the proposed system; however, in problems 1, 2, 4, and 6, alternatives to collective action are available through private markets. Moreover, in problems 1, 2, and 4, coercion probably cannot be used to enforce a collective decision.

Two other desirable properties of institutions that might be used to solve these problems are more difficult to formulate precisely, but can be important: (4) speed and ease of operation; and (5) lack of strategic incentives for the agents.

The economic reasons for wanting institutions that work quickly and relatively cheaply are obvious. Our analysis (1978) of the Station Programming Cooperative (SPC) of the Public Broadcasting Service (PBS) convinced us that decision-making costs are typically quite substantial. We estimated that in the SPC about 5 percent of the total costs of programs was devoted to simply operating the allocational institution.

The fifth requirement—lack of strategic incentives—has been formulated in various ways. One version is that agents have an incentive to report their true (marginal) valuation of the commodities irrespective of the behavior of the other agents. We call this strong incentive compatibility. Other formulations require only that there is an equilibrium at which an efficient bundle of commodities is produced. This we call weak incentive compatibility. Of course, the primary effect of any such axiom is to allow the system to gather the right kind of information to allow the choice of an efficient allocation. A secondary, but still important aspect of nonstrategic behavior is that it can contribute to the "fairness" of the procedure as viewed by the participants, in that certain agents are not perceived as using the system for redistributing income to themselves.

If the strong form of the axiom holds for an institution, the agents have an incentive to report their true valuation of the goods in the system and an easy problem of strategy choice. If only the weak axiom is satisfied by an institution, the problem of strategic choice may be very difficult for the participants. This difficulty may cause, at the least, slow operation and, at worst, nontermination of the procedure.

In the remainder of this paper we shall employ formal versions of properties one through five. In the next section we report some research indicating that no institution exists that possesses certain versions of these properties. Then we give a description of a real problem of institutional design and indicate how various institutions were constructed to solve it. We will then summarize the results of the operation of one mechanism in the field and of various alternative mechanisms in the laboratory. As our theoretical results indicate, all the institutions studied are "second-best" institutions—systems that do not actually possess the five properties but which exhibit them in varying degrees. We think this is likely to be a state of affairs that is typical of attempts to design economic institutions in environments with significant externalities.

II.   THEORETICAL INVESTIGATION OF ALLOCATION PROCEDURES

While the characteristics listed in the previous section appear to be desirable features of an allocation procedure, elsewhere we have shown (1977) that no institution can satisfy all of these axioms. As a background and justification for the remainder of the paper, we summarize this result here.

We assume that there is a set of agents, $N = \{1, 2, \ldots, n\}$, each of whom has a budget, b^i, and a preference relation, R_i, defined on the space of possible allocations. The asymmetric part of R_i is denoted P_i. For the present discussion the space of allocations is written as follows: $X = \{0,1\}^p \times [0,\infty)^n$. The first p components of a vector in X indicate which of p discrete public goods are produced and the last n components indicate how much of the private good (in which the b^i are measured) is possessed by each agent. The cost of producing the ith public good is C_i.

We can write the feasible set for this problem as

$$\Omega = \left\{ x \in X \;\middle|\; \sum_{i=1}^{p} x_i C_i + \sum_{i=p+1}^{p+n} x_i \leq \sum_{i=p+1}^{p+n} b^i \right\}$$

We define an element, x, of Ω as *weakly efficient* if there is no $y \in \Omega$ such that

1. $y_i \neq x_i$ for some $i = 1, \ldots, p$,
2. $y_i \leq b^i$ $\forall i = p + 1, \ldots, p + n$ and such that
3. $yR_i x$ $\forall i = 1, \ldots, n$ and $yP_j x$ for some j

Note that this set is somewhat larger than the set of efficient allocations.

Now each agent may communicate preferences in a language M_i, the size of which we allow to vary with observable data in the process. That is, the message set may actually be a correspondence that depends on the b^i, the C_j, and the messages of all other agents. The message chosen by an agent can depend, at most, on observable quantities in the system $(b^i, i = 1, \ldots, n, C_j, j = 1, \ldots, p$, and the messages of the other agents), and on that agent's own preferences. Thus, if $R_1, \ldots, R_n$ and $R_1', \ldots, R_n'$ are two preference n-tuples and if $R_i = R_i'$ for some i, then $m_i(b^1, \ldots, b^n, C_1, \ldots, C_p, R_i) = m_i(b^1, \ldots, b^n, C_1, \ldots, C_p, R_i')$.

An allocation procedure is a mapping F taking n-tuples of messages into allocations. An allocation procedure is weakly efficient if it maps into the set of weakly efficient allocations which we denote $\hat{\Omega}$. An equilibrium for F is an n-tuple of messages $m = (\overline{m}_1, \overline{m}_2, \ldots, \overline{m}_n)$ with the property that for each i, $(\overline{m}_1, \ldots, \overline{m}_i, \ldots, \overline{m}_n) R_i (\overline{m}_1, \ldots, \overline{m}_i, \ldots, \overline{m}_n)$ for all $m_i \in M_i(b^1, \ldots, b^n, C_1, \ldots, C_p, \overline{m}_1, \ldots, \overline{m}_{i-1}, \overline{m}_{i+1}, \ldots, \overline{m}_n)$.

We have established (1977) for this model that generally there are no dominant strategy equilibria for F. Another way of putting the matter is this: If F is an allocation procedure, then it cannot be nonstrategic and weakly efficient. A corollary of this theorem is, of course, that weakly efficient allocation procedures cannot satisfy the strong incentive compatibility axioms given above.

This result indicates that none of the allocational problems listed above can be solved in the sense that we had hoped. Any institution that could be constructed would necessarily have shortcomings that might in the view of some be critical. One has to be prepared to trade off one virtue against the others when trying to design institutions.

III. THE STATION PROGRAM COOPERATIVE

In the spring of 1974, the American network of noncommercial television stations introduced a decentralized market mechanism—the SPC—to acquire nearly half of the programs that were broadcast over the national network during the 1974–75 television season. The SPC is a decentralized market mechanism for acquiring discrete public goods. A television program is a public good in the sense that its production costs and, for the most part, distribution costs are independent of the number of stations in the network that broadcast it. Programs are discrete public goods in that they are not offered in continuously variable amounts and qualities. Instead, prospective producers propose programs of a fixed duration, format, and composition that with few exceptions are either accepted or rejected as proposed to the network. In current practice, individual stations that choose not to help pay for a program do not broadcast it, although the costs of enforcing this exclusion should a station try to cheat would be quite high. To date, PBS has relied upon stations not to use programs that they do not participate in purchasing and has adopted no formal enforcement mechanism.[1]

The design problem is roughly that given in problem 1, so that the theorem given above suggests that no completely satisfactory system exists. Nevertheless, given the nature of the problem, the stations have a clear incentive to coordinate their program acquisition and production activities and, not surprisingly, coordination has been the rule for many years. The traditional method of coordinating program acquisitions has been through networking (i.e., centralization of the decision-making process) or syndication. The first turned out to be extremely vulnerable to national political forces, while the latter proved to be extremely costly and to sacrifice certain marketing advantages from coordinated scheduling of programs.

For these reasons a marketlike system was designed that allowed the stations to select packages of programs for broadcast over the national network. We give a brief and idealized description of that system (the Station Program Cooperative) here and refer the reader to our other work (1978) for a more complete account.

Except for an attempt to alter the system in 1976, which was quickly abandoned when it proved unsatisfactory, each SPC has followed essentially the same procedures. The station managers participate in a time-sharing, interactive computer system. In each round of the procedure, the center at PBS sends messages to participants about the identity and prices of the programs that remain in the market, and receives from each station a list of the programs that it wishes to purchase at the posted prices. A program is dropped when no station desires to purchase it at the last posted price (or when, with the handwriting on the wall, the producer withdraws the program). Each set of choices by the stations is used until an equilibrium is reached—that is, until so few changes occur in choices by stations that program prices are virtually constant in two consecutive rounds.

The mechanism for achieving a reduction in the number of programs remaining in the system is implicit in the formula for calculating the prices that each station faces for each program. Letting $i = 1, \ldots, s$

---

[1] Ed. note: I am informed by a station executive in Massachusetts that during the first several years of SPC trials all stations have in fact ultimately been given all programs. Clearly this cannot be continued if the process is to have the desired incentive properties.

index the stations and $j = 1, \ldots, p$ index the programs, the price (q_{ij}) of a program j to a station i is:

(1) $q_{ij} = a_{ij}C_j$

where C_j is the cost of the program to the network and a_{ij} is the tax share of station i for program j. The tax share is computed according to the following formula:

(2) $a_{ij} = \sum_{r=1}^{R} \left(\frac{b_r V_{ri}}{\sum_{k \in S_j} V_{rk}} \right)$

where V_{ri} is the amount of some welfare measure possessed by station i; $r = 1, \ldots, R$ indexes the welfare measures entering the tax share computation; b_r is the weight accorded V_{ri} (with the sum of the b_r being unity); and S_j is the subset of the indexes over stations that includes only stations participating in the purchase of program j. In the first round, S_j is assumed to contain 80 percent of all stations. In calculating a_{ij} in subsequent rounds, S_j contains station i and all other stations that in the preceding round included program j in the list of programs they wished to purchase at the last posted prices.

Although the first two markets (SPC I in 1974 and SPC II in 1975) used different welfare measures than were used in SPC III and SPC IV, in all cases the SPC used what amounts to a tax system based upon ability to pay. Both formulas produced tax shares that were highly correlated with the population and income of the area served by a station.

A station is required to pay the price calculated in (1) and (2) only if the program is purchased and the station has listed the program among those it wishes to receive. Otherwise, it neither pays for nor broadcasts the program, even if other stations eventually purchase it and it is included in the final network schedule.

The SPC has certain dissimilarities to the abstract allocation processes discussed in section III. Most important, it is an adjustment process in which the message correspondence for each agent depends on the past messages of all the other agents. In the SPC this dependence is through provisional allocations and computed prices. A natural candidate for a collective choice in such a process is a stationary point—that is, a set of prices and an allocation with the property that the messages sent by the agents lead to the same prices and allocations.

How does the SPC meet the criteria suggested in the previous section? To start with, if a stationary point is reached, both nondeficit and nonbankruptcy are satisfied. As to the remaining conditions, we show elsewhere (1978) that, under the hypothesis that stations exhibit Cournot behavior, the SPC has some shortcomings. First, a stationary point need not exist. Second, stationary points may or may not be Pareto optimal. Third, stationary points may exist but be impossible to reach from various initial prices. Fourth, stationary points may be unstable in the sense that small perturbations from the stationary prices may make the stationary point unreachable.

The SPC also is not incentive compatible in the following sense. In some cases, a station may have the incentive to purchase a program during the procedure even though its price exceeds the station's willingness to pay, given the information communicated by all other stations. In other words, dominant purchasing strategies generally do not exist in the procedure.

The SPC has some desirable properties as well. First, in actual operation the SPC terminates quite rapidly. The system has been modified in various ways that probably speed convergence, as described in our earlier work (1978). Although these modifications are not used in the experimental version, rapid termination still occurs.

Second, participants have difficulty devising a successful strategy that entails misrevealing preferences. Station managers state that they could not see how they could significantly affect the operation of the procedure by their purchasing strategy. And, while a substantial amount of preference misrevelation was observed in the experiments, postsession discussions indicate that participants were not able to achieve desired effects from these actions and in fact usually achieved inferior allocations due to the use of devious strategies. If this result is general, as station managers gain experience in using the system they would probably learn to avoid the use of strategies that involve misrevelation.

Finally, it is generally believed that the decision task facing the station during the operation of the SPC is fairly easy to understand and that the stations are able to produce appropriate responses without difficulty.

Thus, while the SPC seems to achieve the nondeficit and nonbankruptcy conditions, it is not generally efficient, nor is it incentive compatible. On the other hand, field experience indicates that it terminates rapidly and that nontruthful strategies are difficult to find and execute, so the SPC seems to possess a certain kind of strategic simplicity.

IV. EXPERIMENTAL RESULTS WITH ALTERNATIVE INSTITUTIONS

In this section we report on our attempts to construct a more efficient allocation process than the SPC. We require that any candidate institution satisfy nonbankruptcy and nondeficit because these seem to be minimal conditions for the viability of any institution in the absence of government subsidies. We then decided to evaluate the alternatives on three dimensions: (1) relative efficiency, (2) speed of termination, and (3) incentives for strategic behavior.

Three institutions were designed for examination in a laboratory setting: a simplified version of the SPC, a bidding process (the B-procedure) that was similar to certain mechanisms proposed in the literature, and Vernon Smith's (1978) auction process (the A-procedure). Experimental results are available on the first two systems, but only a pilot experiment has been carried out for the auction process.

The three experimental institutions are representatives from two broad classes of decision-making mechanisms. The SPC procedure is one in which the center sends price messages to the agents and the agents must respond in quantities. In the A-procedure and the B-procedure, the center emits quantity information and the agents respond with internal prices. While in some settings this distinction might be inessential, here, because of the discreteness of the quantity space, important differences separate these two classes.

Most salient is that under either the A-procedure or the B-procedure the agents have to be able to compute their willingness to pay for each commodity at each stage of the procedure without knowing the status of the other commodities. That is, agents are asked to give bids when they do not know for sure where they are in the commodity space. In the SPC this problem does not arise. To minimize the effects of this problem, the environment of the experimental series was severely restricted. In particular, substitutes and complements were eliminated from the preferences of the agents by giving them linear monetary payoff schedules.

An additional difference between the SPC and the alternatives is that the size of the message spaces available to the agents is much larger in the A-procedure and the B-procedure than in the SPC. This turns out to be important also. A final difference is that only in the SPC can agents be excluded from acquiring a share in the public good. In the A-procedure and B-procedure, as long as total bids exceed the cost of an alterna-

TABLE 11.   Values of Commodities to Agents
(dollars)

Commodity	Agent				
	1	*2*	*3*	*4*	*5*
A	3.00	1.80	2.40	1.20	4.80
B	1.20	3.60	6.00	1.80	3.00
C	4.80	8.40	6.60	2.40	5.40
D	3.60	6.00	3.60	3.00	7.20
E	1.20	5.40	3.60	4.20	1.80

tive, all agents share in its benefits and costs. The preference distribution that was used throughout the two series is given in table 11.

Table 12 lists the budgets of the agents, the program costs, and the sharing rule (α_i) that were used in both experimental series. Notice that the budgets used in experiments SPC-1, SPC-2, and B-1 were different than those used in the remaining experiments. The change was made because the initial experiments apparently contained an artificially difficult coordination problem. The total group payoff in these experiments was maximized (at $67.20) when commodities C, D, and E were selected and the costs of these commodities equaled the total budgets of all agents ($30.00).

In the SPC procedure, first-round prices were based on the assumption that all agents were purchasing all commodities. These prices were the lowest that could be observed during the experiment. Once the initial purchase decisions were made by the agents, subsequent prices were calculated according to the following formula:

$$p_{ik}(t) = C_k \frac{\alpha_i}{\sum\limits_{j \in S_k(t-1)} \alpha_j} \quad i \in S, \quad k \in P$$

where C_k is the cost of commodity k

α_i is the basic cost share of agent i

and $S_k(t-1)$ is the set of agents purchasing the commodity during the period $t-1$

These new prices were posted on the blackboard in front of the room and the agents were then asked to make new purchase decisions. This process continued until the experiment was terminated.

The termination condition for these experiments was that either (1) the same purchases were indicated by all agents for two consecutive rounds (after round 3) or (2) the round number exceeded some predetermined (secret) number (always ten).

TABLE 12.   Budgets, Costs Shares, and Costs

	Agent					Total budgets
	1	*2*	*3*	*4*	*5*	
Budget (SPC-1 & 2, B-1)	3.00	7.50	9.00	4.50	6.00	30.00
Budget (SPC-3, 4, 5; B-2, 3, 4, 5, 6, 7, 8, A-1)	3.30	8.25	9.90	4.95	6.60	33.00
Share of cost (α_i)	0.10	0.25	0.30	0.15	0.20	

	Commodity				
	A	*B*	*C*	*D*	*E*
Cost	6.00	9.00	12.00	10.50	7.50

In the B-experiments agents were asked to submit their initial bids under the hypothesis that, initially, none of the programs were to be purchased. Each agent's bid vector was required to be nonnegative and to sum to a total not greater than the agent's budget. Bid totals were posted on the blackboard at the conclusion of each round and the experimenter indicated changes in the list of provisional purchasing decisions. In B-1, B-2, B-3, and B-4 changes in the purchasing decisions were made subject to the restriction that at most *one* commodity could enter or leave the list each round. This restriction was placed on the mechanism so that when experiments are designed with preferences exhibiting complements or substitutes, agents could have a basis on which to formulate their willingness to pay. However, this restriction will cause high transactions costs in an environment like the SPC with scores of alternative commodities. In B-5, B-6, B-7, and B-8, no such restriction was employed. In all B-procedure experiments, termination occurred when (1) the round number exceeded some predetermined (secret) number (always ten) or (2) the same messages were sent by all agents for two consecutive rounds.

Agents were able to compute their tax liability according to a table provided to each of them at the beginning of the experiment. [See our other work (1978) for a sample tax table.] The entries in this table were computed according to the following formula:

$$t_i[m(t)] = \min \left\{ \sum_{k=1}^{p} Z_k(t)\left(C_k - \sum_{j\neq i} m_{kj}(t) \right) + \sum_{k=1}^{p} \max\left(\sum_{j\neq i} m_{kj}(t) - \sum_{j\neq i} \alpha_j C_k, 0 \right), b^i \right\}$$

where C_k is the cost of commodity k,

α_i is the basic cost share of agent i,

$Z_k(t) = 1$ if commodity k was purchased in round t, and $Z_k(t) = 0$ otherwise,

$m_{kj}(t)$ is the bid of agent j for commodity k at round t

b^i is the ith agent's budget. (This provision prevents bankruptcy.)

As remarked, this tax rule has the feature that nonbankruptcy and nondeficit are satisfied. It is not, however, nonstrategic because it may sometimes pay agents to overreport their willingness to pay for a program.

In the A-procedure each agent submits a bid $m_{kj}(t)$ for every commodity. The sum of an agent's bids in a round must not exceed his budget. If the sum of the bids for a commodity is at least as great as its cost, the commodity is provisionally purchased. In the last round, the excess of the bid total over the cost is rebated to the agents in proportion to their bids. The procedure terminates if all bids are identical for two consecutive rounds or if a (secret) termination round is reached.

While nondeficit and nonbankruptcy are always satisfied, the A-procedure is not generally incentive compatible nor does it seem to be strategically simple. This version of the process generally exhibits many local Nash equilibria, so the coordination problem for the agents may be quite severe. Smith (1978) has found that in experiments with a single public good, bid prices tend to be closely related to induced valuation of the good. At this time we have not been able even to formulate this relationship for the present class of allocation processes.

The results of several series of five-person experiments on the SPC and B-procedure are reported in some detail elsewhere (1978), and so only a brief summary will be presented here. We have conducted five experiments with the SPC, eight with the B-procedure, and as yet just one with the A-procedure. Obviously the comparisons we give here can only be taken as preliminary to a more complete experimental analysis.

Perhaps the least ambiguous result is in the speed of the procedures. We had been impressed at the relatively quick termination of the real SPC, which generally occurred within twelve rounds even though there were 100 alternative public goods and 150 participants involved. The experimental SPC mechanism terminated rapidly, too. It generally finished in five or six rounds and never lasted long enough to require an artificial termination (round ten). Neither of the alternative procedures ever terminated before round ten, although in some experiments the fluctuations in bid prices became small after about the sixth round.

We think that the major reason for the relatively fast termination of the SPC mechanism is this. During the process the admissible message set for each agent shrinks rapidly. As purchase decisions in the early rounds concentrate on some programs rather than others, the prices of the unpopular programs increase rapidly in relation to the prices of the others. This shrinkage in the message sets limits the amount of strategic flexibility the players have and seems to encourage the choice of simple Cournot response.

In the other procedures, the message set of the agents remains fixed and it seems to be fairly simple to locate insincere bidding strategies that are successful. Our experimental records contain many examples of strategic behavior by the subjects, and such behavior was frequently rewarded. We should point out that in our experiments, unlike those conducted by Vernon Smith on the A-procedure with one discrete public good, there was no real penalty for a failure to terminate prior to round ten.

We computed the relative efficiency of an experimental institution by examining the ratio of actual to potential payout to the subjects. In the SPC the average of this ratio was 60 percent while for the B-procedure the average was about 57 percent. The B-procedure exhibited somewhat more variation around the average than did the SPC mechanism. In the A-procedure experiment, the relative efficiency was zero. The bidding in that experiment exhibited much more round-to-round variation than was observed in the B-procedure experiments. Whether this variability of bidding behavior is a characteristic of the A-procedure in an environment with discrete public goods is unknown at this time.

Our examination of strategy selection is still preliminary but the following conclusions seem warranted. In the SPC, myopic or Cournot bidding is the rule. More than 75 percent of all choices made by subjects in the SPC were consistent with the Cournot hypothesis. If the first two rounds are eliminated, this percentage increases to 84 percent. We did observe some strategic behavior in the SPC, but it was rare and usually futile.

We have been unable as yet to construct a good model of bidding behavior for the other procedures. Preliminary examination of the data indicates that the Cournot hypothesis is not a good model of subject behavior in these institutions. We are still examining the data generated by these experiments to see if a reasonable explanation can be found.

On the basis of the laboratory results, it seems that while the average efficiencies of the B-procedure and the SPC mechanism are about equal, the variability of bids and outcomes seems much higher in bidding institutions than in the SPC. This variability seems to be due to the relative ease of adopting insincere strategies in bidding institutions of the type we have investigated. Perhaps this feature also provides part of the explanation for the very rapid termination of the SPC. In any case, our results suggest that given the design constraints set out earlier, there is no evidence of the availability of a bidding institution that is better, in any natural sense, than the SPC.

V.   DISCUSSION

The investigation has focused on the actual design and construction of allocative institutions in real environments. We have taken the liberty of defining the notion of a real decision-making environment broadly enough to include the ones we construct in the laboratory. The reason for this is simply that we think that many if not all of the features of economic environments can be modeled easily and usefully in laboratory settings.

The environments of interest in this paper are those in which there are several (perhaps many) discrete public goods, not all of which can be feasibly chosen by the agents. While the literature on incentive compatible mechanisms for allocation in economies with public goods is valuable in designing mechanisms for the environments we are interested in, many practical problems of implementing these mechanisms simply do not appear in that literature.

Most important, most of the work in that field is characterized by an examination of equilibrium points of various noncooperative games. In designing a real mechanism, disequilibrium behavior seems to be of preeminent importance. This is not surprising, because in environments with many discrete public goods, the complexity of the search process is enormous even if a centralized programming mechanism is employed.

Except for the experimental work of Vernon Smith (1978), there has been very little study of adjustment processes in environments with public goods. It seems to us that the prospects for making use of the rapidly expanding technical opportunities for implementing decentralized decision-making institutions depend crucially on the study of adjustment processes of the sort examined here.

Edward H. Clarke

Comments

The experiments reported here by Ferejohn, Forsythe, and Noll hold promise of laying a firm groundwork for application of "incentive compatible" mechanisms in the real world. In addition to applauding this effort, I offer some comments on their experimental design and their admittedly tentative findings.

Their objective has been to design a system that will meet five basic criteria, two of which are the avoidance of "bankruptcy" and strategic behavior. I believe, however, that in the pursuit of this objective they may run the risk of throwing the baby out with the bath.

NONBANKRUPTCY

The nonbankruptcy criterion grows out of the recent theoretical literature (Green and Laffont, 1976, 1977; Ferejohn, Forsythe, and Noll, 1977) and the desire to adapt an "incentive compatible" mechanism to the institutional choice setting of public broadcasting (Ferejohn, Forsythe, and Noll, 1977, pp. 29, 30). I will not deal at length with the theoretical concerns here, but will confine my remarks to those aspects of this experimental design which, I believe, are too restrictive, even with the particular features of the potential institutional application(s) clearly in mind. A perfectly reasonable criterion for setting some bound on the extent to which agents can lose resources has been transformed into a virtual "impossibility result" (Ferejohn, Forsythe, and Noll, 1977, pp. 35–43). This is, in my view, unnecessary for the purposes of this experiment.

The theoretical literature has shown that one mechanism, first described by me, retains the desired properties in an environment with consumption lower bounds where agents are making a decision about two alternatives.[1] In the experiment, described by Ferejohn and his coauthors, we are in fact asking the agents to make such a decision—that is, to choose between commodity A and commodity E, for even though there are other commodities, the central choice is between the bundles CDE and CDA.

Even in the much more complex environment of, say, a public broadcasting system which involves choices among *many* alternatives, "a method of 'social' decisionmaking is necessary which allows the station managers the flexibility necessary to accurately reflect the tastes of their potential viewing audiences."[2] Thus, in my view, any experiment aimed at this kind of potential application should give the agents substantial flexibility to exchange a private good (or money) for public (or non-private) good(s).

In the experiment described, however, the experimenters began with zero flexibility by making the total budget ($30) equal to the cost of the most efficient commodity bundle (CDE). They themselves found this too restrictive and relaxed the budget constraint by 10 percent ($33 to spend on a $30 commodity bundle). I would suggest, for reasons described below, that they relax the budget constraint further.

As far as potential station-manager users of such a system are concerned, they can always ask viewers for more contributions or borrow money with the intention of repaying it in the future. Therefore, if the managers and viewers have intense preferences for a particular commodity bundle, let them pay for it rather than force them, unnecessarily, to employ strategy to obtain their desires at the expense of others in a way

[1] Green and Laffont (1976) demonstrate how the Clarke mechanism can remain strategy free while avoiding bankruptcy. In their reply, Ferejohn, Forsythe, and Noll construct a counterexample that practically amounts to a zero sum game (e.g., choice of A would generate an efficiency gain of, say, $1). Here the total incentive taxes will also be $V - 4$ times that potential efficiency gain (e.g., if $V = \$100$, then the agents give up $96 for a gain of $1). I have elsewhere (Clarke, 1978b) suggested the many reasons, other than potential bankruptcy, that we avoid use of demand revelation in such context. The participants would be better off using random selection such as flipping a coin.

If, alternatively, we had 150 program managers rather than 5 agents, and replicated the values for these agents in their table 15 thirty times, then the incentive taxes will be zero. The fact that the taxes decline slowly and will remain positive for a V somewhat greater than 100 is simply a result of their construction of a zero sum game. Where we take a strongly positive sum game, the aggregate incentive taxes will be very small and the probability of "a bankrupt collective," particularly in a larger number setting, will be infinitesimally small.

[2] Green and Laffont (1976, p. 29) recognize the institutional constraints of the public broadcasting setting, but also echo the need for flexibility.

that may reduce the welfare for all. The reason for more budget flexibility is then to make it possible, in the current fashionable usage, to use a "strongly incentive compatible" mechanism so as to avoid strategic behavior.

I continue to believe that a useful experiment can be conducted with the very simple system I proposed. The first experiment with this system was ill designed in some respects and I have explained the problems elsewhere (Clarke, 1975). Although the Ferejohn–Forsythe–Noll experiment avoids these problems, there is a danger of using this experimental method merely to prove the desired results if the advice laid out below is too faithfully followed. I offer the suggestion below, then, not as an experiment to prove my case, but as an observation about the design and results of the particular experiment discussed in their paper.

STRATEGIC BEHAVIOR

The two alternative bidding procedures used in the Ferejohn–Forsythe–Noll experiment display the phenomenon of "budget concentration." In the familiar cases, an individual will not respond to questions about his preferences with honest answers but rather in the manner he perceives will best enhance his goals—in many cases by *overstating* his preferences. Therefore, rational individuals in the experiments described by Ferejohn and his coauthors did indeed exploit the opportunity to employ more or less sophisticated variants of "budget concentration." That such behavior did not always work to the individual's advantage does not mean that the subjects would not learn to do better.

In this respect, I find the SPC procedure particularly vulnerable to more or less sophisticated variants of budget concentration. The B-procedure appears somewhat less vulnerable because it is more akin to the procedure I will describe.[3]

---

[3] The B-procedure is, in fact, more closely related to the *iterative* procedure proposed by Groves and Ledyard (1977) than to the procedure I will describe. The comparative advantages of these procedures are being widely debated in the public choice literature (see Clarke, 1978a; Tullock, 1978).

Ed. note: This is, of course, exactly the opposite of the experimental results reported by Ferejohn and his coauthors. They found that the SPC procedure tended to induce nonstrategic behavior and not to reward such attempts at sophisticated responses as were made, while the B-procedure was *more* subject to insincere strategies.

TABLE 13.   Net Reported Values for Alternative Commodity Bundles;
Calculation of the Incentive Tax[a]

Commodity bundle / agent	CDE	CDA	Incentive tax[b]
1	$ 6.60	$ 8.55	0[c]
2	12.30	9.08	$1.62 = 26.62 - 25.00$[d]
3	4.80	4.05	0
4	5.10	2.32	$1.28 = 33.38 - 32.10$
5	8.40	11.70	0
	$37.20	$35.70	2.90

   [a] The net value is determined by taking the total value for each agent /commodity presented by Ferejohn and coauthors and subtracting the agent's cost share. The net values are then added together for a particular commodity bundle.
   [b] Tideman and Tullock (1976) call it a Clarke tax.
   [c] The incentive taxes for individuals 1, 3, and 5 are zero because their reported valuations do not change the choice which would obtain in their absence.
   [d] To calculate the incentive tax for agent 2, we exclude his reported values and determine what would have happened in his absence. Commodity A would be chosen in lieu of commodity E because the net values from including E would be $25.00 while the net values from including A would be $26.62. This difference is the incentive imposed on agent 2. The analogous calculation determines the incentive tax imposed on agent 4.

A STRONGLY INCENTIVE COMPATIBLE PROCEDURE

   I suggest a very simple procedure that would have each individual pay an *incentive tax* equal to the net cost to others if his vote changes the outcome.

   To see how this procedure might work in the context of this particular experiment, we can simply convert the values of the commodities shown in table 11 in the paper to the values shown in table 13 here. These numbers are simply total values (benefits) less cost shares for each agent for each commodity. We then choose the commodity bundle with the highest aggregate reported value so as to also satisfy the aggregate budget constraint—CDE in table 13. The incentive tax is determined by, in turn, excluding the values reported by each individual. By such a procedure we find that two of the agents—2 and 4 in table 13—report values that change the outcome (i.e., the commodity bundle CDA would have been selected if either of them had not participated). The incentive tax paid by each agent is then the difference between the net values reported by *all others* for CDA compared with CDE.

   As has been observed elsewhere, this procedure is "strongly incentive compatible" in that each individual is motivated to reveal his true net values honestly. However, the taxes must either be "wasted" or at least not returned to the agents in any way that would remove the individual strategy-free properties of the tax. Also, we assume that the agents will not strive collectively against each other by, say, forming coalitions. The problems of "waste" and coalitions in the context of this experiment will be briefly discussed at the conclusion of this comment.

First, however, we must deal with an objection that the participants may have an information problem in identifying the relevant alternatives. Even five commodities generate a large number of possible combinations and 100 potential programs yield a huge number.

However, cooperative information procedures designed to reduce information costs could be used to narrow the issue set down to a few alternatives, even if the potential number of combinations were very great. Station managers, for example, should be able readily to identify the programs which most agree should be included (or excluded) as opposed to those about which they disagree.[4]

Similarly, in the experiment, it should be possible to design procedures to reduce information and decision costs in setting the agenda. In the case just discussed, we are basically choosing only between commodity A and commodity E. We do not need a complicated adjustment process to do this job and, as explained below, the agenda-setting problem should be separated from that of making a straightforward decision on the discrete commodity bundles via the incentive tax.

OTHER CRITERIA: EFFICIENCY AND CONVERGENCE

Of the five criteria laid out by Ferejohn, Forsythe, and Noll, I have dealt briefly with two. A third—nondeficit (or budget surplus)—is satis-

---

[4] Ferejohn, Forsythe, and Noll, p. 180, describe such cooperative information procedures in the context of the existing SPC. Their reply notwithstanding, I would like to stress the general applicability of my procedure to the multialternative setting (see also Tideman and Tullock, 1976, p. 1157). For the practical problem at hand, I suggest a two-step procedure. First, the managers informally agree that, say, two-thirds (67) of 100 potential programs will not be purchased. Given their cost shares, they also agree to purchase 27 of the remaining 33. The incentive tax procedure (step 2) is then used to decide which 3 of the remaining 6, about which they disagree, will be included. In this way, I believe a more informationally efficient decision about the acquisition of 30 of 100 public goods could be made.

My purpose is to clarify the problem of designing institutions to make informationally efficient choices and to distinguish this problem from what I believe to be a trivial one: that an agent does not know his wealth at the time he reveals his preferences, because he does not know how large the incentive tax will be. For a forceful treatment of this point, in relation to the Groves–Ledyard mechanism, see Tullock (1978).

fied by the incentive tax procedure. Although such a procedure will generate a higher budget surplus in the context of this experiment than will the B-procedure, the result could easily be the reverse.[5] In any case, the incentive taxes can be viewed as part of the cost of making decisions that should be traded off against other decision costs in choosing among alternative institutions.

In spite of the potential waste, the incentive tax procedure is likely to lead to the most efficiency, so that this price is worth paying. Setting aside the costs of making decisions, including the surplus, that may arise out of a more complicated adjustment procedure, and using the efficiency measure proposed by Ferejohn and his coauthors, I calculate the expected efficiency of the incentive tax procedure at approximately 93 percent.[6] This compares with the average efficiency in the SPC and B-procedure rounds of 60 percent and 57 percent, respectively. The 93 percent efficiency rate is exceeded in only one of the trials reported by Ferejohn and coauthors.

I would also expect rapid termination or convergence. In fact, if we have an easy way to identify the source of potential conflict (commodity A or E) in the case discussed above, the process terminates after only *one* round.

CONCLUSION

These comments are intended to clarify the issues of experimental design rather than propose a formal experiment which might only be used to prove the case that a "strongly incentive compatible" mechanism would work in the laboratory according to theoretical suppositions —given the required conditions.

---

[5] Clotfelter in this volume provides an example for which the B-procedure would generate a significant budget surplus. If the bids shown in Clotfelter's table were multiplied by any arbitrary constant so as to reflect true valuations (as opposed to admissible bids), then use of the procedure described earlier to make a choice among multialternatives (e.g., ABC, BC, C alone, etc.) would generate zero incentive taxes.

[6] The 93 percent efficiency calculation assumes the consistent choice of the most efficient bundle of commodities (CDE) on every trial and subtracts the incentive taxes calculated in table 13 from the total potential payoff. Also, as indicated below, I assume the absence of coalitions. The efficiency calculation, however, understates what *could* be achieved in small number interactions with the design of procedures to deal with the problem of a budget surplus (e.g., balancing the budget in expectation by returning the expected value of the surplus to agents before they reveal preferences). (See Clarke, 1978a.)

I have expressed some dissatisfaction with such an approach elsewhere, but have also suggested that a more fruitful line of experimentation might be the careful introduction of other information assumptions as well as side arrangements and coalitions (Clarke 1975; 1978a,b).[7] This will take us into a potentially very useful inquiry about which existing incentive compatible procedures (and new ones to be developed) hold the greatest promise of minimizing the sum of all relevant costs—inefficiency arising out of individual strategy or group manipulation, waste (a cost of making decisions), *other* decision costs and information costs.

On a final note, I am fascinated with the potential applications to those other settings (e.g., choosing school textbooks subject to quantity discounts) outlined in the Ferejohn, Forsythe, and Noll paper. I suspect that this work will move us in a direction that will inform demand revelation theory, determine whether or not the incentive compatible mechanisms are just interesting intellectual playthings, and help us find out whether they can be usefully applied in a variety of real world settings.

---

[7] In suggesting the importance of experimentation with potential coalition formation, I have also stressed the importance of *agenda setting* so as to avoid the playing of zero sum games, illustrated by "the bankrupt collective" of Ferejohn, Forsythe, and Noll (reply). The reason is that, in such a setting, all of the new incentive compatible processes are so susceptible to group manipulation.

In the example of "the bankrupt collective," suppose we substitute $V/2$ for $V/4$ in the bids/values for commodity A of any two agents. The result is that the incentive taxes go to zero, thus achieving budget balance and avoiding bankruptcy. Agent 1 may, of course, anticipate this, but the complex game that results carries a very low risk for all players in relation to their potential gains. Procedures that will better assure the use of demand revelation in the context of a positive sum game, including assignments of cost shares more in line with benefits received, can avoid group manipulation. It can also avoid the anomalies illustrated by "the bankrupt collective" of Ferejohn, Forsythe, and Noll.

Charles Clotfelter

Comments

This paper discusses practical aspects of decentralized decision making for a certain class of goods. It is based on a good deal of interesting theoretical and experimental work by the authors and others. Particularly striking is the example they give of the Station Program Cooperative (SPC)—a remarkable success story for decentralized decision making applied to this class of goods.

Before I touch on some of the possible extensions and applications of the paper, let me put in my vote for a revision of the labeling of just what class of goods the paper actually deals with. Following Musgrave and Head, I would maintain that a "public good" is most usefully defined as one that exhibits both nonrivalness and nonexcludability, although the Samuelson definition can be and is often used to require nonrivalness only. Thus the example of fire engines and ambulances in a community would be a public good problem (unless citizens who voted against such items were excluded from service). But the sort of good which is the subject of this paper is simply nonrival; consumers can be efficiently excluded. Television stations collectively purchase programs, but those who do not buy the programs do not show the programs. (The fact that the excludability is institutional rather than technological is not crucial.) To be precise, then, it is *nonrival* goods and not *public* goods which are the subject of this paper.

There seem to be two important characteristics of the institutions described in this paper that are responsible for their apparent success. First, excludability is used to eliminate the free rider problem in the SPC. In the bidding scheme, however, excludability does not eliminate the free rider problem once players have made the minimum necessary bids. The second important characteristic is iteration, or the possibility of successive readjustments. Each allocation process described in this paper goes through a few iterations, in which price and quantity adjustments can be made and in which agents could receive information on aggregate demand for the goods. Which of these two characteristics is responsible for the remarkable success of the decision processes studied? Probably both are, but it would be interesting to discover their individual contributions, perhaps through experimentation. It is possible to imagine, for example, Musgrave-type public goods with possibilities for iterative decision making. Where there are a number of public goods being decided on and a limited budget, an iterative process seems to be central because of the problem of substitutes and complements pointed out by the authors.

As the authors state, the possibility for iteration rests on its technological feasibility or cost. It is difficult to imagine, for example, an SPC process being operated in 1950 using first-class mail and the old mechanical calculators. But even within the traditional technology of voting, it is possible to imagine certain kinds of iteration. For example, two-stage voting in primaries and general elections could serve as a kind of limited iterative voting.

Within the more narrowly defined context where both excludability and iteration are feasible, the paper seems quite useful in its analysis of workable decision processes. The emphasis throughout the paper on the speed of adjustment—or decision costs in general—seems appropriate. The results related to the variability of outcomes for given processes, the apparent existence of multiple equilibria, and the apparent Cournot behavior are all important positive contributions. It would be helpful, however, to have further discussion of the experimental techniques used and the actual numerical results obtained under different processes.

Specifically, more discussion of the bidding and organization processes would be helpful. For example, on page 185 of the paper there is a formula for calculating tax payments for each player in a bidding procedure. As can be calculated from table 14, in a simple three-person, three-good model, this formula may result in significant surpluses as well as the apparent anomaly of the highest bidder with the largest budget constraint not paying the highest tax.

Perhaps it is beyond the scope of this paper, but I would like to see an expansion of a question hinted at near the introduction. It is the notion that incentives to acquire specialized knowledge may exist in a representative government, whereas individual voters, à la Downs, do not have "sufficient" incentive to be informed. The Downs problem is possibly characteristic of these types of direct election as well, as the authors suggest. Further, I agree with the authors that, in considering the efficiency

TABLE 14. Tax Payments Using Bidding Procedure[a]

	Agents			Cost of goods
	1	2	3	
Budget	12	15	20	
Cost share (α)	0.2	0.4	0.4	
Bids:				
Good A	9	0	7	5
Good B	1	5	4	10
Good C	2	8	9	10
Calculated tax payments	12	15	14	

[a] From Ferejohn, Forsythe, and Noll, this volume.

of the systems, we should consider the decision costs of individuals as well as the costs of the adjustment process and conventionally measured costs of misallocation in the resulting allocation. For example, Diamond (1977) suggests that the costs to individuals of obtaining information on old-age insurance would be tremendous because of the complexity of the problem. If Social Security were put to a direct vote by such methods as described in this paper, these costs of individual decision making would have to be considered as well as those of the actual decision mechanism. And how would the resulting allocation from such a direct vote compare with the present allocation?

Returning to the practical aspects of decentralized decision-making systems for Musgrave–Head public goods, it seems to be experimentally possible to test similar decision-making processes using iteration. For example, Bohm-type experiments with several public goods could be conducted allowing "voters" to see the results from previous rounds of voting. Applications to this class of public goods seem to be quite broad. For example, the capability of "instant referenda" by special cable television devices seems to be a growing possibility. Given the degree to which institutional structure is a function of relative costs, as computers and communication systems become more widely acceptable, such direct, decentralized decision making must certainly become a more distinct possibility. By the same token, research such as this will also be of increasing practical importance.

John A. Ferejohn, Robert Forsythe, and Roger G. Noll

Reply to Comments

While we concur with much of the thoughtful commentary by our discussants, we disagree with some of their interpretations. These disagreements are sufficiently important that we are compelled to record our own point of view a bit more explicitly than we did in our paper.

Clarke suggests a strongly incentive compatible procedure when nonbankruptcy restrictions are ignored. While the mechanism he suggests is technically correct, nevertheless if preferences are "intense enough" and "diverse enough," bankruptcy is a substantial drawback to it. Furthermore, he suggests that agents can overcome problems of bankruptcy by borrowing and seeking contributions from viewers (in the television case). This proposal makes sense only if bankruptcy is a relatively rare, nonrecurring phenomenon. Moreover, implementing his suggestion creates further serious complications.

To illustrate how bankruptcy problems may occur, Clarke's table 13 can be reconstructed by assuming a different set of preferences. Here V is the total net reported value for the commodity bundle A. We assume that $V > 4$. If agents value these bundles highly relative to other uses of their funds, V may be arbitrarily large and create an arbitrarily large budgetary surplus ($V - 4$). Likewise, if the net reported values, $V/4$, which agents 2, 3, 4, and 5 place on the bundle A are larger than their respective budgets, the amount each must pay beyond the assigned cost shares, $V/4 - 1$, causes bankruptcy.

Admissible bids may be bounded to cope with the bankruptcy problem. As Clarke points out, Green and Laffont show that with only two alternatives, one of which is costless, if agents are not permitted to submit bids that exceed their budgets, then Clarke's mechanism satisfies non-bankruptcy and is nonstrategic. But if the incentive tax is computed from *two costly* alternatives and if each agent's bid is bounded by the budget, the size of potential bankruptcy is bounded by *twice* the budget. This

TABLE 15. A Bankrupt Collective

Agent	Value of acquiring commodities bundle		Taxes if A acquired		
	A	B	Incentive tax	Cost share	Total tax
1	0	$V - 1 + (1 - \alpha_1)C_B$	0	$\alpha_1 C_A$	$\alpha_1 C_A$
2	$V/4$	$-\alpha_2 C_B$	$V/4 - 1 + \alpha_2 C_B$	$\alpha_2 C_A$	$(V/4 - 1 + \alpha_2 C_B) + \alpha_2 C_A$
3	$V/4$	$-\alpha_3 C_B$	$V/4 - 1 + \alpha_3 C_B$	$\alpha_3 C_A$	$(V/4 - 1 + \alpha_3 C_B) + \alpha_3 C_A$
4	$V/4$	$-\alpha_4 C_B$	$V/4 - 1 + \alpha_4 C_B$	$\alpha_4 C_A$	$(V/4 - 1 + \alpha_4 C_B) + \alpha_4 C_A$
5	$V/4$	$-\alpha_5 C_B$	$V/4 - 1 + \alpha_5 C_B$	$\alpha_5 C_A$	$(V/4 - 1 + \alpha_5 C_B) + \alpha_5 C_A$
Totals	V	$V - 1$	$V - 4 + (1 - \alpha_1)C_B$	C_A	$V - 4 + (1 - \alpha_1)C_B + C_A$

can be seen by examining the total tax paid by, say, agent 2. If agent 2's bid on alternative A was exactly equal to his budget, b^2, then $V/4 - 1 + \alpha_2 C_B = b^2 - 1$. Assuming that both bundles are feasible given the budgets of the agents and that cost shares alone cannot bankrupt an agent, so that $\alpha_2 C_A < b^2$, the total tax paid by agent 2 is bounded because $(V/4 - 1 + \alpha_2 C_B) + \alpha_2 C_A \leq 2b^2 - 1)$.

A major difficulty with any procedure that bounds bids (including our B-procedure) is that if the value of an alternative exceeds ability to pay, the resulting allocation may be inefficient. In other words, collective acquisition of a particular public good can raise the real income of an agent by more than the agent's budget. Such would be the case in our example above if agents 2, 3, 4, and 5 had small budgets and were required to report net values much less than $V/4$, thereby causing bundle B to be chosen.

By arguing that bankruptcy difficulties may be ignored because stations facing bankruptcy may borrow money to be repaid in future time periods, Clarke destroys the nonstrategic properties of his own mechanism. Even if there are no income effects for each commodity initially, allowing agents to borrow when they exceed their budgets induces income effects and, as students of demand revelation know, income effects destroy the nonstrategic property of the Clarke tax.

Clarke also argues that stations can always ask viewers for more contributions if bankruptcy occurs, but this, too, introduces further complications. First, because it is impossible to bound tax liabilities while preserving nonstrategicness, there is no guarantee that sufficient funds may be raised from viewers. Second, if emergency contributions detract from future contributions and if stations discount future allocations, the problem of income effects arises just as in the case of borrowing. Third, the incentive of subscribers to contribute may be affected by the existence of ex post fund-raising activities. Once subscribers realize that they can contribute after these decisions are announced, they may well withhold early contributions and use them as a means of expressing approval of the station's chosen program package. This would cause stations to enter subsequent decision-making periods with smaller budgets, and would further compound the bankruptcy problem to the extent that the ex post contributions were uncertain.

Finally, Clarke correctly points out that if the choice is between two alternatives, a collective does not need a complicated adjustment procedure. This is not very relevant to our practical problem, in which about 30 of 100 public goods are acquired simultaneously. The B-procedure was developed to deal with this more complex case. It is a multialternative analog of the Clarke tax. The only difference between it and Clarke's method is that in the B-procedure agents know that their tax liabilities will never exceed their budgets. This creates strategic possibilities only if an agent is approaching the budget constraint, for then an agent has an incentive to overstate the value of preferred alternatives.

The essence of our view about design criteria is this: in order to apply the existing results on "incentive compatible" mechanisms to a problem in institutional design, a choice must be made with respect to which design features are most significant. Clarke contends that the nonbankruptcy criterion is always of minor importance, but, owing to the difficulties discussed above, we cannot agree. Indeed, collective activities in which agents have a large stake in the outcome of the collective choice process relative to the size of their budgets are most likely to face problems of bankruptcy from a procedure that does not bound taxes. Thus, we believe that many of the most important real world collectivities would make nonbankruptcy a required feature of admissible choice procedures. Certainly our experience with public broadcasters bears out this belief.

Clotfelter makes two points that require a brief response. The first is his discourse on the definition of a collective good. He takes us to task for not adopting Musgrave's definition, which requires both nonrivalrous consumption and the impossibility of exclusion. In the real SPC (and for any real public good that we can think of), exclusion of nonparticipants is technically possible, but requires positive expenditures to accomplish and enforce. The experimental SPC retains this feature, but the two alternatives that we have examined do not. The reason that the SPC does exclude nonparticipants in the purchase of a program is because the people who participate in the SPC want it that way. In fact, one as yet unsolved problem that currently occupies us is to develop extensions of the other procedures that permit exclusion, so that this general approach will be acceptable to the public broadcasting system. Incidentally, station managers are not totally irrational in seeking to introduce expensive excludability; many stations are government entities, and neither legally nor politically can spend money on programs that they do not use or that are supplied without charge to others.

It is important to note that the possibility of exclusion does not eliminate the free rider problem. In fact, excludability coupled with nonrivalrous consumption introduces a source of inefficiency that is absent from a pure Musgrave public good. Excludability in nonrivalrous goods is a dichotomous characteristic: an agent is either in or out. The "ins" still face the same incentives to misreveal preferences in whatever collective choice process they use to decide upon the amount of public good to acquire and the rule for dividing its cost. Meanwhile, if membership in the "outs" is determined by expressing some minimum willingness to pay, some "outs" will be inefficiently excluded if their marginal valuations on the public good exceed the (negative) cost of excluding them, but fall short of the minimum fee for gaining entry to the "ins."

Clotfelter's second point is his observation, backed up by a numerical example, that the demand-revealing process can run a surplus. That is true, but this source of inefficiency should surely have no more status than other sources, such as the costs of operating the system or the failure of a process to reach a Pareto optimal allocation. In fact, this inefficiency is of somewhat lesser concern. It does not represent a loss of real resources (as do the others), but instead is a bundle of cash that can be spent on something else of value as long as incentive compatibility is not affected.

REFERENCES

Clarke, E. 1975. "Experiments with Public Goods Pricing: A Comment," *Public Choice* vol. 23 (Fall) pp. 49–53.

———. 1978a. "Information and Coalitions in a Representative Model of Demand Revelation Under the Rule of Law." Paper presented at the Annual Meeting of the Public Choice Society, New Orleans, La. (March).

———. 1978b. "The Search for Budget Balance in a Theory of Demand Revelation," in Gordon Tullock, ed., *Papers and Proceedings: Annual Meeting of the Public Choice Society (1978)*.

Diamond, P. A. 1977. "A Framework for Social Security Analysis," *Journal of Public Economics* vol. 8 (December) pp. 275–298.

Ferejohn, J., R. Forsythe, and R. Noll. 1977. "Implementing Planning Procedures for the Provision of Discrete Public Goods." Social Science Working Paper No. 156, California Institute of Technology (June).

———, ———, and ———. 1978. "An Experimental Analysis of Decision-making Procedures for Discrete Public Goods: A Case Study of a Problem in Institutional Design," in Vernon L. Smith, ed., *Research in Experimental Economics* vol. 1 (Greenwich, Conn., JAI Press).

Green, J., and J. J. Laffont. 1976. "Satisfactory Mechanisms for Environments with Consumption Lower Bounds," *Journal of Economic Theory* vol. 19, no. 2, pp. 359–375.

———, and ———. 1977. "Characterization of Satisfactory Mechanisms for the Revelation of Preferences for Public Goods." *Econometrica* vol. 45 (March) pp. 427–438.

Groves, T., and J. Ledyard. 1977. "Optimal Allocation of Public Goods: A Solution to the 'Free Rider' Problem," *Econometrica* vol. 45 (May) pp. 783–809.

Smith, Vernon L. 1978. "Incentive Compatible Experimental Processes for the Provision of Public Goods," in Vernon L. Smith, ed., *Research in Experimental Economics* vol. 1 (Greenwich, Conn., JAI Press).

Tideman, T. N., and G. Tullock. 1976. "A New and Superior Process for Making Social Choices," *Journal of Political Economy* vol. 84 (December) pp. 1145–1159.

Tullock, G. 1978. "Demand Revealing, Groves–Ledyard and the Seventh Order of Smalls." Working Paper No. 78-3-4, Center for Study of Public Choice, Blacksburg, Va.

Richard B. Stewart

The Resource Allocation Role
of Reviewing Courts

Common Law Functions in a Regulatory Era

I. THE CONVENTIONAL WISDOM AND ITS DISCONTENTS

It has long been accepted that courts reviewing administrative decisions may not substitute their judgment for that of an administrative agency on policy choices, about which relevant statutes provide no guidance.[1] Under traditional principles of administrative law, the courts' basic function is to ensure that administrative officials adhere to legislative directives (Stewart, 1975, pp. 1669, 1671–1676; and Landes and Posner, 1975, p. 875). However, due to limited knowledge, changing conditions, or political constraints, legislators are typically unable to enact statutes that specify in consistent detail what choices administrators must make. Vague, general, or conflicting statutory provisions, together with the traditional limitations on the scope of judicial review, result in administrators exercising considerable discretion (Stewart, 1975, pp. 1676, 1688). While courts will review for abuse of discretion, inquiring whether an agency's resolution of competing considerations in a particular case was patently unreasonable, in practice courts almost never overrule administrative decisions on this ground.[2] We are concerned here

[1] Courts will also review agency action for conformance to constitutional requirements and the agency's own regulations. However, apart from discussion in section IV of a constitutional right to environmental quality, these aspects of judicial review are not relevant to the subject of this essay.

[2] In *Citizens to Preserve Overton Park* v. *Volpe*, 401 U.S. 402 (1971), for example, the Supreme Court directed the district court to scrutinize closely, for abuse of discretion, an agency's approval of routing a highway through a public park. On remand, the district court concluded that the agency could choose either the park routing or some alternative routing without abusing discretion. 335 F. Supp. 873 (W.D. Tenn. 1971).

with the resulting discretion enjoyed by administrative officials in the allocation of environmental resources.

Agencies with environmental responsibilities are subject in full measure to the contemporary sense of disillusionment with the administrative process (Stewart, 1975, pp. 1681–1687). Environmentalists assert that agencies with development missions in fields such as power, water resources, agriculture, and highways have been "captured" by regulated or client firms, and that they disregard or slight environmental concerns. On the other hand, industry representatives complain that regulatory agencies whose prime mission is protection of environmental quality are insensitive to the economic and social costs of control measures. Both groups have appealed to the courts to abandon traditional limitations on judicial review and to exercise tight control over agency policy choices (Sive, 1970, p. 612). The courts have generally rejected such appeals. For example, in *Scenic Hudson Preservation Conference* v. *FPC,*[3] the court refused to set aside the Federal Power Commission's approval of a pumped storage-generating facility opposed by environmental groups, asserting that in the absence of controlling statutory directives, "this court could not and should not attempt to substitute its judgment for that of the Commission." Similarly, in *Ethyl Corp.* v. *EPA,*[4] the court declined industry's request that it invalidate an Environmental Protection Agency (EPA) order requiring removal of lead additives from gasoline, stating that the established standard of review "forbids the court's substituting its judgment for that of the agency."

Nonetheless, courts have not been heedless of criticisms that bureaucratic administrators, not formally accountable through political or market mechanisms, exercise discretion in ways that may lead to serious resource misallocation or inequitable distributional consequences. The courts have responded, not by substituting their judgment concerning substantive outcomes for that of the agency, but by procedural innovations designed to permit all affected interests access to the process of agency decision and to improve the quality of agency deliberations. For example, courts have required that adjudicatory hearings for licensing power plants be extended to include not only regulated firms but environmental groups.[5] Agencies in turn have reacted to the mounting procedural burdens of expanded trial-type adjudicatory hearings by developing policies through informal legislative-type rulemaking. The

---

[3] 453 F.2d 465 (2d Cir. 1971).
[4] 541 F.2d 1 (D.C. Cir. 1976), *cert. denied,* 426 U.S. 941 (1976).
[5] See *Scenic Hudson Preservation Conference* v. *FPC,* 354 F.2d 608 (2d Cir. 1965).

courts countered this shift by expanding the procedural formalities in rulemaking, requiring that the agency disclose the documentary basis for its proposals and respond in detail to criticisms and additional data submitted by regulated firms, environmental groups, and other private interests.[6] Reviewing courts also began to scrutinize in considerable detail the reasoning advanced by agencies for discretionary policy choices, measuring the agency's justifications against the documentary evidence of record (Stewart, 1977a, pp. 733–740). These requirements have been imposed upon environmental advocate agencies, such as EPA, as well as upon other agencies whose prime role is development (Stewart, 1977a, pp. 717–720).

The courts' response to the problem of agency discretion reflects judicial diffidence in dictating substantive outcomes in given cases, combined with faith that improved processes of decision based on participation by all affected interests, more complete development of data, and decisional rationality as reflected in written opinions will produce desirable and equitable policy choices. This response is fully consistent with jurisprudential assumptions that have been firmly entrenched ever since the New Deal: that the courts should confine themselves to maintaining the integrity of constitutive decision-making arrangements and protecting individual liberties, while decisions about resource allocation should be remitted to the political branches.

This essay questions the conventional wisdom as applied to administrative decision making in the realm of environmental resources. I accept that efforts by courts to improve the process of administrative decision making—particularly the added procedural requirements in rule making and more searching judicial scrutiny of the empirical and analytical basis for discretionary policy choices—have on balance been beneficial. However, these developments have produced costly side effects in added decision-making costs, delay, and sometimes perverse effects on substantive policies.[7] Some of these costs might be avoided by more explicit judicial reexamination of the merits of agency policies. More-

---

[6] The cumulative result of these requirements is a "paper hearing" which yields a record for decision based on the parties' documentary submissions rather than the oral testimony of witnesses. See Stewart (1977a, pp. 713, 729–733).

[7] For example, the Atomic Energy Commission, in order to avoid the delays involved in full-fledged adjudicatory hearings to license individual nuclear power plants, decided to deal with reactor safety issues on a generic basis by utilizing more informal rule-making procedures to define safety requirements for all plants of a given type, thus avoiding the need to retry safety issues in individual licenses. However, as the safety regulations were repeatedly tightened in the face of mounting concern with reactor safety and technological advance, this generic approach required repeated and costly retrofit of plants in the process of construction in order to conform with the new regulations.

over, in some cases judicial control of substantive choices may be essential to secure important societal interests in allocation of environmental resources.

II. RESOURCE ALLOCATION BY COMMON LAW COURTS

Common lawyers and judges in the first two-thirds of the nineteenth century would be astonished at the procedural cul-de-sac in which reviewing courts today operate in relation to environmental resource decisions. In that earlier era, it was the judges who directly shaped resource allocation decisions through developing common law rules of tort and property. The courts of that day combined the functions of an EPA, a department of energy, and a zoning board, together with many other functions that today are primarily exercised by administrative officials.

In recent years there has been a dramatic growth of scholarly interest in the role of U.S. common law courts in resource allocation in the nineteenth century, when the market was the predominant form for the organization of economic life, and legislative and administrative intervention was far less frequent than it is today. Numerous scholars of quite different persuasions have concluded that the dominant thrust and effect of common law court decisions was to structure property relations and market arrangements to secure an efficient allocation of resources or to promote economic growth and development.

Several students, most notably Richard Posner, have applied welfare economics analysis to a variety of common law rules, concluding that they promote efficiency by reducing or countering transactions cost barriers to private negotiation of efficient outcomes (Posner, 1977, pp. 1–191). One version of this view holds that judges are led to adopt efficient laws because of their institutional independence and the tendency of the adjudicatory process to generate impersonal rules of general applicability (Posner, 1977, pp. 399–405). Another regards the common law judges' selection of decisional rules as purely random with respect to efficiency, but asserts that those rules that promoted efficiency tended to be accepted by the affected private actors and thus hardened into precedent, whereas those rules that were inefficient were repeatedly challenged in litigation until they were eroded or replaced. In this latter view, the litigation process is a form of social Darwinism ensuring that the rules that survived were efficient (Rubin, 1977, p. 51; and Priest, 1977, p. 65).

Legal historians such as Morton Horwitz (1977) and James Willard Hurst (1956) have emphasized the role of common law courts in promoting economic development by devising rules of contract to accommodate more extensive and complex commercial and financial arrangements, and by altering rules of tort and property to foster industrial growth.[8] Their thesis is that judges self-consciously adopted and nurtured economic development as a dominant value.

There are difficulties in these various accounts, as well as conflicts among them, which I do not wish to labor here.[9] The essential point for present purposes is the growing recognition that the resolution by courts of individual common law cases through the development of general

---

[8] Both Horwitz (1977) and Hurst (1956) assess common law rules in terms of economic growth and development rather than in terms of either static or dynamic allocative efficiency. At one point (p. 100) Horwitz suggests that legal rules may have promoted an inefficient "overinvestment in technology," but concludes that it is not possible to resolve this question.

[9] Posner's basic technique in attempting to demonstrate that the common law was efficient is to employ partial equilibrium analysis indicating that various common law rules would tend to promote efficiency under simplified hypothetical factual situations. This is a long way from showing that the common law system, either as a whole or in particular instances, promoted efficient outcomes under any actual set of historical conditions, especially when second-best problems are considered. Moreover, Posner fails to offer a consistent theory of judicial behavior that would account for the courts' asserted pursuit of efficiency. At one point, Posner characterizes judges as displaying "aloof disinterest," but at another he asserts that judges are driven by a desire to impose their subjective preferences on the rest of society (Posner, 1977, pp. 401, 422). At several points, the efficiency of the common law is attributed in part to judges' disregard of the parties' individual characteristics, viewing them as representative of broad classes of economic activity (Posner, 1977, pp. 401, 405). But later the asserted tendency of courts to promote efficiency is attributed in part to standing rules that allow only particular plaintiffs rather than interest groups the right to sue. At another point, Posner seems to adopt the theories advanced by Rubin (1977) and Priest (1977) (Posner, 1977, pp. 439–440).

The Rubin and Priest theories are also hypothetical and axiomatic in character, based on *ceteris paribus* assertions that litigation will be more frequent in character if particular legal rules are inefficient. Even if their arguments were accepted, they do not demonstrate that the dominant thrust of the common law was the generation of efficient rules, because the incentives cited by Priest and Rubin may have been swamped by countervailing tendencies. For example, one consequence of industrialization was to generate harms (such as pollution) that are diffuse and cause relatively small amounts of harm to individuals. Common law rules limiting class actions and requiring each party to bear its own litigation expenses meant that industrial defendants would have strong incentives to litigate while individual plaintiffs would not, a situation well calculated to lead to inefficient aggregate outcomes.

The difficulties in the accounts by Horwitz (1977) and Hurst (1956) are of a different sort. Neither explains how judges came to internalize economic development as a dominant value, or why legislatures permitted courts such a dominant role. These issues have particular interest in the context of Horwitz's work, which depicts the courts' decisions as advancing the interests of a wealthy commercial and industrial elite at the expense of other interests.

decisional rules had a pervasive and systematic impact on resource allocation. Some scholars, such as Hurst, have applauded the courts' perceived
tendency to promote economic efficiency or industrial development.
Others, such as Horwitz (1977), have stressed the assertedly inequitable
distributional consequences of these tendencies. But none gainsays the
pervasive and inescapable power of the courts over resource allocation.[10]
Why in the twentieth century should courts have largely abdicated that
role to administrative agencies?

III.   THE PREEMPTIVE IMPACT OF ADMINISTRATIVE REMEDIES

This section of the essay considers three potential reasons why legislative creation of administrative agencies with environmental resource
responsibilities might lead courts to exchange the premier resource allocation role which they occupied in common law for the "process" oversight role that they occupy today. While each is persuasive, none of these
reasons is so compelling as to justify total judicial renunciation of
resource allocation responsibilities.

Legislative Reallocation of Roles

The creation of administrative agencies might be interpreted as an
authoritative legislative reassignment of resource allocation responsibilities from judges to administrators, based on the legislature's judgment
that courts are not competent to secure efficient outcomes under conditions of urban industrialism, or that courts are inescapably biased in favor
of certain social interests, such as manufacturers or developers, resulting
in distributional inequities. But such judgments are not logically entailed
by the mere creation of administrative agencies with environmental
responsibilities.

Courts are handicapped in responding to problems of environmental resource allocation both by their institutional characteristics and
(a related circumstance) the limited remedies at their disposal. For
example:

- Environmental harms are very often diffuse and the amount suffered
  by any individual small. Litigation, however, is a highly imperfect

---

[10] The resource allocation function of common law rules was established in
pioneering work by Ronald H. Coase (1960) and Calabresi (1970).

mechanism for securing more efficient resource use by "collecting" small harms through damage or injunctive remedies.

- Many forms of environmental degradation are most appropriately dealt with through prophylactic measures applied consistently on a broad basis. Courts, however, are hostage to the happenstance of private initiative in bringing litigation, their decisions are ad hoc in character, and they are ill equipped to exercise continuing management and oversight functions.

- Environmental resource conflicts are often best resolved through a variety of incentives, including subsidies, effluent fees, creation of transferrable emission rights, and government expenditures for research. Courts, however, have a quite limited range of remedies to deploy.

- Many contemporary environmental problems are presented in the management of resources owned by the government (such as land or minerals), the disbursement of government funds for provision of collective goods (such as highways), and the regulation of private activities (such as power production or airline service) for ends other than environmental quality. Courts, however, lack the management capabilities needed in the allocation of public funds or resources or regulation of broad sectors of the economy.

These institutional shortcomings on the part of courts provide a logically sufficient basis for legislative creation of administrative agencies with managerial capability and the self-starting, specialized capacity to take prophylactic measures and deploy a broader range of incentives. But the creation of agencies to remedy certain institutional shortcomings in the courts does not necessarily imply that such agencies should supplant the courts in exercising ultimate authority over environmental resource allocation policies. It is logically just as plausible to view the administrative agencies as legislatively created auxiliaries of the courts, analogous to special masters, affording an increased range of institutional tools and capabilities that would be deployed by judges in discharging their traditional resource allocation function.[11]

---

[11] In *Crowell* v. *Benson*, 285 U.S. 22 (1932), the Court explicitly utilized the special master analogy in sustaining the creation of an administrative system of compensation for workplace accidents against the charge that it improperly transferred lawmaking powers from judges to administrators.

Under such a model, the agency bears responsibility for implementation of resource allocation decisions made by the court. The political and operational necessities of implementation will, however, constrain the resource allocation choice in

However, the foregoing argument does not take us very far toward restoring the courts' resource allocation function. For even if legislative creation of administrative agencies does not *logically* entail a shift of resource allocation from courts to agencies, the legislature may, as a matter of historical fact, have wished to effect such a transfer. Because (constitutional questions aside) the legislature has plenary authority to allocate decision-making responsibility among various organs of government, any such wish on the legislature's part must be respected by the courts. The inference of such a legislative mandate would be strengthened if we followed the view, advanced by scholars as diverse as Louis Jaffe (1965, pp. 3–10) and George Stigler (1971), that the legislature's creation of administrative agencies is often designed, not to secure more efficient resource allocation by remedying courts' institutional defects in redressing "market failure," but to redistribute wealth to politically powerful groups by shifting decisional responsibility from judges to administrators more sympathetic to such groups' interests.

There are indeed instances where such redistribution purposes underlay the creation of an agency, or an extension of its powers; examples include the Transportation Acts of 1920 and 1940, the National Labor Relations Act, the Civil Aeronautics Act, the Robinson-Patman Act. But the redistribution rationale does not carry us very far in most contemporary environmental controversies. Too often the legislative mandate is conflicting and ambiguous.[12] In many cases where a sharp shift in policies is mandated, as in the 1970 Clean Air Act Amendments or the 1972 Federal Water Pollution Control Act Amendments, the creation of administrative authority can as plausibly be attributed to the correction of market inefficiencies beyond the courts' capacity to remedy as to redistribution objectives.[13] Even if some past legislature did on one

---

various ways, and it may be difficult for a court to inform itself about implementation issues (see Horowitz, 1977). Accordingly, the court may have to defer to the agency insofar as resource allocation choices appear to be seriously constrained by implementation problems. Note that in common law, "implementation" was left to the parties and their counsel; it is presumably easier for judges to inform themselves about implementation issues in this context.

[12] Even where Congress attempts to specify policy in great detail, as in the Federal Water Pollution Control Act Amendments of 1972, the statute is often the checkered product of compromise within and between the two houses; the resulting lack of consistent logic in the statute's structure and provisions has created serious difficulties for reviewing courts. See, for example, Hunciker and Pagano (1976, pp. 59, 62–71) and Parenteau and Tauman (1976, p. 1).

[13] Legislators, of course, have little concern with efficiency in the abstract, and are likely to take action only in response to some constituency that stands to gain from legislative intervention. But this mechanism could be perfectly consistent

ground or another intend an ultimate shift in resource allocation authority from court to agency, it is not obvious that such an intent should be respected if relevant conditions have changed substantially; an updated statutory response is hindered by impasse or pursuit of other priorities in the legislature, and there are systematic deficiencies in the designated administrative agencies' discharge of resource allocation responsibilities.[14] Without offering detailed proof here, I would accordingly claim that neither the statutory record nor legitimate political understandings inevitably require us to interpret the creation of administrative agencies as shifting primary resource allocation responsibilities from courts to administrators.

This conclusion is fortified by the general rule that the creation of administrative agencies does not preempt common law remedies (Stewart and Krier, 1978, ch. 5). If judicial resource allocation judgments were hopelessly inept under modern conditions or were systematically at odds with the legislature's distributional objectives, one would expect administrative remedies to preempt the entire field. Since they generally do not, any justification of the prevailing conventional wisdom regarding judicial review of administrative action must somehow distinguish resource allocation issues in that context from those in private litigation.

---

with the advancement of efficiency through legislative intervention to correct "market failure" (more properly, "judicial failure"), particularly if we assume that advocacy for legislative intervention is correlated with exposure to losses generated by market inefficiencies. However, the currently prevailing analysis of regulatory legislation is less sanguine. See Stigler (1971).

[14] William Landes and Richard Posner (1975) argue that reviewing courts should limit themselves to enforcing administrative conformance with legislative "deals" among interest groups embodied in statutes. See also Posner (1977, pp. 408–417, 480–481). However, they do not address the question of what the courts should do when the legislative "deal" is ambiguous or otherwise unhelpful in resolving a given decision. Nor do they offer reasons why courts should limit themselves to enforcing legislative "deals" beyond suggesting that (a) the constitutional scheme so requires and (b) if courts go too far in enforcing their own views of sound policy, the legislature will curtail their independence. But these considerations have little relevance where conditions have changed in such a way as to make a statutory "deal" obsolescent or irrelevant, and the agency's discharge of its responsibilities does not invite the confidence that justifies deference.

For example, Congress in enacting and subsequently modifying the Federal Power Act in 1920 and 1935 may not have intended aesthetic values to be a mandatory consideration in power plant siting. But the development thirty years later of environmental concerns, coupled with legislative inertia and the Federal Power Commission's disregard of those concerns in the pursuit of a power development mission, justifies judicial intervention to require the Commission to give weight to adverse environmental impacts in considering the resource allocation implications of a proposed project. See *Scenic Hudson Preservation Conf.* v. *FPC*, 354 F.2d 608 (2d Cir. 1965).

The Courts' Technical Incompetence

A shift of decisional responsibility for environmental resource allocation from courts to agencies is arguably justified by the difficult technical questions characteristically involved. Whatever may have been the case in the nineteenth century, the development of modern industrial processes, the growth of scientific knowledge, and the complexity of economic arrangements in contemporary society may far exceed the capacities of lay judges and the adversary process. If so, these difficulties would not adequately be met by the "special master" theory which views administrative agencies as adjuncts to the judicial process designed to rectify the courts' institutional shortcomings. All too frequently, environmental resource decisions are shot through with medical and technical issues, problems of evaluating statistical data, and judgment in the face of limited information. Unless the judicial process can master such issues, courts cannot realistically make the ultimate resource decisions.

These objections to a direct resource allocation role for reviewing courts have considerable force, but are far from decisive. It is easy to overstate the technical incompetence of the judicial system. That judges do not have technical training is hardly compelling, for most top administrators also lack such training. Nor is it clear that the judicial reviewing process is far inferior to the administrative in collecting and analyzing technical data, at least where judges are sufficiently willing to probe technical issues to give the litigants (including the administrative agency) strong incentives to marshal and analyze the relevant data. The recent performance of courts reviewing environmental controls imposed by EPA (for example) reflects considerable technical sophistication.[15]

The circumstance that ordinary trial courts are not only permitted to continue hearing private litigation, but have also played a considerable role in resolving environmental controversies initiated by government regulatory agencies[16] is also evidence that the technical issues presented in environmental resource decisions are not beyond the judicial system's competence. Moreover, there are steps that could be taken to enhance the judicial system's ability to deal with such issues (Leventhal, 1974, p.

---

[15] See, for example, *South Terminal Corp.* v. *EPA,* 504 F.2d 646 (1st Cir. 1974); *Texas* v. *EPA,* 499 F.2d 289 (5th Cir. 1974); *International Harvester Co.* v. *Ruckleshaus,* 478 F.2d 615 (D.C. Cir. 1973).

[16] See, for example, *Reserve Mining Co.* v. *United States,* 514 F.2d 492 (8th Cir. 1975) (EPA court action to abate water and air pollution from an industrial facility).

509), including the alleviation of burdens on the courts by creating a "quality control" body within the executive branch that would be independent of the agencies whose analysis it would review. In short, the problems of technical competence are real but not disqualifying.

The Defects of Courts as Instruments of Social Choice

The context in which common law courts decided resource allocation issues is quite different from the context in which such issues are presented to courts reviewing administrative action. The differences may support a conclusion that courts should not make resource allocation choices in the context of administrative decision making, at least so long as efficiency is our goal.

Common law courts facilitated decentralized decision making by firms and individuals through adoption of tort and property rules defining boundaries and contract rules defining the framework of exchange. Judges did not themselves decree the ultimate resource allocation outcome, but laid down the ground rules for such decisions by others. Contract law most obviously, but even tort and property law, can be understood as a set of constitutive arrangements, defining rules of procedure and agendas channeling decision making by private "administrators"[17] (Hayek, 1974; Heymann, 1973, p. 797). It is arguably far less difficult to devise rules that will generate productive outcomes over the long run in such circumstances, than to determine the most efficient outcome in a given case. Also, if a court adopted a general rule tending to promote seriously inefficient outcomes, its effects might be avoided through private bargaining, or the rule might be supplanted through a litigative form of natural selection (Rubin, 1977, p. 51; Priest, 1977, p. 65).

When called upon to provide a remedy in particular cases by determining the appropriate amount of damages or awarding injunctive relief, the common law courts faced greater difficulties from the viewpoint of achieving efficient outcomes, because the decision was particularistic, and the court was required to ascertain preferences for environmental quality in order to weigh the harm to be avoided or compensated. Since there is no ready market or other yardstick for measuring such prefer-

---

[17] In this view there is no basic distinction between private and public law; both are means by which society delegates the authority to make resource allocation decisions to individuals operating under specified constraints. Cf. Kelsen (1970, pp. 280–284).

ences, courts might be quite likely to err. But a judicial effort to avoid this hazard by refusing ever to provide any remedy would likely produce even greater inefficiencies, because market processes of bargaining generally fail to respond at all to preferences for collective goods such as clean air.

The problem of resource allocation is quite different in the context of judicial review of administrative decision making. As we have seen, one of the basic explanations for the creation of the administrative process is to remedy the shortcomings of the court system in "adding up" diffuse preferences for collective goods such as environmental quality. While the administrative/political process may be a highly imperfect barometer of such preferences, the courts, lacking any form of direct political accountability, are likely to be an even more imperfect register. Because of the pervasive importance of such preferences in determining the efficiency of environmental resource allocations, this circumstance argues strongly for judicial deference to agencies in resource allocation judgments. Moreover, if reviewing courts did intervene and erred in their assessment of efficient resource allocation, there is little opportunity for the "correction by the market" that existed in the common law context. Administrative decisions about resource allocation typically involve very large commitments of resources in a single decision involving multiple parties, and their precedental significance is limited. The transaction costs of changing a particular result by private bargaining are very high. Common law rules, by contrast, typically governed multiple transactions, each involving a few individuals who often could adjust their behavior and the terms of exchange to avoid the otherwise inefficient consequences of given rules.

Distributional considerations may also counsel judicial deference to environmental resource allocation decisions by administrators. Given the apparent lack of widely accepted principles for establishing a just distribution of income, questions of equity should presumptively be resolved through the political process. There are two alternative bases for such a presumption. First, the distribution of income can be viewed as a collective good whose production should be determined by citizens' preferences; if so, the superiority of political over judicial processes for adding up preferences would be decisive. Second, one could perceive the distributional consequences of political choices as the by-product of factional struggle for economic advantage, and view this process as the intended mechanism for resolving distributional issues within the Constitution.

Either view argues against the courts making resource allocation choices in either the common law or administrative context. However, the objection is less weighty in its common law context because the gains and losses generated through the rules defining tort and property rights and conditions of market exchange can be more readily captured and measured in money terms, facilitating centralized redistribution through the tax system. By contrast, the gains and losses visited through administrative regulation, particularly as they relate to collective goods or bads, are less susceptible to market valuation, are more often interstitial in character, and less amenable to centralized redistributive efforts. Moreover, in the context of judicial resolution of particular controversies, it is at least plausible that equity should not be measured in terms of the overall distribution of income, but in terms of the competing moral claims of the particular parties (Fletcher, 1972, p. 537; Epstein, 1973, p. 151). It is difficult to transpose the latter view of equity to administrative choices affecting a wide range of inchoate interests.

These efficiency and distributional objections to the courts' exercise of a direct resource allocation role in judicial review of administrative action are weighty, but not decisive. As developed in section IV, there are important societal values implicated in environmental resource decisions that go beyond efficiency or equitable income distribution, and that are likely to be better served by courts than by the political/administrative process. Moreover, the argument that the political/administrative process is in general better equipped than the courts to reach efficient resource allocation decisions about collective goods does not exclude the possibility of defining a subclass of decisions in which courts may have a comparative advantage. This possibility is also developed in section IV.

IV. TOWARD A COMMON LAW FUNCTION FOR COURTS IN THE REGULATORY ERA

The preceding section of the essay argued that legislative creation of administrative agencies should not necessarily be held to oust courts from their traditional resource allocation role. However, no affirmative argument that courts *should* discharge such a role in reviewing administrative action was offered. This section of the essay suggests three different grounds for such a role, and then briefly considers potential objections, based on distributional considerations, to such a role.

First-Order Preconditions of Individual Autonomy

Our prevailing understanding of political and economic life presupposes a community of relatively autonomous, choosing individuals. This understanding is made quite explicit in welfare economics and associated theories of public choice. Such an understanding implies that certain minimum conditions of individual autonomy must be satisfied before arrangements for mutual bargaining and collective policies can be determined. In terms of legal arrangements, this implication translates formally into first-order rules securing minimum conditions of individual autonomy, and second-order rules defining the mechanisms of mutual or collective choice. While these second-order rules may be selected with a view to efficiency or aggregate distributional equity, the first-order rules that secure the preconditions of exchange and social choice cannot logically be devised on the basis of such criteria.[18]

This lexical ordering is reflected in crude form in the common law divide between tort and property law, which defines the initial boundaries between individuals, and contract law, which specifies the arrangements for subsequent bargaining and exchange. In the administrative state, however, this lexical ordering is destroyed in collective decisions about the allocation of environmental and other resources, creating the danger that political and administrative arrangements guided by criteria of efficiency or the struggle for distributional advantage could yield policies that failed to secure minimum preconditions of individual autonomy.

Bodily Integrity. Bodily integrity is clearly one of the minimum conditions of individual autonomy and is enshrined as such in the common law of tort.[19] One can at least envision a society in which political and administrative policies reflected a persistent marginal willingness to trade off bodily integrity for increased production of goods and services carried to the point where our current conception of human integrity would be seriously degraded (Fabricant, 1971, pp. 139, 148–149). The recent history of Japan contains examples suggesting such possibilities.

This danger might justify judicial intervention in administrative resource allocation decisions to protect first-order interests in bodily integrity. Such intervention would be analogous to constitutional decisions in which courts today intervene to protect certain other prerequi-

---

[18] This argument is elaborated in Fried (1978).

[19] It seems difficult to conceive of a community of individuals each attempting to realize a relatively well-ordered set of purposes over time under a regime in which, for example, each person's body was subject to free appropriation by others.

sites to individual autonomy (such as First Amendment freedoms), which may be slighted in the short-run political and administrative pursuit of expanded social output or the distributional struggle.

There are several obvious objections to this suggestion. First, the common law analogy is weakened by the circumstance that an individual might waive rights to bodily integrity protected by common law by contracting to engage in hazardous activity or by accepting money in return for relinquishing the right to enjoin a neighbor's hazardous activity. If an individual could thus waive common law rights protecting bodily integrity, why cannot the community decide to incur serious hazards when environmental policies are administratively selected? But this line of argument is not decisive. In common law the decision to incur risks was individual, whereas administrative decisions about environmental quality may expose many risk-averse individuals to greater hazards than they would willingly incur. Particularly where environmental policies are geographically uniform, as they frequently are, they may in effect constitute a coerced invasion of bodily integrity. Moreover, administrative decisions about environmental quality create a more serious danger of collective, possibly irreversible, degradation in standards of individual integrity than does a system of individual waivers of common law rights.[20]

A second objection to the suggested judicial reexamination of administrative resource allocation decisions is the lack of a basis for such a practice in the federal Constitution. The Constitution does not by its terms or history convey a judicially protected right to avoid exposure to "excessive" environmental hazards. However, the matter is not quite so simple. Common law rights (including rights to bodily integrity) may have been understood by the Framers as included in the "life, liberty, or property" protected by the due process clause of the Constitution. This understanding is reflected in current decisions that the government may not deprive an individual of common law rights without adequate procedural due process.[21] Why should not courts also exercise a measure of substantive review as well? The expectation of the Framers was that environmental resource decisions would be made by an independent

---

[20] A system of common law rights may distribute entitlements and, correspondingly, wealth in such a fashion that a substantial percentage of the population may be forced to endure hazardous activities or environments as a condition of existence. See, for example, *Versailles Borough* v. *McKeesport Coal & Coal Co.,* 83 Pittsburgh Legal Jl. 379 (1935). But administrative policies are likely to be even more inclusive.

[21] See *Fuentes* v. *Shevin,* 407 U.S. 67 (1972); *Board of Regents of State Colleges* v. *Roth,* 408 U.S. 564 (1972).

judiciary. The creation of administrative agencies arguably should not be permitted to destroy this constitutional understanding by limiting court review to questions of the agency's statutory authority.[22]

However, judicial control of resource allocation decisions through doctrines of substantive due process would force courts to confront the difficult problem of determining, usually in the face of considerable uncertainty, what level of hazard to bodily integrity should be permitted. The difficulty in resolving that question is complicated by distributional issues raised by variations in individuals' susceptibility to environmental insult. If environmental quality is established at a level adequate to protect the most susceptible individual, tremendous costs will be visited on other members of the society. A decision to establish environmental quality at any lower level will extend basic protection to some persons but deny it to others.

These difficulties argue against recognition of a constitutional right to bodily integrity that would override explicit legislative determination of the competing considerations. But they do not appear so weighty as to bar judicial reassessment of administrative policies where relevant statutes provide no guidance and the agency's policies (e.g., adoption of a radiation standard posing grave long-run genetic hazards) seriously threaten bodily integrity. Judicial decisions invalidating such policies in the absence of specific legislative warrant for them might be termed "quasi-constitutional." While basing its decisions on grounds analogous to those underlying constitutional rights, the court would not invalidate the agency's action as unconstitutional, but rather construe narrowly its otherwise broad statutory mandate as not including discretion to infringe on basic interests in bodily integrity.[23] Alternatively, such intervention by the courts could be viewed as a logical adaptation of common law functions to a regulatory era. Under either rationale, the courts' intervention

---

[22] Cf. Crowell v. Benson, 285 U.S. 22 (1932), asserting that Congress lacks constitutional authority to transfer from the federal courts to administrative agencies the entire resolution of controversies, between private citizens, formerly governed by common law principles. Crowell acknowledged that administrative agencies might be given fact-finding responsibilities in resolving such controversies, but insisted that reviewing courts retain power to resolve all questions of "law."

The presumption that common law remedies continue to be available following the creation of administrative schemes also suggests constitutional overtones in the protection of common law interests (Stewart and Krier, 1978, ch. 5).

[23] See Stewart (1977a, pp. 713, 750–758). The approach suggested here might be framed in terms of clear-statement doctrine: that bodily integrity is such a basic value that a statute should not be read to authorize administrative decisions which seriously compromise that value unless the legislature explicitly so provides. For use of this approach in other contexts, see Kent v. Dulles, 357 U.S. 116 (1958); Greene v. McElroy, 360 U.S. 474 (1959).

could be reversed by the legislature on an explicit determination that the health risks in question were justified in the pursuit of other societal objectives.

At present in the United States, however, there seems little prospect that courts need often intervene to counter serious administrative laxity in setting environmental quality standards. Most such standards aim at environmental quality levels considerably higher than plausible minimum guarantees of bodily integrity would dictate.[24] There are instances, however, where administrative standards and controls are incomplete. In some such instances, common law damage remedies may provide an adequate response in the case of injuries which have already occurred and whose causal origin is unambiguous. Such remedies have been particularly important in the evolution of environmental policy in Japan.[25] However, where harm is threatened but has not yet occurred, prophylactic administrative measures may be required. In at least one decision, *Environmental Defense Fund* v. *Ruckleshaus,*[26] American judges have required administrators to undertake such measures on a showing of serious hazard. This decision is consonant with the judicial role urged here.

Environmental Diversity. Another set of first-order values which courts would be justified in protecting through quasi-constitutional lawmaking revolves around the generation of choice preferences. Conventional economic analysis does not address the origin, content, or formative significance of the preferences whose satisfaction individuals strive to maximize. Such preferences are simply an exogenous "given." However, individual opportunity to explore and critically evaluate different preferences or values is basic to any tolerable conception of individual autonomy. If individuals' preferences or values were simply a reflex function of their environment, we could hardly be justified in according, as we do, positive normative weight to the realization of those values or preferences. Individual self-development and, with it, a firm sense of individual identity, depends upon the potential for experiential heterogeneity. Indi-

---

[24] The hazard to interests in bodily integrity rarely lies in the setting of standards, but in the failure to implement standards because of limited agency resources, lack of cooperation by state and local authorities, and citizens' resistance to governmentally required changes in established patterns of conduct. There may be little that courts can do to remove these obstacles beyond generous construction of the enforcing agencies' legal authority. See Stewart (1977b, p. 1196).

[25] See *The Itai-Itai Case*, 635 Hanrei Jiho 17 (Toyama Dist. Ct. 1968); *Mitamura* v. *Suzuki*, 669 Hanrei Jiho 26 (Sup. Ct., 3rd Petty Bench, 1972); *The Yokkaichi Air Pollution Case*, 672 Hanrei Jiho 32 (Tsu Dist. Ct. 1972).

[26] 439 F.2d 584 (D.C. Cir. 1971).

viduals' capacity to assume a critical stance toward their existing preferences and beliefs, and to explore a variety of alternative life-styles and values would remain in large degree simply formal if the social and material conditions upon which the growth of new forms of perceiving, judging, and living were impoverished or homogeneous. Environmental diversity, and particularly the preservation of relatively unspoiled environments, can be an important element of this necessary diversity in potential experience (Stewart, 1977a, pp. 750–754).

In common law in the last century, the sheer size and physical diversity of the nation, the relatively restricted reach of industrialization, and judges' adaptation of law to local circumstances all combined to maintain considerable geographical, economic, and cultural variety. This variety has been threatened by pervasive industrial and commercial development, and the resort to political and administrative systems of resource allocation that are often biased against environmental diversity. In these circumstances, the courts are justified in intervening to protect environmental diversity by reversing otherwise discretionary administrative resource allocation decisions that destroy important sources of such diversity.

In our federal system of government, there are, as developed in the next subsection, powerful political and administrative incentives for the adoption of geographically uniform regulatory measures—such as the ambient standards in the Clean Air Act—that would permit degradation of high quality environments. In the *Sierra Club* litigation,[27] the courts intervened by reading into the Clean Air Act a nondegradation requirement that restricted the administrator's discretion to adopt policies that destroy high quality environments. Other threats to experiential diversity are posed by the increasing use of efficiency yardsticks in management of public resources (Hirsch, 1977, pp. 84–114). Joseph Sax (1976, p. 239; 1977, p. 565) has recently suggested that managers of public lands should not emulate market measures of efficiency, but should strive to provide opportunities for forms of experience not readily available in the market sector.[28] Administrative disregard of these nonmarket opportunities could be an appropriate basis for judicial intervention to require alternative resource allocations. Courts have already intervened

---

[27] See *Sierra Club* v. *Ruckleshaus,* 344 F.Supp. 253 (D.D.C. 1972), *aff'd per curiam,* 4 ERC 1205, *aff'd by an equally divided Court,* 412 U.S. 541 (1973).

[28] *Izaak Walton League* v. *Butz,* 522 F.2d 945 (4th Cir. 1975); *Sieske* v. *Butz,* 9 ERC 1061 (D. Alaska 1976); *Sierra Club* v. *Department of Interior,* 376 F.Supp. 90 (N.D. Cal. 1974).

to prevent clear-cutting in national forests and road building through public parks[29] in situations where administrators operated under financial incentive systems that underplayed diversity. In doing so, the courts are instinctively performing a valuable and legitimate institutional function that should be explicitly acknowledged.[30]

Second-Order Efficiency Values

Even if courts are in general less institutionally competent to advance efficiency interests in the context of administrative regulation than are administrators, it may be possible to identify subcategories of resource allocation decisions in which the political/administrative process displays structural defects that result in serious inefficiencies which the courts are equipped to correct.

Our current political system characteristically relies upon relatively inflexible, uniform regulatory controls to deal with problems of environmental resource allocation. Use of regulation, as opposed to other incentive systems, may be inevitable given the political necessity of whipping up public support for legislation on the part of otherwise apathetic citizens by portraying polluters as evil wrongdoers (Ingram, 1978). Legislators, fearing that nonuniform standards may lead to industrial relocation, and reluctant to grant discretion to administrators on such a fundamental matter, tend to insist on uniform measures. National administrators operate under bureaucratic incentives to adopt uniform controls, and are encouraged in this by environmental advocates who fear that local flexibility will lead to weakening of environmental policies.

In these circumstances, courts may usefully advance efficiency by mitigating the rigors and inflexibility of regulatory controls when they come to be applied and enforced. For example, courts have set aside administrative decisions imposing sweeping pollution controls on existing industrial sources without apparent regard to the benefits to be

---

[29] *Citizens to Preserve Overton Park, Inc.* v. *Volpe,* 401 U.S. 402 (1971).

[30] Can judges be counted upon to discharge a defined institutional role? This question has clearly posed difficulties for analysts who have attempted to apply a relatively crude self-interest maximization to an independent judiciary with no apparent monetary or career incentives to decide cases for one side or another. Both casual empiricism and the historical practice of the federal judiciary in the United States suggest that professional socialization (with incentives such as peer group and public prestige) of judges is the most important factor in their behavior, leading them to play a more or less well-defined role. The means by which their professional socialization might be modified to alter that role presents subtle but tractable questions.

achieved[31] or the costs imposed[32] with respect to older plants; have required administrative postponement of rigid controls deadlines when the costs of imminent enforcement in a particular instance far outweighed benefits;[33] and have also set aside a general agency policy of requiring continuous emission controls as applied to a given plant when the agency failed to establish that it was feasible for that plant to utilize such controls.[34] In each case, the costs of enforcing inflexible regulatory requirements in a given context appeared to far outweigh the benefits. By and large the courts, while appearing to address only procedure, have promoted more efficient outcomes at the stage of implementation by finding that the administrative record was deficient in not containing adequate information about costs or that the agency's opinion did not deal adequately with cost objections, and remanding for further proceedings. However, the courts' application of the procedural scalpel often reflects a substantive concern with seemingly arbitrary agency policies. Administrative agencies will often heed this concern in proceedings on remand by not insisting upon measures that cannot plausibly be justified by an analysis of costs and benefits.[35] Thus the functional impact of judicial review is to dampen rigidities in regulatory implementation in instances where they generate costs that greatly exceed apparent benefits. This efficiency-promoting function of the courts could likely be enhanced and extended if it were explicitly acknowledged as such.

In addition to this moderating role at the "micro" level of implementation and enforcement, courts might also intervene to promote efficiency at the "macro" level of basic policy or standard setting. They have in fact done so by requiring administrators to give consideration to costs that an agency would, because of its institutional mission, tend to disregard or discount. For example, agencies whose basic mission is to promote the construction of electric generating facilities or highways have been required to give greater consideration to the environmental costs of such developments (Stewart, 1977a, pp. 717–720). Similarly, agencies whose prime mission is environmental protection have been required to pay greater attention to the resource costs involved in securing improvements in environmental quality (Stewart, 1977a, pp. 727–740).

---

[31] See *Appalachian Power Co.* v. *Train,* 545 F.2d 1351 (4th Cir. 1976).

[32] See *American Iron & Steel Institute* v. *EPA,* 10 Envir. Rep. [BNA] 1689 (3d Cir. 1977).

[33] See *International Harvester Co.* v. *Ruckleshaus,* 478 F.2d 615 (D.C. Cir. 1973).

[34] See *Bunker Hill Co.* v. *EPA,* 10 Envir. Rep. [BNA] 1401 (9th Cir. 1977).

[35] See, for example, the decision of the Environmental Protection Agency on remand from the *International Harvester* decision, 38 Fed. Reg. 10317 (1973).

These requirements—which tend to promote efficiency by countering a form of "government failure" that is generated by tendencies of special-purpose bureaucracies to systematically skew the counting of relevant costs and benefits—are expressed in procedural form but are calculated to have substantive impact. Courts require administrators to provide for formal participation by representatives of major interests affected by a proposed decision. The administrative record must document the relevant impacts and the administrative decision discuss these impacts in analyzing the issues at stake and justifying the choice ultimately made. These measures give a degree of bargaining power to the interests formally represented, expose administrative decision makers to impacts that might otherwise be disregarded, and furnish courts with tools to set aside decisions that appear to generate large costs for limited or dubious benefits (Stewart, 1977a, pp. 717–720 and 1975, pp. 1711–1760).

However, these procedural requirements are costly, particularly where an agency's failure to meet them leads, as it typically does, to a remand by the reviewing court for further administrative proceedings. Why do not reviewing courts instead simply dictate the ultimate result, or set bounds on acceptable outcomes? Courts generally refuse this course, in part, perhaps, because it is far more difficult for judges to identify inefficient "macro" policies than to identify "micro" instances where a particular application of a general requirement generates excessive costs.[36] For example, one might plausibly argue that the nature of regulatory politics, the media's concern with hazards that can be dramatized as life-threatening, the institutional biases of environmental protection agencies, and the use of regulatory controls that tend to disguise the costs of such controls all lead to adoption of environmental standards that are excessively stringent from the viewpoint of efficiency.[37] But whether such standards are indeed inefficient is a function of individual preferences for a collective good—a more healthful environment—which a reviewing court is extraordinarily ill equipped to measure. It is a real and even plausible possibility that many in society would prefer to strive for a world that is free of contaminants whenever it is possible to elimi-

---

[36] Judicial "fine tuning" at the stage of enforcement or application of a general policy could be carried to the point where the more general policy was effectively undermined. Agencies with developmental missions and those with environmental missions do not hesitate to raise this specter in judicial review. But judges sensitive to the problem are capable of moderating regulatory rigidities without encroaching on the central core.

[37] Ingram (1978). As previously discussed, these standards are also in most instances far more stringent than those required to preserve first-order values of individual autonomy.

nate them through means that are not socially disruptive (even if expensive). Because of the courts' institutional deficiencies in "adding up" fuzzy, inarticulate preferences, they are poorly situated to review the efficiency of general administrative policies relating to environmental resource allocation.

Might the problem of measuring preferences be cured by the development of indexes, based on property values or wage rate differentials, of the value placed by individuals on various aspects of environmental quality? This is at best an uncertain prospect. Preferences for collective goods such as environmental quality are strongly conditioned by the availability of information concerning the adverse effects of diminished environmental quality—and such information is itself in many respects a collective good whose production is a function of social choice. Moreover, preferences for collective goods are likely to be powerfully conditioned by the perception that the production of such goods is a matter of collective choice, and by the mechanisms of collective deliberation and decision on such choices. The value citizens place on clean air, for example, is not simply a "datum" or exogenous "given" which can be fed into a mechanism of collective choice.[38] The valuation of clean air is instead at least in part the endogenously conditioned outcome of any such mechanism. Courts can play a valuable role as part of that mechanism by ensuring that consideration is given to relevant values by administrators and legislators, and that procedures are available for the representation of divergent views. Rarely would courts be justified in shortcircuting the evolving collective process of valuation by dictating certain environmental resource allocations on grounds of efficiency.[39]

This analysis would not exclude a more forward judicial role in reviewing, on grounds of efficiency, administrative resource allocation decisions that do not present the special problems of valuation posed by collective goods such as environmental quality. For example, in its recent

[38] To borrow Charles Lindblom's terminology, environmental quality choices are rarely a matter of "simple preference"; they involve elements of "volition" involving analysis and judgment. See Lindblom (1978, pp. 134–135).

[39] There may nonetheless be extreme cases where an agency's zeal carries it beyond any plausible accounting of costs and benefits. *Reserve Mining Co.* v. *Herbst*, 10 Envir. Rep. [BNA] 1114 (Minn. Sup. Ct. 1977) may be such a case. There the court set aside the denial by environmental protection agencies of a permit for an on-land disposal site for wastes generated by a taconite iron-ore processing plant; prior litigation had resulted in decisions requiring the plant to cease its present practice of discharging these wastes into Lake Superior. The court explicitly took responsibility for the ultimate decision, finding that the environmental risks of disposal at the on-land site were small, and that denial of the permit would probably entail shutdown of the plant and massive economic dislocation.

Home Box Office decision, the District of Columbia Circuit Court of Appeals departed from normal principles of deference to agency policy making to invalidate Federal Communication Commission regulations restricting the ability of cablecasters to compete with established over-the-air television broadcasters.[40] The regulations were a classic instance of protecting established firms against competitive inroads generated by new technologies.[41] Common law courts in the early nineteenth century United States refused to protect such firms, favoring the collective efficiency benefits of competition (Horwitz, 1977, pp. 31–53, 109–139). Given the contemporary ossification of legislative and administrative policies in a form of "special interest politics,"[42] there is an appropriate role for the courts in countering the tendency of administrators to protect the established position of organized interests at the expense of the community's interest in efficient resource use. Given the apparent intensification in the United States of short-term, defensive distributional struggle at the expense of long-run productive efficiency, this judicial role may become increasingly important.

Distributional Considerations

Even if it is otherwise justified as serving first-order values of personal integrity or experiential diversity, or second-order values of

---

[40] *Home Box Office, Inc.* v. *FCC,* 567 F.2d 9 (D.C. Cir. 1977), *cert. denied,* 434 U.S. 829 (1977).

[41] The court found no substantial justification for the FCC's restriction on entry, and concluded that accordingly, the FCC's imposition of such restrictions exceeded its statutory authority and also infringed free speech rights in violation of the First Amendment. The First Amendment issue raises special questions not relevant here. The statutory ruling displays a new willingness by courts to construe narrowly vague legislative grants of authority to agencies. Compare *FCC* v. *National Citizens Committee for Broadcasting,* 555 F.2d 938 (D.C. Cir. 1977), *cert. granted,* 98 S.Ct. 52 (1977), where the court invalidated an FCC policy permitting continuation of previously established cross-ownership relations between television stations and newspapers because the policy contravened a judicially developed principle favoring diversity of broadcast sources. This diversity principle might be explained in terms of efficiency or, possibly, first-order principles of individual autonomy.

[42] See Drew (1978, p. 64). As pointed out in Lindblom (1978, p. 348), in the common-law market system there is wide freedom for parties to agree to achieve more efficient outcomes beneficial to society as a whole even though some third parties may suffer financial loss through the operation of pecuniary externalities. Political and administrative systems of resource allocation, by contrast, facilitate veto of changes in the status quo by threatened interests, even though the changes may be efficient and desirable from the viewpoint of the community. Accordingly, the displacement of the common law by administrative regimes seriously threatens efficiency. [Ed. note: This is the burden of a recent line of research and writing by Mancur Olson. See, for example, Olson (1976).]

efficiency, judicial modification of administrative resource allocation decisions could be undesirable if the distributional consequences were seriously at odds with policies explicitly or implicitly reflected in legislative decisions. Particularly in the context of global distributional equity, courts engaged in case-by-case decisions are far less competent than legislatures to decide upon and implement appropriate distributional judgments.

While the distributional consequences of second-order "fine tuning" to promote efficiency at the "micro" level seem indeterminate, judicial efforts to promote first-order integrity and experiential diversity would probably have substantially regressive distributional consequences. Courts might well carry protection of bodily integrity beyond what the poor would voluntarily pay for in preference to other goods and services. It is quite clear that preservation of pristine environments heavily benefits the wealthy, who have both the income and acquired taste to place a high value on such amenities, and can afford the incidental expenditures needed to enjoy them (Stewart, 1977a, pp. 715–717, 719). But these consequences need not deter the courts from intervening to protect first-order values.

In the analysis presented here, global considerations of income distribution are a question of second-order arrangements concerning the appropriate division of goods and services, rather than first-order arrangements securing the personal integrity of the individuals who consume those goods and services. Accordingly, distributional considerations are, strictly speaking, irrelevant in framing first-order arrangements. But even if distributional consequences are relevant, the environmental policies emerging from legislatures also tend to be globally regressive, so that the consequences of judicial intervention would not be out of line. Congress has displayed a lively concern with geographical variations in the impact of environmental control, and has been particularly concerned to avoid incentives for industrial relocation. Judicial intervention to secure first-order values of bodily integrity and experiential diversity is unlikely to threaten this concern. Moreover, "micro" level judicial "fine tuning" of geographically uniform controls at the stage of application or enforcement would probably advance Congress' objective in avoiding relocation because the effect would be to moderate environmental controls on older facilities with high abatement costs, which might otherwise be shut down. At the "macro" level, judicial invalidation of administrative policies designed to protect entrenched firms at the expense of community interests in efficiency might run contrary to the design of some statutes; but in most instances the discernible legislative intent is too ambiguous or open-ended to find square conflict.[43] Accordingly, there does not appear to be serious conflict between the judicial role in resource allocation decisions outlined here and the distributional concerns embodied in legislation.

V. CONCLUDING REMARKS

The aim of this essay is modest. It emphasizes the important re-source allocation role of the courts in common law and argues that the creation of administrative agencies should not entirely displace the courts from responsibility for resource allocation decisions. Political and admin-istrative processes tend in characteristic ways to neglect certain first-order values of individual autonomy and to make unjustified sacrifices of second-order efficiency values. The reviewing courts can play an appro-priate role in checking those tendencies. The particular content of that role will vary depending upon the subject matter of the relevant admin-istrative scheme. For example, review of policies with respect to "fuzzy" collective goods such as environmental quality may justify a larger judi-cial role in promoting first-order values, and a smaller role in furthering efficiency, than review of administrative price and entry regulation, where the alternatives are more susceptible to market-type evaluation. The analysis offered here need not entail drastic changes in the current prac-tice of reviewing courts; this essay has already indicated that a number of contemporary judicial decisions are best explained in terms of the role suggested here. However, explicit acknowledgment of that role should enhance its discharge. The contentions sketched here are only the poten-tial beginnings of a more general theory of the resource allocation func-tion of courts in an era of administrative regulation.

[43] For example, the Federal Communications Act, on which the ruling in *Home Box Office* was in part based, directs the FCC to regulate radio communica-tions in the "public convenience, interest, or necessity" 47 U.S.C. §307(a). This broad delegation to an agency of authority to deal with problems of conflicting uses of a limited resource—the radiomagnetic spectrum—contains no mandate for pro-tection of those firms presently deriving economic benefit from use of the spectrum. Indeed, there is positive evidence in the statutory scheme of intent to deny such protection. See *FCC v. Sanders Bros. Radio Station*, 309 U.S. 470 (1940).

In the nineteenth century, efficiency may have been achieved by the common law by throwing the burdens of dislocation on those least prepared to bear it. See Horwitz (1977). Such distributional impacts are far less likely if regulated firms are deprived of administrative protection against dynamic change.

A. Myrick Freeman III

Comments

This is not like most papers in social choice theory. It does not use mathematical tools to deduce theorems about the consequences of alternative sets of axioms and value judgments. Nor does it use models to derive hypotheses about the real world and subject them to empirical testing. So I cannot comment on possible biases in Stewart's estimating technique nor discuss the robustness of his conclusions, given minor changes in axioms and assumptions.

Rather, Stewart's paper is more like a lawyer's brief. Perhaps this is not surprising. But it means that as a discussant, I will have to judge his paper on these terms. He has done an excellent job in marshalling the legal and philosophical arguments in favor of his position. But despite the grace and skill with which he has presented his argument, I am inclined to decide the case against him, even though I have not heard the opposing team's presentation.

His argument goes as follows. He says that there is general agreement among legal scholars that, historically, courts, through common law, played a major role in the development and evolution of the principles of contract and property. In this way, courts had a major impact on resource allocation. The general tendency was for the law to promote the efficient allocation of resources. However in recent times (the past thirty to forty years or so), as the legislative branch has become increasingly involved in resource allocation, the courts have adopted a more restricted role, at least with respect to decisions made in the executive branch. That has been one of oversight, with emphasis on due process rather than substance. He observes that the courts in reviewing administrative decisions have been very reluctant to substitute their own judgment for that of responsible administrative officers following established procedures for reaching decisions.

Stewart would like to see courts take a more activist role in reviewing administrative decisions, especially to protect what he has elsewhere called quasi-constitutional rights such as the right to bodily integrity, the right to experiential diversity, and to promote economic efficiency where it is threatened by the regulators' emphasis on uniformity in standards.

To evaluate the argument, let us consider a hypothetical example. Suppose Congress has authorized EPA to regulate certain kinds of chemicals so as to "protect the public health with due regard to technical feasibility and cost." It is proposed to regulate a certain chemical, and the issue is which of two levels of control is to be imposed. The administrator has before him statements of the expected reduction in mortality for each control level as well as the expected costs of achieving that control.

There are at least two important characteristics of the problem posed. The first is that there is almost surely going to be uncertainty regarding the estimates of the magnitude of benefits and costs. The statements are either implicitly or explicitly expected values. And the administrator's way of dealing with that uncertainty may be an important part of the choice problem. Second, the choice of a regulatory standard typically involves a tradeoff along some continuum. It is rarely a question of "bodily integrity or not," but rather a question of how much bodily integrity one wishes to buy by giving up other goods and services. Whatever the choice, it reveals a marginal willingness to pay or marginal rate of substitution between benefits and costs.

Stewart is talking about two alternative regimes for making the regulatory and judicial decisions. Let me call them the *administrative* law regime and the *common* law regime. Under both regimes, the administrator of EPA would gather the relevant data, make findings of fact, reach a decision by making some judgment on the tradeoffs involved, and publish his reasons for doing what he did. Under the administrative law regime, anyone unhappy with the decision could ask for court review. But this review would be limited, more or less, to an examination of the procedures used to reach the decision, and the determination as to whether the decision was consistent with the congressional directive and the information available to the administrator.

Under the common law regime, courts would be allowed to go further in their review. If there were two alternatives which were both supportable with the evidence at hand, under the common law regime the court would be allowed to substitute its judgment for that of the administrator if it could offer certain justifications for doing so.

Which regime is to be preferred? I don't think one can deduce an answer to that question except on the basis of some value judgment about the basic principles of government. One value judgment is that governmental decisions affecting people should only be made by officials who are politically accountable to those people. On the basis of this value judgment, one would prefer the administrative law regime, since the administrator of EPA is accountable to the people by virtue of his being appointed by an elected president and in a less direct but more tangible way through his relationship with Congress.

The common law regime places the ultimate decision-making authority with a judge who has been removed as much as possible from direct political accountability for his decisions. Now, I can't say that this is wrong. But I can say that I don't like it.

Having discussed Stewart's paper, let me comment on a paper that he didn't write—but that I think would have been valuable to have. The participants in this forum would, I think, have been interested to learn how the body of legislative and case law governing administrative procedures and practices has affected social choice processes, especially in the area of economic regulation. There has been some interesting work on the economic theory of regulation which has applied the assumption of rational behavior and the principles of maximization to understand better the behavior of the various parties involved in the regulatory process. At least to my knowledge, none of this work has taken into account in an explicit way the effects of the typically broad delegation of authority by Congress along with the limits on discretion and the safeguards provided by administrative law—and especially changes in the body of law over time—on the way regulatory decisions are made and carried out. I think that there are some interesting and important positive and normative questions here. Some of them may be important in evaluating alternative forms of regulation, for example, charges versus standards for pollution. I hope that some of these questions will find a place on the research agenda for applied social choice theory.

Alvin K. Klevorick

Comments

Stewart's paper discusses an interesting issue: the role of courts under different economic—more accurately, different political/economic —structures. As his point of departure, he takes the view that "numerous scholars of quite different persuasions have concluded that the dominant thrust and effect of common law court decisions was to structure property relations and market arrangements to secure an efficient allocation of resources or to promote economic growth and development."[1] He then asks why courts should have largely abdicated the "pervasive and inescapable power . . . over resource allocation" that they had under laissez-faire to the administrative agencies created to regulate the market in a more "mixed system," a system in which such agencies play an important role.

In Stewart's view, the current stance of courts in reviewing administrative decision making in the realm of environmental resources is "fully consistent with jurisprudential assumptions that have been firmly entrenched ever since the New Deal: that the courts should confine themselves to maintaining the integrity of constitutive decision-making arrangements and protecting individual liberties, while decisions about resource allocation should be remitted to the political branches." He wants to question this conventional wisdom—which is sometimes attributed to a "legal process school"—as applied to environmental resource decision making. In particular, the paper argues that the creation of administrative agencies should not displace courts entirely from direct responsibility for resource allocation, and it outlines a number of poten-

[1] Just as Stewart does not wish to labor the difficulties with the several accounts of the common law courts' resource allocation functions he mentions, I do not wish to labor here the difficulties with his point of departure. He does cite scholars of diverse persuasions who have emphasized the courts' resource allocation role. But the "emerging scholarly consensus" on the role of common law tort and property rules which he identifies is not as universal as he suggests.

tial functions for reviewing courts in making resource allocation decisions.

I want to argue that there is a tension between what Stewart sets out to do and what he eventually does. To be sure, he calls for more explicit judicial reexamination of the merits of agency policies and for judicial control of substantive choices in some cases. But, in the end, he makes an important distinction—namely, that between first-order values and second-order values—and assigns roles to institutions in accord with that distinction in a way which places him not as far from the legal process school as he makes out to be the case.

Stewart begins by considering several possible efficiency and distributional objections to a direct resource allocation role for courts reviewing administrative agency actions about the environment. These relate to: (1) institutional shortcomings of courts and the possibility that the legislative creation of administrative agencies was in direct response to those shortcomings and represents an authoritative, determinative reallocation of responsibilities from judges to administrators; (2) technical shortcomings of courts; and (3) social preference revelation shortcomings of courts in cases involving collective goods. Stewart finds each of these objections interesting and of some merit, but not decisive. (Though I shall not try to elaborate on these objections, one might question whether Stewart has presented them as cogently as their advocates would.)

Having blunted what he sees as the principal objections to a direct resource allocation role for courts in reviewing administrative actions, Stewart argues that important social values are affected by environmental resource decisions, values that go beyond concern with efficiency or income distribution. And, he argues, these values "are likely to be better served by courts than by the political/administrative process." Furthermore, he believes it is possible to define a subclass of resource allocation decisions about collective goods—and, in particular, the environment—which courts may be better at making compared with the political/administrative process.

It is noteworthy that in discussing the resource allocation decision-making ability of courts, Stewart repeatedly contrasts the courts with "the political/administrative institutions" and "the political/administrative process." This conflation of the distinction between the legislature and the administrative agencies which are its creation is problematic. It ignores the difference in the direct political accountability of legislators and administrators, a difference which is crucial when one is contrasting the relative responsiveness to social preferences of courts and the administrative agencies they review.

Early on, Stewart's paper notes the contemporary criticisms of "bureaucratic administrators not formally accountable through political or market mechanisms," and indeed his entire paper concerns the appropriate way for reviewing courts to respond to these criticisms of administrative agencies. But then in discussing "the defects of courts as instruments of social choice," Stewart declines to distinguish between the legislature and the administrative agencies. He writes, "While the administrative/political process may be a highly imperfect barometer of such preferences [for collective goods such as environmental quality], the courts, lacking any form of direct political accountability, are likely to be an even more imperfect register," and "Distributional considerations may also counsel judicial deference to environmental resource allocation decisions by *administrators*. Given the apparent lack of widely accepted principles for establishing a just distribution of income, questions of equity should presumptively be resolved through the *political process*." [my emphasis]

This move, compressing the legislature and the administrative agencies into *one* institution and the legislative process and the administrative process into *one* process, is at best unhelpful, and at worst potentially misleading, in the context of the interesting issue Stewart is discussing. This move portrays the choice between administrative agencies and courts as decision-making units as a choice between a set of deciders who are readily accountable to the collectivity and a set who are fully insulated from public reactions. Of course this is not the case. The choice is rather between two sets of institutions, neither of which is directly politically accountable, and both of which stand in sharp contrast to the legislature, which is subject to direct accountability.

What then are the resource allocation functions Stewart advocates for courts reviewing administrative agency decisions about the environment? The responsibilities he suggests can be divided into two categories: (1) protection of "quasi-constitutional" interests in bodily integrity and environmental diversity; and (2) "fine tuning" of agency implementation and enforcement decisions on environmental standards.

The first function derives from Stewart's basic proposition that "Our prevailing understanding of political and economic life presupposes a community of relatively autonomous, choosing individuals. . . . Such an understanding implies that certain first-order rules securing minimum conditions of individual autonomy" must be established before one addresses the choice of second-order rules governing conditions of inter-action and exchange among such individuals. The first-order rules are lexically prior preconditions, and while the "second-order rules may be selected with a view to efficiency or aggregate distributional equity, the first-order rules that secure the preconditions of exchange and social choice cannot logically be devised on the basis of such criteria."

Stewart then *identifies* bodily integrity and experiential diversity as two first-order conditions (certainly not the only first-order conditions) of individual autonomy. I would stress that the word "identifies" (my word, not his) might be replaced by the words "asserts that" because Stewart presents us with no theory of justice from which his lexicographi-cal ordering or, a fortiori, the contents or subject matter of the first-order rules, can be derived. He gives us no systematic way of deriving these lexically prior preconditions. We are, instead, launched on a sea of intuitionism without an anchor.

Suppose we accept Stewart's lexical ordering. How do we ascertain what minimum conditions are required for the autonomy of individuals in society? For example, Stewart recognizes that potential objections, grounded in distributional considerations, might be raised against judicial intervention to protect interests in bodily integrity and experiential diversity. He thinks such objections are likely because such protection would probably have substantially regressive distributional consequences. In response to these concerns, he offers as a defense that "global consid-eration of income distribution are a question of second-order arrange-ments concerning the appropriate division of goods and services, rather than first-order arrangements securing the personal integrity of the indi-viduals who consume those goods and services." Why are income distri-bution issues second-order matters? One could well argue, to the contrary, that a minimum income is critical to securing personal integrity and autonomy of choosing individuals.

Without a theory of why there should be a lexicographical ordering of interests and what the composition of each level of that ordering should be, how can we decide what arguments to accept about which interests are to be protected? And, how can we determine to what extent those interests should be protected? For example, how broad should be the class of preferences or values which individuals should have the oppor-tunity to explore and to evaluate critically? How much experiential diver-sity is important?

It is also interesting to note the limitations Stewart imposes on the court's protection of these "quasi-constitutional" interests, rights which he views as analogous to but not identical with interests explicitly protected by the Constitution, such as First Amendment rights. In his schema, the courts' intervention can be reversed by the legislature if the latter explicitly determines that the threats to those "quasi-constitutional" interests were justified in the pursuit of other societal interests. Hence, these "quasi-constitutional" interests are lexically prior only to the extent that the legislature as a collective decision mechanism says they are. But then the sense in which these are first-order interests *necessary* to establish and preserve individual autonomy becomes rather nebulous.

Let us, however, make a temporary leap of faith with Stewart to the world where first-order and second-order interests are well defined. It is very interesting to see who is responsible for protecting which interests and for making which rules in Stewart's world. The reviewing courts are given the role of protecting the quasi-constitutional, first-order interests. The *basic* decisions about the second-order rules concerning the allocation and distribution of goods and services are to be made by the legislative/administrative institutions. Compare this division of roles with that espoused by the "legal process school" with whose views the paper initially took issue. Stewart's allocation of responsibilities seems quite similar to that made according to what he calls "the conventional wisdom."

To be fair, though, we should note—and Stewart emphasizes—that he also perceives a fine-tuning role for courts with regard to the second-order rules. He views the legislature as having a strong proclivity for uniformity and national administrators as being subject to great pressures for uniformity. The fine-tuning role he would assign the courts would help restore the flexibility of legal rule making undercut by these tendencies and pressures in the legislative/administrative process. As Stewart puts it, "In these circumstances, courts may usefully advance efficiency by mitigating the rigors and inflexibility of regulatory controls when they come to be applied and enforced."

One wonders whether, although Stewart does not discuss it, there is not a role for courts to fine tune in the other direction as well. After all, uniform standards may be too weak in some circumstances just as they are too strong in others. Perhaps the *Izaak Walton League* and *Overton Park* decisions could be viewed as fine tuning in the opposite direction of greater environmental protection rather than, as Stewart interprets them, as judicial protection of the quasi-constitutional interest in experiential diversity.

But, more important, one wonders whether courts are well suited to make the fine-tuning adjustments Stewart proposes they should. Are they really well suited to take into account the general equilibrium effects of the measures they require, of the (subtle?) impacts of their decisions? Will the courts be able to judge accurately whether their fine tuning will necessarily move the economy to a more efficient position?

Stewart closes by looking back upon his contentions as "the potential beginnings of a more general theory of the resource allocation function of courts in an era of administrative controls." He has made a beginning, and an interesting one. But there are, as we have seen, some stumbling blocks even in the early going on this path—stumbling blocks which the use of social choice theory might help remove.

REFERENCES

Calabresi, Guido. 1970. *The Costs of Accidents* (New Haven, Conn., Yale University Press).

Coase, Ronald H. 1960. "The Problem of Social Cost," *Journal of Law and Economics* vol. 3, no. 1 (October).

Drew, Elizabeth. 1978. "A Reporter at Large, Phase: Engagement with the Special Interest State," *The New Yorker* (February 27) pp. 64–82.

Epstein, Richard. 1973. "A Theory of Strict Liability," *Journal of Legal Studies* vol. 2, no. 1 (January) pp. 151–221.

Fabricant, Solomon. 1971. "Economic Growth and the Problem of Environmental Pollution," in Kenneth Boulding et al. *Economics of Pollution* (New York, NYU Press).

Fletcher, George P. 1972. "Fairness and Utility in Tort Theory," *Harvard Law Review* vol. 85, no. 3 (January) pp. 537–573.

Fried, Charles. 1978. *Right and Wrong* (Cambridge, Mass., Harvard University Press).

Hayek, Friedrich. 1974. *Law, Legislation and Liberty* (Cambridge, England, Cambridge University Press).

Heymann, Phillip B. 1973. "The Problem of Coordination: Bargaining and Rules," *Harvard Law Review* vol. 86, no. 5, pp. 797–877.

Hirsch, Fred. 1977. *The Social Limits to Growth* (Cambridge, Mass., Harvard University Press).

Horowitz, Donald L. 1977. *The Courts and Social Policy* (Washington, D.C., Brookings Institution).

Horwitz, Morton J. 1977. *The Transformation of American Law* (Cambridge, Mass., Harvard University Press).

Hunciker, Kurt M., and Vincent Pagano. 1976. "Federal Environmental Litigation in 1976: The Federal Water Pollution Control Act," *Harvard Environmental Law Review* vol. 1, pp. 59–101.

Hurst, James Willard. 1956. *Law and the Conditions of Freedom in the Nineteenth Century United States* (Madison, University of Wisconsin Press).

Ingram, Helen. 1978. "The Political Rationality of Innovation: The Clean Air Amendments of 1970," in Ann Friedlander, ed., *Approaches to Controlling Air Pollution* (Cambridge, Mass., MIT Press).

Jaffe, Louis. 1965. *Judicial Control of Administrative Action* (Boston, Little, Brown).

Kelsen, Hans. 1970. *Pure Theory of Law* (Berkeley, University of California Press).

Landes, William M., and Richard A. Posner. 1975. "The Independent Judiciary in an Interest-Group Perspective," *Journal of Law and Economics* vol. 18, no. 3 (December) pp. 875–911.

Leventhal, Harold. 1974. "Environmental Decisionmaking and the Role of the Courts," *University of Pennsylvania Law Review* vol. 122, no. 3 (January) pp. 509–555.

Lindblom, Charles E. 1978. *Politics and Markets* (New York, Basic Books).

Olson, Mancur. 1976. "Statement" and "Response," Hearings before the Joint Economic Committee, Congress of the United States, 94th Cong., 2nd sess., November 10, pp. 50–53 and 79–83.

Parenteau, Patrick A., and Nancy Tauman. 1976. "The Effluent Limitations Commentary: Will Careless Draftsmanship Foil the Objectives of the Federal Water Pollution Control Act Amendments of 1972," *Ecology Law Quarterly* vol. 6, no. 1, pp. 1–62.

Posner, Richard A. 1977. *Economic Analysis of Law* (2nd ed., Boston, Little, Brown).

Priest, George L. 1977. "The Common Law Process and the Selection of Efficient Rules," *Journal Legal Studies* vol. 6, no. 1 (January) pp. 65–82.

Rubin, Paul H. 1977. "Why Is the Common Law Efficient?" *Journal of Legal Studies* vol. 6, no. 1 (January) pp. 51–82.

Sax, Joseph. 1976. "Helpless Grants: The National Parks and the Regulation of Private Lands," *Michigan Law Review* vol. 75, no. 2 (December) pp. 239–274.

————. 1977. "Freedom: Voices from the Wilderness," *Environmental Law* vol. 7, no. 3 (Spring) pp. 565–574.

Sive, David. 1970. "Some Thoughts of an Environmental Lawyer in the Wilderness of Administrative Law," *Columbia Law Review* vol. 70, no. 4 (April) pp. 612–651.

Stewart, Richard B. 1975. "The Reformation of American Administrative Law," *Harvard Law Review* vol. 88, no. 8 (June) pp. 1667–1813.

————. 1977a. "The Development of Administrative and Quasi-Constitutional Law in Judicial Review of Administrative Decisionmaking: Lessons from the Clean Air Act," *Iowa Law Review* vol. 62, no. 3 (February) pp. 713–769.

————. 1977b. "Pyramids of Sacrifice? Problems of Federalism in Mandating State Implementation of National Environmental Policy," *Yale Law Journal* vol. 86, no. 6 (August) pp. 1196–1285.

———— and James E. Krier. 1978. *Environmental Law and Policy* (2nd ed., Charlottesville, Va., Michie).

Stigler, George. 1971. "The Theory of Economic Regulation," *The Bell Journal of Economics and Management Science* vol. 2, no. 1 (Spring) pp. 3–21.

Oran R. Young

International Resource Regimes

Some natural resources lie outside national jurisdictions or cut across existing jurisdictional boundaries in such a way that effective management by any one state is infeasible. For example, the principal concentrations of manganese nodules in the Pacific Ocean are in areas that lie beyond even the most expansionary claims to national jurisdiction. Many stocks of fish and other renewable marine resources (e.g., marine mammals and oceanic birds) range over extensive areas without regard for the jurisdictional boundaries of sovereign states. The airwaves employed in intercontinental broadcasting are not subject to effective control by individual states. By its very nature, maritime commerce commonly makes use of sea lanes that pass through two or more sovereign jurisdictions.

It would not be utterly infeasible in some cases to redefine jurisdictional boundaries in such a way as to bring a given natural resource effectively under the control of a single sovereign state. Here it is pertinent to consider the desirability of some form of national management (e.g., the emerging regime for marine fisheries established under the American Fishery Conservation and Management Act of 1976, PL 94-265)[1] in contrast to open-to-entry arrangements or management through supranational institutions. In other cases, there is little prospect of bringing the relevant resources or stocks of resources wholly under the jurisdiction of individual states (e.g., deepsea minerals, oceanic birds). Under these circumstances, the real choice is between unrestricted open-

[1] American Fishery Conservation and Management Act of 1976, PL 94-265, 90 Stat. 331 codified at 16 USCA §§ 1801–1882 (W. Supp. 1977). Hereafter referred to as AFCM.

to-entry utilization (i.e., a common property regime) and some sort of supranational institution.

No doubt gray areas between these polar cases are common in real-world situations. Attempts to extend effective national jurisdiction are sometimes only partially successful. I expect the current American effort to gain full control over commercially harvested salmon of North American origin in the North Pacific will fall into this category. Similarly, the introduction of supranational institutions quite often proves ineffectual in practice. This has been the fate of some of the regional authorities set up to manage marine fisheries, and worries along these lines are often expressed in discussions of the proposed International Seabed Authority for deepsea mining.

Even allowing for these intermediate cases, however, it is possible to identify two distinct questions about institutional frameworks or regimes for the management of natural resources at the international level.[2] Are supranational institutions of any sort desirable in connection with a given natural resource? The critical issue here concerns the merits (i.e., the costs and benefits) of supranational institutions in comparison with other feasible managerial arrangements for the same resource. In those cases where it does seem desirable to introduce supranational institutions, what specific institutional arrangements seem most promising? This is essentially a matter of designing institutional frameworks or regimes to accommodate the natural, economic, and political features of the resource management problem at hand.[3]

In this essay, I propose to examine these questions in some detail. I shall draw heavily on several specific cases—marine fisheries and deepsea mining—in order to lend concrete empirical content to the discussion. But the issues are general ones relevant throughout the international relations of resource management. My thesis is that the details of institutional design will typically have far-reaching consequences with respect to both the distribution of wealth and the allocation of factors of production in the realm of resource management.

[2] A resource regime is an interrelated set of institutional arrangements (formal or informal) which structures the incentives of the actors involved in the exploitation of a given natural resource or group of natural resources. For further discussion of this concept, consult Young (1977, ch. 2).

[3] In this essay, I assess the performance of alternative resource regimes in terms of the following criteria: (1) economic efficiency, (2) nonmarket objectives (e.g., conservation of species, environmental quality, international cooperation), and (3) distributive equity. These criteria are spelled out in some detail in Young (1977, pp. 47–50).

I. ARE SUPRANATIONAL INSTITUTIONS DESIRABLE?

It is not self-evident that supranational institutions are desirable in conjunction with the management of any given natural resource at the international level. Even when resources are distributed in such a way that they cut across existing or initial national jurisdictions, there are management options that do not require the development of formal institutions at the supranational level. The task of this section, then, is to examine the conditions under which the introduction of supranational institutions constitutes a preferred strategy in the international relations of resource management. To lend substance to the discussion, I shall focus on the case of marine fisheries.[4]

There is now general agreement that unrestricted common property or open-to-entry arrangements will typically lead to highly unfortunate results in the marine fisheries (Gordon, 1954; Crutchfield, 1964; Christy and Scott, 1965). The major problems arising from the absence of exclusive rights in this realm include: (1) overfishing and severe depletion of stocks, (2) the dissipation of economic profits or rents, (3) over-capitalization and the acquisition of gear that lies idle large parts of the year, and (4) low wages and underemployment in the pertinent labor force. A rising demand for fish products on a worldwide basis has obscured the most severe *economic* implications of this situation. But it has done nothing to alter the fact that common property arrangements are fundamentally inadequate for the management of marine fisheries.[5] To be accurate, this conclusion applies with full force only to cases where fish stocks are subjected to heavy usage. But this restriction is not of great importance since heavy usage has become the rule rather than the exception in the marine fisheries, and there is every reason to expect that worldwide demand for fish products will continue to rise. In consequence, many commentators now argue that virtually any alternative would be preferable to a common property regime for the management of the marine fisheries.

---

[4] The stakes in the marine fisheries are high. In 1975, the latest year for which figures are available, worldwide landings of fish from the marine fisheries amounted to 69.7 million metric tons (live weight) (UN, 1977a, pp. 146–417). For the United States in 1975 the total catch was 2.8 million metric tons, with a total value of $971 million or an average value of $347 per ton (Bell, 1978, p. 362).

[5] As Crutchfield puts it, "The basic theory of a high sea fishery, whether exploited by a single nation or by more than one nation, suggests a bleak economic existence, to say the least" (Crutchfield, 1964, p. 212).

What are the alternatives to common property arrangements in this realm? While numerous variations are possible, the principal alternatives fall into three broad groups or families. The first involves the expansion of coastal state jurisdiction coupled with the establishment of some sort of exclusive fishery conservation zones. A second type of alternative rests on the idea of creating a global fisheries organization with sufficient power and authority to manage the marine fisheries of the world on an integrated basis. An intermediate solution would be to organize a system of regional supranational authorities for marine fisheries demarcated in terms of meaningful ecological units or domains. Selecting an alternative from the first group implies that the introduction of supranational institutions is not desirable in efforts to manage the marine fisheries while a choice of some alternative from either of the other groups suggests the opposite conclusion.

Coastal State Jurisdiction

Though we are currently moving rapidly toward expanded coastal state jurisdiction in the marine fisheries, I have serious reservations about the probable consequences of this jurisdictional option. No doubt it is too early to arrive at definitive conclusions concerning this sort of regime for the marine fisheries. Nevertheless, an examination of the American Fishery Conservation and Management Act of 1976 will allow me to pinpoint my reservations about regimes of this type.

The FCMA establishes a fishery conservation zone (sec. 101) within which the United States claims exclusive fishery management authority (sec. 102). This zone extends "200 nautical miles from the baseline from which the territorial sea is measured," except in the case of anadromous species in which management authority is claimed "throughout the migratory range of such species. . . ." Though the practical implications of this effort to expand coastal state jurisdiction in the marine fisheries are substantial, they are less dramatic than they may at first appear. The FCMA does not attempt to extend exclusive fishery management authority to highly migratory or pelagic species. It merely reaffirms and solidifies the existing situation with respect to sedentary species, that is, crustaceans and mollusks (Young, 1977, ch. 4). And it is doubtful whether the asserted claims to extended jurisdiction over anadromous species can be implemented fully and effectively in the critical case of salmon in the North Pacific. The major change heralded by the FCMA relates to the large stocks of demersals or groundfish located within the 200-mile limit. Here it is reasonable to expect the act will lead to fundamental changes in the preexisting situation.

The FCMA sets up an elaborate institutional apparatus to carry out the responsibilities arising from the claim to exclusive management authority in the marine fisheries off the coasts of the United States. The distinctive feature of this apparatus is the creation of a system of eight regional fishery management councils (sec. 302). These councils are responsible for the formulation of detailed fishery management plans (sec. 303) and will presumably play a major role in the actual implementation of these plans with respect to specific fisheries. At the same time, the act allocates a major role in fisheries management to the secretary of commerce, as represented by the National Marine Fisheries Service (NMFS). In many cases, NMFS is expected to operate either in conjunction with the regional councils or on a concomitant basis (sec. 304). In fact, it is not entirely clear where effective power will lie in this system,[6] and it will require additional experience with the FCMA to determine the nature of the balance of power that will emerge between the regional councils and NMFS (U.S. Office of Technology Assessment, 1977, ch. 4).

Let me turn now to my reservations concerning this regime. It is a little simplistic but not, I think, inaccurate to say that the basic problem of conservation in the marine fisheries is to prevent severe depletions of stocks arising from overfishing. In unregulated, open-to-entry fisheries, this problem stems from the intrinsic characteristics of a common property regime. Where conscious regulation is present, the key issue is to establish total allowable catches (TACs) on an annual basis and to administer them effectively. The FCMA proposes to deal with this issue through the use of the criterion of *optimum yield* [sec. 3(18)].[7] But unlike the concepts of maximum sustained yield (MSY) and economic efficiency, the concept of optimum yield has no intrinsic analytic content. As Larkin has succinctly put it, "optimum is whatever you wish to call it" (Larkin, 1977, p. 8). It is true that the FCMA appears to designate maximum sustained yield as an upper boundary in the computation

[6] The FCMA also provides significant roles for the secretary of state under secs. 204 and 205 and for the U.S. Coast Guard under sec. 311.

[7] Specifically, sec. 3(18) states that, "The term 'optimum,' with respect to the yield from a fishery, means the amount of fish—(A) which will provide the greatest overall benefit to the Nation, with particular reference to food production and recreational opportunities; and (B) which is prescribed as such on the basis of the maximum sustainable yield from such fishery, as modified by any relevant economic, social, or ecological factor."

of total allowable catches. Unfortunately, however, this has little practical significance, since the concept of MSY is notoriously difficult to operationalize under real-world conditions (especially in cases involving multiple species such as the major ground fisheries of the fishery conservation zone). Consequently, the concept of optimum yield "is potentially subject to abuse, and would almost certainly be used as a way of justifying a political course of action" (Larkin, 1977, p. 8). To say the least, I do not find the implications of this reassuring. The decision-making processes established under the FCMA are weighted heavily toward the concerns of the American fishing industry. This industry, however, can hardly be said to have an impressive record of concern for its own long-term interest in the continuing viability of fish stocks, much less for the preservation of healthy fish stocks as a valued goal in its own right.

What of the implications of the FCMA for economic efficiency conceptualized in terms of equalizing marginal revenue and marginal costs across the fishing industry as a whole?[8] To begin with, the act is vague on the extent to which economic efficiency is to be taken as an important goal in the management of marine fisheries. Optimum yield is not fundamentally an economic criterion; economic considerations constitute only one of a list of factors to be taken into account in computing optimum yield. When it does turn more directly to economic guidelines, the act articulates a rather ambiguous standard to the effect that "Conservation and management measures shall, where practicable, promote efficiency in the utilization of fishery resources; except that no such measure shall have economic allocation as its sole purpose" (FCMA sec 301(a) (5).

It is probable that the FCMA will produce at least a temporary reduction in the annual harvests of certain stocks of groundfish (e.g., Alaskan pollock) due to limitations on foreign fishing.[9] This will result in *de facto* improvements in economic efficiency in the short run.[10] But

---

[8] In principle, the formula $MR = MC$ is sufficiently general to encompass all benefits and costs, however conceptualized. In practice, most analyses confine the application of the formula largely to those benefits and costs arising from private-good transactions in markets or from other situations where "prices" are easily assignable. I use the phrase "*economic* efficiency" to mean exactly this. Such computations largely ignore nonmarket phenomena such as social costs (and benefits), collective goods, and various political values. For a helpful general discussion of the criterion of economic efficiency, see Dorfman and Dorfman (1977, pp. 7–25).

[9] But note that foreign fishing is not being abruptly terminated. See, for example, *Washington Post* (1977, A3) and Samuelson (1977b, D 7–8).

[10] This is because the single most important source of inefficiency in the marine fisheries has been overinvestment (and therefore excess harvesting) arising from the common property character of the resource.

the FCMA does not take a strong stand on the development of effective entry restrictions, generally regarded as the key to the problem of economic efficiency in the marine fisheries.[11] Entry restrictions are relegated to the category of "discretionary provisions" under sec. 303(b). Numerous factors are to be taken into account in establishing systems of entry restrictions, including a catchall factor called "any other relevant considerations." Further, secs. 303 and 304 are written in such a way that the whole subject of entry restrictions seems likely to become a bone of contention between the regional councils and NMFS.[12] All this suggests that political considerations, rather than the criterion of economic efficiency, will dominate the specification and implementation of entry restrictions. In this connection, I see no reason to expect that politics will yield results similar to those that would be required for the achievement of economic efficiency.

In addition, the FCMA virtually guarantees the introduction of a new form of economic inefficiency in the marine fisheries of the American zone. It strongly sanctions efforts to expand the role of high-cost American operators and to reduce the role of more efficient foreign operators in these fisheries [e.g., sec. 2(7)].[13] In short, the act sets up an explicit form of protectionism for the marine fisheries of the fishery conservation zone. While the actual impact of this feature of the FCMA will depend upon the way in which the act is administered in specific regions, there is no escaping the fact that this represents a movement away from rather than toward economic efficiency.[14] Frankly, I do not find the arguments for protectionism (e.g., guaranteeing employment, helping an industry in temporary trouble, promoting American national security) compelling in this case. It is true that this feature of the FCMA is compatible with the concurrent rise of economic protectionism in other areas and may seem perfectly acceptable to some. At the very least, however, it seems that those who take this position should accept the political implications of their views explicitly rather than cloaking them under the banner of conservation.

[11] For an extensive discussion of this point, see Christy and Scott (1965).

[12] The key point is that both the regional councils and NMFS are authorized to prepare fishery management plans. There is reason to expect that the interests of individual regional councils and NMFS will sometimes conflict, and the FCMA does not make it clear how such conflicts are to be resolved. See also U.S. Congress, Office of Technology Assessment (1977, ch. 4).

[13] Thus, sec. 2(7) FCMA states that "A national program for the development of fisheries which are underutilized or not utilized by United States fishermen, including bottom fish off Alaska, is necessary to assure that our citizens benefit from the employment, food supply, and revenue which could be generated thereby."

[14] For evidence concerning initial patterns of administration, see *Washington Post* (1977) and Samuelson (1977b).

I do not find the distributive implications of the FCMA any more reassuring, though this is admittedly an area where value judgments are unavoidable. There can be little doubt that the initial effect of the FCMA will be to redistribute at least some of the proceeds from the marine fisheries toward coastal state (though not necessarily local) fishermen.[15] No doubt, the government could intervene to offset this initial effect through systems of taxation, price setting, or transfer payments. But I am convinced that the probability of any coherent program along these lines is low. This raises several more specific distributive issues that I find troublesome. To begin with, where foreign operators are engaged in well-established fisheries in the fishery conservation zone (e.g., Japanese operators in the eastern Bering Sea) the act promotes what amounts to a form of expropriation without compensation.[16] In this case, it is rights rather than assets which are subject to expropriation, but I cannot see that this makes the change any more palatable.[17] Next, there are problems of equity in the allocation of permits for foreign fishing as well as permits for domestic fishing in the event that meaningful entry restrictions are developed.[18] The act leaves the allocation of permits for foreign fishing to a rather open-ended administrative process [see sec. 201(e)], and it is virtually silent on processes for allocating allowable catches among domestic fishermen. My judgment is that outcomes in this area will be heavily influenced by the actions of the regional councils. As I have already suggested, I view these regional councils as highly politicized entities, and I am certainly not confident that their decisions in this area will meet any reasonable standards of distributive justice. Finally, should the managerial system introduced under the FCMA succeed to the point where it becomes possible to reap significant economic returns from the marine fisheries, questions will arise concerning the allocation of these

---

[15] Ironically, the FCMA provides no firm guarantees for truly local fishermen. In the Alaskan case, for example, it may well be that larger Seattle-based firms (some of which are partially owned by Japanese interests) will increasingly dominate the marine fisheries of the region.

[16] A possible response to this situation is for foreign interests to invest directly in American fishing operations or processing plants. Some direct investment of this type has already occurred. But this is a politically sensitive subject, and the U.S. government is likely to come under severe pressures to place restrictions on investment of this type. For some illustrative data on this subject, see Heggelund (1977, pp. 1–2, 8–9).

[17] For helpful discussions of the general concept of property rights, consult Demsetz (1964) and Dales (1968).

[18] Under this system, permits conveying rights become factors of production in their own right. There are numerous methods of allocating such rights, with widely differing consequences.

returns. As far as I can tell, the FCMA is silent on this issue. It sets up no procedure (e.g., a leasing system for the use of specified fishing grounds) through which some of the proceeds from the exploration of fish stocks might find their way into the public domain. I take this to mean that the state is not viewed as a proper beneficiary of the harvest of fish in the marine fisheries (in contrast to the exploitation of oil on the outer continental shelf).[19] Though this issue may seem academic given the current unprofitable condition of the marine fisheries, I find the distributive implications of this posture impossible to justify in any persuasive way.

I am further troubled by the fact that the FCMA treats the management of marine fisheries in a highly compartmentalized fashion. That is, it fails to recognize interdependencies among marine resources (e.g., fisheries, hydrocarbons, sea lanes, natural environments), and it makes no effort to fit the management of marine fisheries into the larger picture of ocean policy. Yet, it is clear that we are moving into an era of heavier and heavier usage of many marine resources and that conflicts in this realm are already becoming prominent in the arena of public policy. To take an illustration that strikes close to home, how are we to resolve conflicts between the interests of fishing operators and the interests of those who wish to proceed as rapidly as possible with the extraction of oil from the outer continental shelves?[20] I have no general solution to offer for these problems; I believe they raise ultimate political questions that cannot be resolved through the application of technical procedures like cost–benefit analysis.[21] But it seems to me that a managerial system that focuses on individual resources in a compartmentalized fashion leaves much to be desired under contemporary conditions.

Finally, I want to argue that the implications of the FCMA are highly unfortunate from the perspective of international cooperation and coordination in a highly interdependent world. In essence, the act represents a unilaterally declared and imposed redistribution of rights at the

[19] The question is whether the state as the owner or manager of a valued factor of production should not receive "normal" economic returns from the use of this factor. For a discussion of this question in the context of outer continental shelf oil, see Devanney (1975).

[20] Consider, for example, the controversy over the oil and gas lease sale for Kachemak Bay in the Lower Cook Inlet of Alaska (Munro, 1975). Interestingly, the state of Alaska, under pressure from fishing interests, eventually bought back the oil and gas leases it had sold in Kachemak Bay.

[21] This is because the problem turns on what should be conceptualized as benefits and costs to begin with, quite apart from the difficulties involved in assigning numerical values to some of them.

international level.[22] It is simply not true that the marine fisheries were previously unowned (or *res nullius*) so that the promulgation of exclusive fishery management authority amounted to the assertion of rights where none existed before.[23] On the contrary, this action entailed the extinction of a number of existing rights together with the proclamation of a new set of rights on a unilateral basis. Moreover, I find it hard to escape the conclusion that this transition has been effected in a harsh and discriminatory fashion. Let me illustrate this point. The punishments for criminal offenses set forth in the FCMA (sec. 309) discriminate sharply between American fishermen and foreign fishermen. The act adopts a discriminatory position on the issue of historic or traditional fishing rights, appearing to ignore them where the activities of foreign operators are concerned [sec. 201(d)] while insisting that they be recognized in the case of American operators [sec. 202(e)]. The act enunciates what turns out to be a self-serving position on the regulation of highly migratory species. In fact, the phrase "highly migratory species" is construed to mean tuna [sec. 3(14)], and the act goes to some lengths to deter foreign interference with this important American fishery. [See, for example, sec. 205(a).] The FCMA lays out an extraordinarily complex system of administrative procedures for the issuance of permits for foreign fishing [sec. 204(b)], which cannot fail to curtail the operations of foreign fishermen beyond what is contemplated under the terms of sec. 201(d). The contrast between this bureaucratic maze and the relative absence of such complications for domestic fishermen [sec. 303 (b)(1)] is striking.

The point of emphasizing these details is simple. In a highly interdependent world, a policy that not only imposes redistributions of rights in a unilateral fashion but also does so in a harsh and discriminatory way has dangerous implications. Other states with the capacity to do so (e.g., Japan) are likely to consider seriously taking retaliatory measures of various types. Such retaliatory actions need not of course be confined to the realm of marine fisheries; they might well deal with other economic or even political issues. Further, American positions on other issues relating to marine policy (e.g., freedom of navigation, flag state predominance in dealing with marine pollution, freedom of scientific research) are likely to be received with growing coolness on the part of

---

[22] This is so even though the Law of the Sea Conference has been moving in the direction of sanctioning expanded coastal state jurisdiction for the marine fisheries. See, for example, Samuelson (1977a).

[23] For a review of the relevant literature on rights, see Furubotn and Pejovich (1972).

other states. And in general, harsh and discriminatory unilateralism raises the specter of a new round of protectionist moves leading to economic warfare. While it is not clear that all forms of coastal state management for the marine fisheries will exhibit this drawback, I find this concern deeply troubling in connection with the regime for marine fisheries laid out in the Fishery Conservation and Management Act of 1976.

Global Organization

It follows from the preceding discussion that both unrestricted common property arrangements and coastal state jurisdiction leave much to be desired as methods of managing the marine fisheries under contemporary conditions. This suggests that the alternatives involving supranational institutions are at least worthy of serious consideration in this realm. Let me proceed then to these options, turning first to the idea of a global organization capable of managing the marine fisheries of the world on a unified basis. What I have in mind here is an agency resembling the Department of Fisheries of the FAO but endowed with effective power and authority. While many specific variations of this institutional option are possible (Miles, 1974), I think it is feasible to arrive at some general conclusions about this sort of regime without going into the details of these variations.

Of course this option runs immediately into the objection that it would not be acceptable politically to many powerful members of the international community. Some states would not be willing to agree, even on paper, to the creation of a global organization endowed with adequate power and authority to manage the marine fisheries of the world effectively. Further, there is every reason to conclude that such an organization would be ineffectual in practice, even if the members of the international community were to subscribe to the arrangement in principle. However, I do not view this as a particularly shocking or distressing conclusion. I think it is easy to show that the introduction of a global organization would not constitute a preferred strategy for the management of the marine fisheries, even if it were feasible.

To begin with, global organization is not required for the achievement of either conservation or economic efficiency in most of the marine fisheries of the world. This is because most marine fisheries involve regional rather than global commons.[24] While the boundaries of the

[24] For a selection of essays on various types of commons, consult Hardin and Baden (1977).

relevant ecological systems are often difficult to subsume under the jurisdiction of individual states, they do not begin to approach the global level in most cases. This is true even if we are sensitive to interdependencies among intersecting marine fisheries. There are a few exceptions to this general rule. The obvious example is the case of whales, where management is clearly a worldwide problem (Small, 1971). A somewhat less impressive case can be made for treating tuna as another exception (Saila and Norton, 1974). In such cases, efforts to manage the relevant fisheries on a global basis may well be justified. But the general rule is that neither conservation nor economic efficiency requires extending the scope of management schemes beyond the boundaries of the relevant ecological systems. And the application of this rule does not suggest global organization for most of the important marine fisheries of the world.

Nor am I persuaded that there is a strong case for global organization in the marine fisheries on grounds of distributive justice. This is partly because I believe such an organization would be ineffectual and incapable of producing decisive outcomes in many instances. Consequently, it would often become embroiled in activities tending to reduce the size of the pie to be distributed rather than concentrating on distributing obtainable proceeds from the marine fisheries in an equitable fashion. In my judgment, this has been the fate of the International Whaling Commission during much of its history.[25] In addition, I am not convinced that a global organization would yield equitable outcomes with respect to the allocation of total allowable catches or the distribution of economic returns from the marine fisheries. Decisions about such matters would inevitably be made through some sort of bargaining processes undertaken in a highly politicized atmosphere. In many ways, they would resemble the negotiations we have witnessed over the past several years in the context of the United Nations Law of the Sea Conference. Frankly, I have little confidence that such processes would lead to results capable of meeting even the most modest standards of distributive justice.

Should any doubts remain at this point, the problem of transactions costs also looms large in conjunction with the option of global organization for the marine fisheries. Such costs (e.g., decision costs, administrative costs, compliance costs) must be taken into account in assessing any regime for the marine fisheries other than simple common property

---

[25] For a detailed description, see Small (1971, ch. 8). For various reasons, the regulatory achievements of the IWC have improved somewhat in recent years.

or unregulated open-to-entry arrangements. But there is widespread agreement that transactions costs exhibit a clear tendency to increase rapidly as a function of areal domain, functional scope, and size of membership (Mishan, 1971, pp. 21–24). As a result, a truly global organization for the marine fisheries of the world would be extraordinarily expensive to operate. In fact, the transactions costs might well reach a level that would prohibit the promulgation of well-defined and effective management schemes in this realm. This is one way to interpret the debacle of the ongoing Law of the Sea negotiations, and I can see no reason to conclude that a global organization for marine fisheries would fare much better in these terms. My conclusion, therefore, is that supranational institutions in the form of an all-purpose, global organization do not constitute a preferred option for the management of the marine fisheries of the world.

Regional Authorities

There remains for consideration the other group of alternatives involving supranational institutions. The essential idea here would be to create a collection of regional authorities, each of which would have responsibility for the management of the marine fisheries of some geographically demarcated area. Thus, each individual authority would take the form of a "supranational fishing entity with exclusive rights over a geographic area that encompasses an appropriate ecological unit" (Crutchfield, 1964, pp. 214, 215). While it is true once again that many variations on this theme are possible, let me attempt to formulate some general arguments about regimes of this sort for the marine fisheries.

Past experience with regional authorities for marine fisheries undoubtedly leaves much to be desired. But I think it would be a serious mistake to draw unduly pessimistic conclusions from this observation. Some regional arrangements have clearly yielded real successes; examples like the International Halibut Convention, the Fraser River Salmon Convention, and the Fur Seal Convention come to mind (Christy and Scott, 1965). Further, many regional arrangements have operated under distinctly unfavorable conditions. Either the members have failed to convey adequate managerial authority to the supranational agency, or one or more of the members have attempted to make use of the arrangement to impose some preferred outcomes on the others. Experience with schemes such as the International North Pacific Fisheries Convention reflects both of these problems (Kasahara and Burke, 1973). Consequently, extrapolating from past experience is hazardous in this realm, though it does serve to sensitize us to the political problems involved in efforts to organize effective supranational institutions for the management of any natural resource.

In fact, regional authorities have great advantages as regimes for the management of marine fisheries. There can be no doubt that they constitute, in principle, the preferred option from the perspective of efforts to achieve conservation and economic efficiency in the marine fisheries. Unlike global organization and coastal state jurisdiction, regional authorities can be demarcated in such a way as to make their boundaries congruent with the ecological units and economic systems associated with complexes of marine fisheries (Crutchfield, 1964, p. 215). The aereal domain of any given authority could be extended to encompass the range of the relevant species of fish. Similarly, functional scope could be adjusted to take into account complexes of interdependent fisheries (e.g., the ground fisheries of the eastern Bering Sea or the northwestern Atlantic Ocean). And it would be possible to include all those states with a serious interest in the relevant fisheries as members of the authority without (in most cases) running into the problems associated with collective action in large groups.[26] Under the circumstances, it would not be difficult to endow individual regional authorities with adequate managerial authority to perform well with respect to the achievement of conservation and economic efficiency in their respective areas. This would of course require the development of effective systems of entry restrictions and reasonable methods of dealing with new entrants, but there are no insuperable technical problems in this realm. Whether individual states would find management schemes of this type for the marine fisheries politically acceptable is undoubtedly another matter. Past experience certainly does not sustain easy optimism about this issue. On the other hand, it is well worth noting that definite indications are now emerging of a serious willingness to try the regional authority approach for at least some of the marine fisheries of the world. For example, thirteen nations are currently engaged in negotiations aimed at the development of a regional arrangement for the fisheries of Antarctica, and twelve South Pacific states have announced plans for a joint regional authority to manage their combined fisheries zones (Nossiter, 1977; *Christian Science Monitor*, 1977).

[26] The classic modern work on collective action problems of this sort is Olson (1965).

I believe a case can also be made for the attractiveness of regional authorities from the point of view of distributive justice. The allocation of shares of total allowable catches and the handling of economic returns would certainly be matters for hard bargaining within each regional authority, and I do not wish to claim that outcomes would conform to some ideal standard of distributive justice in every case. But no individual member would occupy the driver's seat on distributive questions, as is inevitably the case under regimes based on capital state jurisdiction. In most cases, moreover, regional authorities (unlike a global organization) would be sufficiently wieldy so that there would be some expectation of bargaining leading to outcomes on something resembling the production possibility frontier rather than producing a drift toward inconclusive or Pareto inferior results of the type that commonly occur when the number of participants is too large. It is true that regional authorities might exhibit some tendency to slight the just claims of new entrants from outside the original group and of consumers of fish products on a worldwide basis. Though efforts could be made to combat these tendencies (e.g., through the creation of markets in fishing rights), I doubt whether they could be eradicated altogether. In my judgment, however, these distributive drawbacks are mild compared with the distributive problems of the other regimes for marine fisheries I have been examining.

Finally, let me comment briefly on the issue of transactions costs in conjunction with regional authorities for marine fisheries. I have no doubt that these costs would be significant. I also assume that they would exhibit a distinct tendency to increase at the margin as efforts were made to expand any given regional authority with respect to group size, areal domain, or functional scope. Moreover, I think it is fair to assume that at some point declining marginal gains would set in from such expansions. Without attempting to make these concepts operational for the moment, let me draw some simple conclusions from this scenario.[27] There will be an optimal size for any given regional authority. This size (defined in terms of some combination of group size, areal domain, and functional scope) will occur at the point where the marginal gains from expansion are just offset by the marginal costs (defined in terms of the pertinent set of transactions costs). The exact point at which this occurs will be determined by the shapes of the curves depicting marginal gains and marginal costs. All this is portrayed in figure 24 in which optimality

---

[27] A somewhat similar argument is advanced in Sandler and Cauley (1977).

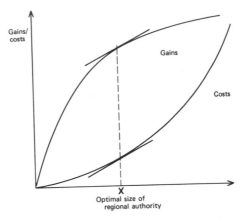

Figure 24. Optimal size of regional resource management authority.

occurs at the point labeled X_1. Obviously, manipulations of the shapes of
the relevant curves can lead to great variations in recommendations concerning the appropriate size for any given regional authority (including
opposition to the initial creation of such an authority in extreme cases).
At this time, my judgment is that such analyses will justify considerable
expansions of regional authorities for marine fisheries, though there can
be no doubt that marginal costs will increase sharply with group size and
areal domain after some point.

Are supranational institutions desirable in conjunction with the
management of natural resources at the international level? The argument of this section does not license any simple answer to this question.
It is illusory to expect any regime to yield results in practice that measure
up to our ideal standards of performance. Nevertheless, the preceding
discussion of marine fisheries is instructive in this regard. There is general agreement that unrestricted common property arrangements are
inadequate for most marine fisheries under contemporary conditions.
Coastal state jurisdiction leaves much to be desired, not only on grounds
of distributive justice, but also on grounds of conservation and economic
efficiency. This suggests that regimes involving the introduction of supranational institutions are at least worthy of serious consideration. Though
I find the idea of a global fisheries organization unattractive, supranational arrangements based on the development of regional authorities
exhibit a number of attractive features in the realm of marine fisheries.
Therefore, I conclude that it is worthwhile to proceed to an analysis of
the principal issues of institutional design which arise in conjunction

with the development of supranational institutions for the management of natural resources.

II.   TYPES OF SUPRANATIONAL INSTITUTIONS

The conclusion that introducing supranational institutions is desirable in efforts to manage any given natural resource only opens up a new range of questions. With respect to most natural resources, numerous varieties of institutional arrangements are feasible. Further, the selection of a specific set of arrangements will ordinarily have far-reaching consequences both in terms of private costs and benefits and in terms of social costs and benefits. That is, the choice of institutional arrangements can be expected to have a significant impact on the interests of the relevant actors. The objective of this section is to explore these consequences of institutional design, with special reference to the development of supranational institutions for the management of natural resources. This time I shall focus on the case of deepsea mining as a substantive base.[28] This will broaden the scope of my inquiry into the character and consequences of international resource regimes. At the same time, the principal implications of what I have to say about deepsea mining should be pertinent to the marine fisheries and other natural resources as well.

In fact, some have argued that an open-to-entry regime without exclusive rights would be adequate (or even desirable) for deepsea mining, especially from the point of view of the United States.[29] In essence, the case for such a regime rests on the following line of reasoning. There are fundamental differences between manganese nodules on the one hand and stocks of fish or pools of oil on the other. Accordingly,

[28] It is not easy to calculate the stakes in deepsea mining at this time. Estimates of the magnitude of the nodules themselves are highly speculative and vary widely; the range 1.5 to 3 trillion tons is currently mentioned frequently (source: private communication from staff of the Merchant Marine and Fisheries Committee of the U.S. House of Representatives). Estimates of the value of the minerals recoverable from these nodules are even harder to come by since all such estimates are nothing but projections of future revenues and costs, and numerous factors (both economic and political) may interfere to alter current estimates dramatically before hard minerals from the deep ocean come on the market. It is interesting to note, however, that "The mining firms estimate cumulative expenditures of at least $109 million to develop deep seabed mining technology and cumulative investments of from $1.5 to $2.4 billion to achieve commercial operations" (U.S. Congress, Office of the Comptroller General, 1976, p. 5).

[29] The argument is expressed with clarity and force in Eckert (1974).

it is not evident that the absence of exclusive rights to manganese nodules would reduce the economic efficiency of deepsea mining by encouraging either underinvestment arising from free-rider problems or overinvestment stemming from common pool problems (Eckert, 1974, pp. 154–163). As Eckert (1974, p. 163) puts it, economic analysis suggests that "a policy favoring regulation cannot be supported on grounds of economics until more is known about the industry's operating conditions, costs, and incentives." To the extent that this argument holds, there is no reason to conclude that the investment climate with respect to deepsea mining would be severely damaged by the absence of exclusive rights in nodule deposits per se. Those who take this position also typically maintain that there is no persuasive reason to interfere with market forces in determining the rate of exploitation of manganese nodules. To do so would be to jeopardize the achievement of economic efficiency, the topmost value posited by this line of thinking.[30] Finally, an unrestricted open-to-entry regime for deepsea mining would avoid the transactions costs associated with the operation of supranational institutions as well as the dangers of economic distortion actually caused by the activities of such institutions (Eckert, 1974, pp. 174, 175). In short, those who advance this line of reasoning assert that supranational institutions are unnecessary for the achievement of economic efficiency in the realm of deepsea mining and that the introduction of such institutions might well generate large and avoidable costs.

Unfortunately, this line of reasoning has serious drawbacks. There is a widespread feeling in the relevant communities that exclusive rights to manganese nodules and security of tenure are necessary to call forth large-scale investment in deepsea mining. For example, an officer of the Chase Manhattan Bank has recently testified that "A firm concession with security of tenure to a specific mine site would appear to me to be an absolute requirement for the project financing of an underseas mining venture—without it, a lender could assume neither the reserve nor production risks" (U.S. House of Representatives, 1977, p. 21). And many would concur in the following conclusions concerning this issue: "*Economic efficiency* in production will require, first of all, the ability of the entrepreneur to acquire security of investment. He must be able to obtain exclusive rights to a sufficiently large area for a sufficient length of time to capture a fair return on his investment. While it is conceivable

---

[30] Thus, Eckert (1974, p. 144) states explicitly that "The general criterion will be the efficient allocation of scarce resources—including nodules and the allied resources required to gather and process them."

that an entrepreneur could undertake such an investment and operate it effectively in the absence of rules guaranteeing tenure of rights, most writers believe that the risk would be too high to do so" (Christy, 1968, p. 229, emphasis in original).

Beyond this, the argument for an unrestricted open-to-entry regime for deepsea mining fails to deal with issues other than efficiency in a somewhat narrow economic sense. It makes no provisions, for example, for the regulation of the social costs of deepsea mining relating to such matters as the quality of the marine environment. Nor does it allow for the achievement of political goals such as the protection of existing copper and nickel operations in developing countries or the use of deepsea mining as a device for transfering certain types of technology to developing countries. Similarly, an unrestricted open-to-entry regime would raise serious distributive questions pertaining to deepsea mining operations. Initially, all economic returns (true economic rents as well as "normal" profits) would fall into the hands of the mining companies themselves under a regime of this sort. It is no doubt true that this outcome could be altered through the intervention of governments and the negotiation of agreements concerning suitable international transfer payments (U.S. House of Representatives, 1977, p. 39). I have little confidence, however, that the governments of the relevant countries (e.g., the United States) would pursue such a policy vigorously, and I have no difficulty understanding the objections of the less developed countries to this method of handling the distributive questions associated with deepsea mining.

Perhaps even more decisive is the point that the argument for an unrestricted open-to-entry regime for deepsea mining rests on a misconstrual of the distinction between *res communis* and *res nullius* in this realm. There can be no doubt that the deposits of manganese nodules are at present owned and that they are not literally unowned. This is the import of the general view that marine resources are common property, and it was explicitly reaffirmed by the United Nations in General Assembly Resolution 2749(XXV) (1971) which specifically describes the deposits of nodules as forming part of the "common heritage of mankind" (a resolution voted for by the United States and other developed countries).[31] As it happens, the owner of the nodules is the international community as a whole rather than certain individual members of the community. But this certainly does not imply an absence of ownership

[31] Consult the discussion of GA 2749 in Hardy (1977, pp. 313–315).

or of property rights any more than public ownership does in municipal systems. Now, the international community may wish to allow individual members of that community to exploit the nodules without restrictions in the form of rules concerning use or the payment of fees.[32] But it need not do so. Surely, the owner of a given natural resource has the right to specify the conditions under which it will be available for exploitation. In this case, the owner (i.e., the international community) has expressed its desires concerning the use of the relevant resource quite clearly (Hardy, 1977, pp. 313–315). Thus, GA 2749 requires the establishment of "appropriate international machinery" to govern the exploitation of the manganese nodules. It lays down goals to be pursued in this connection [e.g., paying "particular consideration (to) the interests and needs of the developing countries"]. It specifies that the details of the regime for deepsea mining are to be incorporated into an "international treaty of universal character." And it clearly implies that individual members of the international community are not free to proceed with the exploitation of the nodule deposits unilaterally, pending the establishment of the relevant supranational institutions. Under the circumstances, the fact that there has been disagreement concerning the details of this regime and, therefore, delay in formulating the required treaty, can hardly justify individual members of the community taking matters into their own hands and proceeding with the exploitation of the nodules unilaterally.[33] To do so would be roughly equivalent to mining firms simply going ahead with the extraction of hard minerals on national interest or publicly owned lands when there is disagreement within the community that leads to delays in the formulation of specific rules governing the exploitation of the minerals.

Let us assume, then, that some sort of supranational institutions for deepsea mining will come into existence, whether or not these institutions meet with universal approval. For convenience, label this set of institutions the International Seabed Authority (ISA), following the usage of the Revised Single Negotiating Text (UN 3rd Law of Sea Conference, 1976) and the Informal Composite Negotiating Text (UN 3rd Law of Sea Conference, 1977a) of the United Nations Law of the Sea Conference. What would (or should) such a regime be like? It turns

[32] This has traditionally been the position of the international community concerning marine fisheries. But even in the fisheries, there can be no question that the international community has the authority to introduce rules placing limits on use.

[33] For a conflicting view, see U.S. House of Representatives (1977, pp. 24–25).

out that there are numerous variations on this theme, many of which would yield substantially different outcomes. To lay the groundwork for a discussion of the principal issues of institutional design arising in this connection, let me clarify several key distinctions at the outset.

There are, initially, questions relating to the nature and distribution of property rights to the manganese nodules.[34] Would the ISA actually own the nodules or would it merely be vested with managerial authority in this area by the international community? If it is treated as a manager or steward, what will be its obligations to the actual owner (i.e., the international community) of the nodules, and how or in what ways would the community be able to intervene to review or revise the regime? I assume that the international community is not likely to transfer to the ISA formal property rights to the nodules, but I also expect that it is unlikely to interfere with the day-to-day operations of the ISA, owing to the unwieldy character of the international community and the consequent problems of reaching purposeful decisions on major issues at the international level. Beyond this, there is the question of whether the ISA becomes an operating authority (i.e., what is called the Enterprise in the documents referred to in the preceding paragraph) or remains a regulatory authority supervising (perhaps closely) the activities of private companies that undertake the actual work of extracting, transporting, and processing the manganese nodules (Hardy, 1977, pp. 321–328). The underlying issue here concerns the extent to which deepsea mining proceeds in the fashion of a (closely supervised) private enterprise system or in the fashion of a socialized system operating through something analogous to a state corporation.[35] Current discussions in the Law of the Sea Conference tend to emphasize the idea of a mixed system in which some combination of these options is pursued (Hardy, 1977, pp. 323–325). I assume, however, that little deepsea mining undertaken in the foreseeable future will be carried out by the Enterprise. At the same time, I have little doubt that the ISA (if and when it is formally established) will want to supervise closely the activities of individual corporations engaged in deepsea mining operations.

Bearing these preliminary points in mind, let me identify three separable (though interconnected) groups of institutional issues which

---

[34] For background material on property rights in general, consult Dales (1968, ch. 5) and Furubotn and Pejovich (1972).

[35] For a discussion of the less familiar, socialized alternative, see Lange and Taylor (1938). In fact, several individual states (e.g., Mexico, Indonesia, the Soviet Union, China) have socialized their petroleum industries.

arise in conjunction with the establishment of an ISA. One set of issues encompasses constitutional provisions dealing with the basic institutional structure of the authority. What actors should be included as members of the ISA and should all members of the organization have equal weight? What major organs (e.g., assembly, council, secretariat) should the authority have and how should these organs relate to one another? What decision-making processes should be set up to deal with questions requiring collective or group choices? What procedures should be established to govern efforts to change or restructure the regime itself? A second set of issues pertains to the scope of the authority and power to be accorded to the ISA. Regardless of the constitutional structure of the authority, should the ISA be granted the authority and power to determine such things as rates of use of manganese nodules, rules governing entry into specific nodule tracts, the allocation of shares of nodules among mining firms, and the raising and disposing of revenues? Should there be some specified procedure through which dissatisfied parties can appeal the decisions of the ISA? The third group of institutional issues concerns the specific managerial mechanisms and policies the ISA should adopt in dealing with those matters with respect to which it possesses authority and power. So, for example, if the authority is to allocate shares among interested parties, what specific mechanism should it employ to achieve this objective? If the ISA is to lease nodule tracts or to license individual mining firms, what system of leasing or licensing should it use? Or again, if it is agreed that the ISA should be entitled to raise revenue on its own, what institutional mechanism(s) should it introduce to generate these revenues?

An examination of these three groups of issues suggests several general observations. While questions of constitutional structure have often been analyzed in detail with respect to supranational institutions, (Nicholas, 1962; Bailey, 1961; Hadwen and Kaufman, 1962) they turn out to be remarkably unimportant in this context. This may seem surprising to those who have worked primarily with domestic institutions, but there is in fact a perfectly straightforward explanation of this situation. By and large, the members of the international community have little trust in autonomous supranational institutions, and they are unwilling to entrust their fortunes to the unrestricted deliberations of such institutions, especially when it comes to matters they regard as important. This produces the following results. In the typical case, strenuous efforts are made during the process of creating new supranational institutions not only to resolve questions pertaining to constitutional structure but also to spell out both the scope of the authority and power to be accorded the institutions and the character of the specific managerial mechanisms and policies to be adopted. All this places a heavy burden on the phase of "constitutional" bargaining preceding the establishment of any given set of supranational institutions and it goes far toward explaining the underdeveloped character of many institutions at the international level. But it is not a mysterious or puzzling situation in the context of a highly decentralized sociopolitical system in which there are severe conflicts of interest and a low level of generalized trust or "good will."[36]

Further, when controversial or contentious issues arise in an area "governed" by some set of supranational institutions, there is no presumption that the issues will be resolved in an orderly fashion through a routinized exercise of the procedures established under the constitution of the relevant authority. Instead, efforts to deal with such issues typically emerge as complex bargaining processes in which all available bargaining "chips" are brought into play and in which the details of formal institutions are soon lost from sight. In fact, somewhat similar situations are common even in domestic systems; it is a typical error to overestimate the extent to which formal institutional arrangements determine substantive outcomes, especially in cases where powerful interests are pitted against each other.[37] However, this phenomenon is far more marked at the international level. In effect, the "decisions" emerging from supranational institutions are generally the products of broader bargaining processes, frequently accompanied by the calculated use of coercion. While constitutional structure is not altogether irrelevant in this context, the impact of the institutions themselves on substantive outcomes is severely limited.

All this leads to the conclusion that it will not be particularly illuminating to proceed with a detailed examination of alternative constitutional provisions for the proposed ISA on the assumption that these provisions will have a profound effect on actual policy outcomes. But it certainly does not indicate that we should ignore questions relating to the scope of the authority and power accorded to the ISA and the specific managerial mechanisms and policies adopted. Choices concerning these

---

[36] For a sophisticated discussion of the contemporary international system which clarifies the background of the argument presented in this paragraph, see Bull (1977).

[37] I take it that this is one of the lessons to be learned from the so-called bureaucratic politics perspective on public policymaking. See, for example, Allison (1971).

matters can be expected to have far-reaching consequences for the interests of the relevant actors. The ultimate character of the ISA with respect to such matters will reflect a series of bargains struck among the members of the international community. In the case of deepsea mining, the stakes are high, and the conflicts of interest among the principal actors or groups of actors are severe. This does nothing to reduce the importance of bargaining over the institutional character of the proposed ISA. But it does suggest that agreement is apt to be slow in coming in this area and that the players may resort in the course of the bargaining to highly coercive practices, with little concern for considerations of fairness or equity.

The implication of this argument is that there is more to be learned from a careful examination of the probable course of bargaining over the institutional character of the ISA than from a sophisticated analysis of the likely consequences of alternative constitutional structures for the ISA.[38] In the remainder of this section, then, I shall identify and discuss what I regard as the principal substantive issues of institutional design at stake in the bargaining over the creation of supranational institutions for deepsea mining. Bear in mind that no institutional arrangement is intrinsically correct and that alternative arrangements will typically have substantially different effects on the interests of the pertinent parties. I shall try to indicate the most important arguments for and against alternative arrangements as well as to convey some sense of the bargaining positions relating to these issues. In the process, I shall feel free to develop and to express my own judgments or preferences about these matters. If I am successful, however, the discussion will help others to frame their own positions on the major questions of institutional design relating to deepsea mining.

How rapidly should the manganese nodules of the deep seabed be extracted? Should the ISA be given the authority to make binding decisions about this matter and how actively should it intervene to determine rates of harvest of these nodules? Several preliminary points require immediate emphasis in this context. The nodules do not constitute a renewable resource (within any relevant time frame) so that it is not important to worry about problems of maintaining healthy stocks in this realm.

---

[38] Existing formal theories of bargaining are analyzed and evaluated in Young (1975). A collection of essays oriented explicitly toward international bargaining is Zartman (1976). An examination of these volumes should make it abundantly clear that we do not now have any highly developed theories which can be applied systematically to the case of negotiations relating to the institutional character of the proposed ISA.

Moreover, it appears that existing stocks (i.e., inventories) of nodules are so extensive that they are likely to be essentially inexhaustible within any pertinent time frame.[39] Therefore, worries about the supply literally running out are less meaningful in the case of manganese nodules than in the case of certain other nonrenewable natural resources (e.g., oil and natural gas). Under the circumstances, the issue at stake boils down to the questions of whether there is some specifiable socially desirable rate of use for manganese nodules and whether the unregulated activities of private actors can be expected to approximate this socially desirable rate of use.

Actually, these questions raise a profound problem of managerial philosophy. What is it that we wish to maximize in the realm of deepsea mining? Are we content to let the markets for the relevant private goods (i.e., copper, nickel, cobalt, and manganese) operate in an unregulated fashion so that the rate of use of the manganese nodules is set by the interplay of supply and demand in these markets (Scott, 1973, ch. 8)? Or do we wish to bring to bear various nonmarket (or "political") criteria to replace or supplement these market considerations in settling on the rate of use for manganese nodules? Not surprisingly, there is no shortage of proposals concerning nonmarket criteria to be applied in this context. The Informal Composite Negotiating Text (UN 3rd Law of the Sea Conference, 1977), for example, requires the ISA to limit production of minerals from nodules "so as not to exceed for the first seven years . . . the projected cumulative growth segment of the world nickel demand." This and other proposals like it are protectionist devices designed to safeguard the financial health of competing mineral producers already operating in the less developed countries of the world (or elsewhere?). Similarly, there are those who wish to restrict the exploitation of manganese nodules to minimize social costs that will not be reflected in market prices. The critical argument here concerns the extent to which deepsea mining is likely to generate negative externalities affecting the quality of the marine environment.[40] On the other hand, some commentators have argued that the rate of use of manganese nodules resulting from market

---

[39] Hammond (1974, pp. 502–503). Of course, this does not mean that all (or even a high percentage) of the nodules can be exploited economically under current conditions with respect to technology and world demand. See also Eckert (1974, pp. 144–151).

[40] This subject has been investigated, in a preliminary way, by the Deep Ocean Mining Environmental Study (DOMES) project of the National Oceanic and Atmospheric Administration (NOAA). See U.S. Congress, Office of the Comptroller General (1976).

forces will be too low and that steps should be taken to accelerate this rate. There is some reason to believe that the industries involved in deep-sea mining will not be highly competitive so that there may be a need to combat production restrictions designed to reap monopolistic profits.[41] Further, certain American leaders wish to accelerate the production of minerals from nodules in the interests of achieving what amounts to hard mineral independence for the United States (U.S. House of Representatives, 1977, pp. 17–19). The pros and cons of this view bear a distinct resemblance to the arguments concerning the parallel idea of achieving energy independence.

There are no doubt numerous other nonmarket criteria that could be brought to bear on discussions of the socially desirable rate of use for manganese nodules. In general, however, it is important to bear in mind that the employment of any nonmarket criterion will necessitate some sort of political choice and that the transactions costs of reaching such choices may be high in specific cases. This is the chief virtue of market mechanisms; they yield social choices while minimizing the transactions costs of doing so. I do not find this point compelling, at least with respect to the issue of making decisions on rates of use for manganese nodules. Though this is admittedly a matter involving value judgments, I have a strong interest in the preservation of the marine environment and in the success of certain industrial enterprises in the less developed countries. In any case, I can see no compelling reason to deny the ISA the authority to make binding decisions concerning the rate of use of manganese nodules. To do so would be to attempt to settle in advance certain "ideological" issues concerning which there are fundamental and legitimate differences of opinion.

Rules Governing Entry

What rules should govern the activities of firms extracting nodules from the deep seabed? The issue here concerns the rules under which deepsea mining should proceed rather than the allocation of shares or tracts among those desiring to extract nodules. To the extent that the ISA becomes an operating authority (i.e., engages in extraction activities itself through the Enterprise), this issue becomes irrelevant. But I have

[41] There is, however, some disagreement about this subject. For an argument deemphasizing problems arising from imperfect competition, see Eckert (1974, pp. 150–151). Nevertheless, I believe it is reasonable to conclude that the international markets for the relevant hard minerals are unlikely to be as competitive as the international market for oil was prior to the winter of 1973–74.

already expressed the view that most efforts to extract nodules will be carried out by private firms rather than the Enterprise during the foreseeable future. Beyond this, there is the argument, discussed earlier in this section, that an open-to-entry regime with no rules governing access would not be particularly harmful in the realm of deepsea mining. Such a system would allow each individual firm to dredge for nodules at places and times of its own choosing without regard to the concurrent activities of other firms or standards designed to promote an orderly pattern of development in deepsea mining. I find it hard to believe that the relevant mining firms themselves would favor a system of this sort, and I think the potential social costs of such an arrangement would be substantial. Therefore, the issue of rules governing entry is a serious one which deserves careful consideration in the process of setting up the ISA.

I can see at least five differentiable questions in this realm. The first concerns the identification of nodule tracts. What size should individual tracts be? How should they be demarcated? Who should determine which tracts to make available for exploitation during any given time period? These are largely technical issues.[42] While they are by no means unimportant, I cannot see any reason why they should become sources of severe conflict. The same cannot be said, however, of a second question: whether firms interested in extracting nodules should have guaranteed access to the nodule deposits (Samuelson, 1977a, p. 1342). It is generally accepted that the ISA would have the authority to issue licenses for deepsea mining, and it seems reasonable to require that firms not be allowed to undertake dredging without licenses. The real issue concerns the criteria and procedures associated with the issuance of such licenses. Should individual firms be guaranteed the right to receive licenses upon filing the required applications? Is there any way to ensure that the licensing procedures would never be abused in the interests of pursuing political objectives? If the ISA is to manage deepsea mining effectively, it seems to me that it must be given the authority to grant individual licenses and to establish procedures for the issuance of these licenses. No doubt this means that the possibility of political abuse cannot be eliminated altogether, but I find nothing unusual or remarkable about this.

Beyond this, there are three questions relating to the rights firms would obtain under licenses granted by the ISA. Should individual firms be given exclusive rights to dredge within the boundaries of specific

---

[42] On these technical questions, see Hardy (1977, pp. 315–321). For a discussion of the way similar issues are handled in the United States in connection with outer continental shelf development, see U.S. Senate (1977, pp. 48 *et seq*).

tracts? As I have already said, there is some debate about the economic significance of exclusive rights in the realm of deepsea mining. However, I have little doubt that firms will demand exclusive rights to dredge within specific tracts, and I can see no reason why the ISA should refuse to accommodate such demands. Much the same can be said about the issue of security of tenure. Should individual firms be guaranteed exclusive rights to dredge in specific tracts over time? There is, I think, a case to be made for placing some time limits on the duration of claims (ten years, twenty years?), for demanding some economic activity as a requirement for retaining a claim, and for requiring that holders of claims comply with the general rules of use formulated by the ISA.[43] But beyond this, security of tenure strikes me as a reasonable demand on the part of the firms engaged in deepsea mining, and I can see no reason to oppose it. Finally, there is a question concerning investment guarantees. Is it desirable to set up some sort of program to guarantee the investments of private firms engaged in deepsea mining? In my judgment, such guarantees could only be justified under conditions involving an absence of exclusive rights and security of tenure.[44] They seem entirely unwarranted in connection with the other arrangements suggested in this paragraph.

Allocation of Shares

How should shares in the deepsea nodules be apportioned among those firms wishing to extract them? In practice, this issue boils down to an examination of alternative methods of assigning rights (or licenses conveying rights) to clearly demarcated nodule tracts. Assuming that decisions have already been made about the number and identity of tracts to be made available during any given time period and about the rules governing entry, it remains only to devise a method of apportioning exclusive rights to individual tracts among those desiring to engage in deepsea mining. But this turns out to be a complex issue in its own right.[45] There are several different methods of apportioning rights, none of which is without real drawbacks under the conditions likely to prevail in the realm of deepsea mining. In the following paragraphs, I identify

[43] Current proposals envision the formulation of contracts between the ISA and individual mining firms to deal with these issues. See, for example, article 151 of the Informal Composite Negotiating Text.

[44] They are also envisioned under the proposed U.S. Deep Seabed Hard Minerals Act (H.R. 3350) to compensate for losses caught by the adoption of an international treaty. See, for example, U.S. House of Representatives (1977, pp. 19, 20).

[45] The pros and cons of various alternatives are surveyed in connection with American outer continental shelf development in Devanney (1975, pp. 68–118).

and comment upon what strike me as the most pertinent of these methods of apportionment.

There is, to begin with, the idea of proceeding on a first-come, first-served basis. The first company to stake a claim to a given nodule tract would receive priority in filing for a license to dredge in that area. To preserve the exclusivity of rights under this system, individual claims would have to be patented by the ISA. But this could be accomplished easily in connection with the licensing procedure. In essence, the whole arrangement would resemble the American system of dealing with terrestrial claims to hard minerals established under the Mining Act of 1872.[46] Unfortunately, it would also have all the drawbacks of this system. Severe inefficiencies would be predictable in such forms as stampedes to stake extensive claims and overcapitalization. Nor is there any reason to expect that the resultant distribution of patented claims would conform to even the most modest standards of equity. It is also helpful to distinguish between two variants of this system. The ISA could proceed to patent claims without charging fees (or levying only nominal fees to cover operating expenses), in which case the nodules themselves would become free goods for the exploiting firms and fundamental distributive questions would arise. Alternatively, the ISA could levy nontrivial charges in conjunction with the issuance of licenses; this would raise major issues that I shall confront directly later on in this section.

A second method of allocating shares involves administrative decisions and the issuance of work obligation permits. Under this arrangement, firms interested in specific nodule tracts would submit proposals for exploitation to the ISA officials of the ISA would select the "best" of these proposals and grant licenses or work obligation permits on this basis. The problems afflicting this method, however, are severe: individual firms have incentives to submit unrealistic proposals, there is scope for political abuse in the administrative decision processes, it is not easy to ensure compliance with the terms of work obligation permits, and the transactions costs of the system are apt to be high (Devanney, 1975, pp. 80–82). It is true that this system facilitates serious consideration of nonmarket objectives such as maintaining the quality of the marine environment, but it is questionable whether this advantage is sufficient to offset the drawbacks spelled out here.

Various procedures involving bargaining have also been suggested for the apportionment of nodule tracts among mining firms. One idea is

---

[46] An Act to Promote the Development of the Mining Resources of the United States, 42nd Cong. 2nd sess., 10 May 1872. (U.S. Statutes at Large, March 1871–1973, 91–96).

simply to allow the relevant firms to strike private bargains (formalized in enforceable contracts) in which they would agree among themselves concerning who is to exercise exclusive rights to specific tracts (Eckert, 1974, pp. 157–158, 160–161).Bargaining of this sort does not always lead to mutually acceptable outcomes, and there is no guarantee that any outcomes reached will be equitable. Quite apart from these problems, however, such an arrangement would bypass the ISA with respect to the critical issue of apportioning nodule tracts among users. It would therefore be inappropriate in conjunction with the type of regime for deepsea mining under examination in this section. On the other hand, individual firms might be allowed to engage in what would amount to private bargaining with the ISA concerning the issuance of licenses covering specific nodule tracts. Such a system would constitute a kind of intermediate method between work obligation permits and a full-fledged system of competitive bidding (see below). My guess is that, in practice, it would have most of the drawbacks of the method of work obligation permits. The scope for political abuse would be substantial, so that serious problems of equity would arise. Further, the transactions costs of this system would be high, especially if the ISA allowed several firms to become involved in individual bargaining sessions in the interests of keeping complaints about injustice and unfairness to a minimum.

A final alternative would be to establish a full-fledged market in rights to exploit individual nodule tracts (Dales, 1968, ch. 6). The ISA would periodically select tracts to be made available for exploitation and announce a license (or lease) sale at a specified time.[47] Exclusive rights to make use of a given tract would then go to the firm making the highest bid at the time of the sale. It turns out that there are numerous methods of organizing markets of this type. The current debate over the allocation of oil and gas tracts on the American outer continental shelf is full of acrimonious arguments about the alleged advantages and disadvantages of the various methods of organizing lease sales (U.S. Senate, 1977, pp. 158–161). As I see it, the basic problems with this system are to maintain a reasonable level of competition in the bidding and to provide some opportunity for smaller firms to play a role in deepsea mining. At the same time, a market in rights to exploit individual nodule tracts has real attractions: it could be used to promote economic efficiency in deepsea mining, it could provide the ISA with substantial revenues, and the transactions costs of operating such a mar-

----

[47] A similar system is now used by the United States in connection with the leasing of oil and gas tracts on the outer continental shelf. For a clear description, see Devanney (1975, pp. 68–79).

ket need not be exorbitant. I suspect the ISA would want to consider seriously undertaking preliminary exploration of nodule tracts on its own prior to placing rights to them on the market (cf. the analogous debate concerning the leasing of oil and gas tracts on the outer continental shelf by the U.S. government) (Devanney, 1975, pp. 96–118). Moreover, I would advocate a policy under which the ISA would incorporate stringent restrictions into all licenses issued for nodule tracts to minimize social costs relating to such things as the quality of the marine environment. Nevertheless, I am persuaded that a carefully organized market in rights would constitute the preferred method for the allocation of rights to exploit nodule tracts.

Nonmarket Effects

I turn now to the issue of nonmarket considerations I raised earlier in this discussion. Though I have stressed the virtues of a market system once the ISA has decided to make specific nodule tracts available for current use, I can see no objection to a policy under which the ISA is authorized to devote attention to nonmarket effects in the management of deepsea mining. Nor do I see any conflict between such a policy and the development of the market in rights I described in the preceding paragraph. An examination of several specific problems will make this position on nonmarket effects more concrete.

I think it would be entirely appropriate for the ISA to include social costs explicitly in calculations relating to the management of deepsea mining. The social costs of greatest concern in this connection are those pertaining to the quality of the marine environment, but other types of social costs might be relevant as well. There is some debate concerning the probable environmental consequences of deepsea mining, and there is reason to believe that environmental problems will be less severe here than in the case of offshore oil and gas operations.[48] Nevertheless, the ISA ought to have the authority to make independent assess-

---

[48] Since the mining operations will take place in the deep ocean, the resultant environmental problems are not likely to be of great concern to fishing interests or to resort operators worried about the preservation of beaches. But see the comments in U.S. House of Representatives (1977, p. 35), to the effect that "there is a real concern about the possible adverse impact which deep seabed mining may have on the environment. But this concern is tempered by the generally widespread recognition that these impacts are, at this point, unpredictable. Nobody can determine what the actual impacts will be until a substantial amount of evidence is accumulated from actual exploration and commercial recovery activities. Clearly, deep ocean mining will have an effect upon the existing physical-chemical environment of the marine ecosystem. But the precise impacts which occur cannot fully be determined at this time."

ments concerning these matters and to take effective steps to regulate social costs. In some cases, this may require withholding specific nodule tracts from exploitation regardless of the desires of the mining companies. In other cases, the formulation of well-defined standards and the development of a system of charges would probably suffice to control the pertinent dangers to environmental quality (Kneese and Bower, 1977).

Further, I see no inherent objection to efforts on the part of the ISA to achieve political goals through the management of deepsea mining.[49] So, for example, it may seem desirable to withhold certain choice nodule tracts from current use in the hope that firms from the developing countries will be able to bid for them at a later date. Similarly, the ISA may wish to withhold some tracts for its own use in the event that it decides to experiment with the idea of becoming an operating agency in its own right. Further, there have been suggestions that the ISA should attempt to promote technology transfers through the management of deepsea mining by compelling mining companies to make full disclosures concerning the technology employed in their mining operations (UN 3rd Law of the Sea Conference, art. 144, UN, 1977a). Many efforts along these lines will undoubtedly be opposed on the ground that they promote economic inefficiency and, therefore, yield suboptimal results. But it is important to note that the conception of economic efficiency underlying most complaints of this type is a rather narrow one resting on the idea of achieving an outcome on the production possibility frontier defined largely in terms of standard private goods. While efforts to achieve specific political goals should no doubt be examined critically on their merits, I do not find such complaints about economic inefficiency compelling.

This discussion of nonmarket effects suggests one additional observation about institutional design relating to the ISA. It seems clear that the ISA should have legal standing in the same way that government agencies do in judicial systems. In fact, it would be important not only for the ISA to be able to bring suits but also for others to be able to file suits against it. On the one hand, this would enable the ISA to employ legal sanctions against mining companies violating the terms of their

[49] My earlier criticism of the American FCMA of 1976 on grounds of politicization should not be confused with this argument about the legitimacy of political goals. There my claim was that the decision-making apparatus established under the FCMA permits special interest groups with no particular claim to legitimacy to influence outcomes decisively. Here I am suggesting that there is no inherent reason why the relevant community should eschew political goals in contrast to or in conjunction with economic goals in managing deepsea mining.

licenses, failing to pay charges levied in conjunction with efforts to regulate environmental damage, or refusing to disclose information about pertinent technologies. On the other hand, it would allow for two other significant types of litigation: (1) suits brought against the ISA by individual mining companies alleging specific breaches of contract, and (2) suits brought against the ISA by outside groups claiming that the agency had failed to enforce its own rules and standards vigorously. The principal complication that would arise in this realm stems from the fact that the International Court of Justice is simply not capable of handling the relevant litigation.[50] Under the circumstances, I would advocate giving the ISA legal standing in the courts of the individual members of the international community.[51]

Revenues

Should the ISA manage the extraction of manganese nodules in such a way as to generate revenues? There are three differentiable issues embedded in this question. To begin with, there is the issue of whether the ISA should levy user's fees on the mining firms in order to cover its own operating expenses. I think the answer to this question is a decisive "yes," and it seems clear that the problem can be handled in a simple fashion through the device of licensing fees. Next, there is some question whether the ISA (acting as the agent of the actual owner of the manganese nodules) should take steps to recover "normal" returns from the nodules treated as a factor of production. This is clearly what any private owner of a natural resource would do, and I think there is a trend in this direction within nation states (e.g., most governments certainly want to collect "normal" returns from deposits of oil and natural gas under their jurisdiction).[52] The idea of proceeding in the same way at the international level has been hampered by the absence of authoritative institutions as well as by the "law of capture" traditionally associated with common property arrangements. (The marine fisheries undoubtedly constitute the most striking case in point.) But the whole idea of creating

[50] For a study that is sympathetic to the Court but that nevertheless clearly substantiates this conclusion, see Rosenne (1973).

[51] In addition, the ISA could consider creating a judicial mechanism of its own along the lines of the European Community's Court of Justice.

[52] Interestingly, many governments still do not seem to think in terms of collecting "normal" economic returns from publicly managed fisheries and forests. I would not be surprised, however, to see this posture begin to change in the near future.

supranational institutions to manage deepsea mining represents a break with past practices concerning the international relations of resource management. I for one can see no reason why the ISA (on behalf of the international community) should not collect "normal" returns on manganese nodules extracted by the mining companies. Finally, there is the question of whether the ISA should share in any true economic rents (i.e., scarcity rents and surplus returns to factors of production arising from market imperfections) resulting from deepsea mining (Hughes, 1975). Admittedly, this is an issue on which it is impossible to escape value judgments. But I would advocate allocating a large portion of any such rents to the ISA. This position is analytically equivalent to the argument for transferring economic rents into the public sector when they occur within national systems.[53]

If it is agreed that it is desirable for the ISA to raise revenues, it follows that it is important to consider ways of obtaining such revenues. In fact, there are numerous methods of achieving this objective: cash sales, bonus bids, license fees, royalties, taxes of one sort or another, and combinations of the preceding mechanisms. The choice of specific institutional arrangements in this realm is clearly a highly technical matter requiring expert analysis. However, I think the basic principle to be followed is simple enough. The ISA should endeavor to obtain its share of the proceeds from deepsea mining in such a way as to distort the economic calculations of the mining firms as little as possible. With respect to "normal" returns, I see nothing wrong with a straightforward system of royalties (computed as a percentage of market price). "Normal" returns are after all part of any economic enterprise; it should not be undertaken at all if they are not forthcoming.[54] The question of true economic rents is somewhat more complex. I think there is a strong case for something like an excess profits tax in this realm, but I do not feel competent to offer any definitive judgment on this matter.

To the extent that the ISA accumulates funds in excess of its operating expenses (and this would almost certainly occur under the scheme I have suggested), it would become necessary to deal with the distribution of these funds. There are, I think, three basic alternatives in this context. The funds could be set aside or placed in escrow to be used for international emergencies at the discretion of the ISA itself or some other

[53] See also Devanney (1975) in which the issue is discussed in terms of the distinction between national income and public income.

[54] This is the system now employed in the United States in the case of oil. See, for example, Resources for the Future (1968).

international body like the United Nations.[55] As an alternative, the funds could be distributed among the "shareholders" of the ISA (i.e., the individual members of the international community). This would mean dividing the funds among the signatories to the ISA treaty according to some agreed-upon formula (e.g., on the basis of population). Or the funds could be used to achieve various redistributive goals through the mechanism of international "transfer payments." Numerous goals of this sort come to mind, but it seems relevant at this point to recall the injunction of GA 2749 (UN General Assembly, 1971) to pay particular consideration to the "interests and needs of the developing countries." Once again, we have arrived at a point where value judgments are inescapable. I personally would favor some combination of the first and third alternatives on this distributive question. While the case for planned redistribution is strong, I find much that is appealing in the idea of establishing at least a modest international emergency fund to be used for disaster relief on a worldwide basis.

Costs

It seems clear, then, that the ISA would be capable of raising revenues. In fact, it seems reasonable to conclude that it would not only be able to cover its own expenses but also to accumulate a surplus as well. But what about the costs of introducing supranational institutions to manage deepsea mining? What would be the magnitude of these costs, and would the benefits attributable to the existence of the ISA exceed these costs? Several differentiable types of costs require consideration in any attempt to deal with these questions.

To begin with, there would be the start-up costs involved in setting up the ISA. These would be substantial if the ISA were to become an operating agency engaging in deepsea mining in its own right; initial capital investments to organize an efficient operation would run to several hundred millions of dollars (Hardy, 1977, p. 316). If the ISA acts primarily as a regulatory agency, however, start-up costs should be quite modest. The largest item would be for a physical facility and various types of equipment, and this could hardly assume exorbitant propor-

---

[55] The question of an appropriate decision-making procedure for the allocation of these funds would no doubt be controversial. I would not advocate turning the matter over to the General Assembly of the United Nations. Reliance on a specialized agency staffed by professionals seems to me likely to produce results that are both more efficient and more equitable.

tions. Once the ISA became operative, there would also be operating expenses to consider. These would take such forms as: (1) decision costs, (2) administrative costs, and (3) compliance costs. We might group these loosely under the rubric of transactions costs (compare Sandler and Cauley, 1977). Though such costs would certainly not be negligible, it is hard to make confident estimates of their magnitude. They would depend on such things as the intensity of conflicts of interest among the members of the ISA, the willingness of individual members to acquiesce in the use of various procedural devices to resolve conflicts of interest, and the willingness of the mining companies themselves to comply with the decisions of the ISA. Moreover, there can be little doubt that these costs would rise as a function of such things as the number of members included in the ISA, the degree to which individual members were accorded anything like a veto power in the decision processes of the agency, and the extent to which the ISA pursued political goals in managing deepsea mining (c.f., Mishan, 1971). Though I shall not attempt to come up with a specific figure, my judgment is that the running costs of the ISA would be substantial.

In addition, the regulatory activities of the ISA might prove costly in the sense of interfering with the economic efficiency of deepsea mining. As Eckert (1974, pp. 174–175) puts it, "regulation could harm economic efficiency by raising the costs of entry into ocean mining, limiting output, and introducing monopoly to protect terrestrial producers of metals." Similarly, the ISA might experience so much difficulty reaching clear-cut decisions that it would severely curtail the pace of deepsea mining, thereby keeping investments in this area below what would be required for the achievement of economic efficiency.

Several observations about these dangers of economic distortion strike me as pertinent at this juncture. These forms of inefficiency would certainly be possible under the aegis of the ISA, but they would not be necessary. There would be nothing to prevent the ISA from singlemindedly pursuing the goal of economic efficiency if the members chose to do so. Next, the achievement of economic efficiency would certainly not be guaranteed in the absence of the ISA. In fact, the general view is that an unregulated open-to-entry regime in the realm of deepsea mining would encourage relatively serious forms of economic inefficiency. Again, economic inefficiency under the ISA would generally take the form of underinvestment in deepsea mining. I for one would prefer some risk of this type of inefficiency to the risk of overinvestment under an open-to-entry regime.[56] Finally, it is important to note that these costs of economic distortion would typically be offset by benefits arising from the pursuit of political goals. That is, economic distortions would ordinarily arise from efforts on the part of the ISA to achieve political goals of one sort or another in the management of deepsea mining.[57] Whether the resultant political benefits would outweigh the economic costs is not easy to say; conclusions about such matters must rest heavily on value judgments. As I have already indicated, however, I myself see nothing inherently objectionable in the adoption of policies requiring certain economic sacrifices to achieve political goals.

This leads me to two additional observations concerning the costs of managing deepsea mining through supranational arrangements. It is not possible to arrive at any simple answer to the question of whether the total benefits attributable to the existence of the ISA would exceed the total costs. This is partly because it is difficult to conduct a controlled experiment in this realm, managing some deepsea mining activities through a regulatory agency while leaving the operation of others to an open-to-entry regime. Even more important, the problem stems from the absence of a clear-cut metric to be used in computing the costs and benefits flowing from the development of supranational institutions to manage deepsea mining. This will continue to be the case unless and until the difficulties associated with the construction of social welfare functions are solved in global terms.[58] In the meantime, let me simply say that I personally have no difficulty in supporting the creation of the ISA on cost–benefit grounds. Given my value system, the political advantages of this form of management are sufficient to outweigh any economic costs of regulation likely to occur. This sets the stage for my final observation about costs. I think it will be possible to avoid severe conflict relating to the *incidence* of the costs of operating the ISA. This is

[56] The probability of overinvestment occurring in the absence of exclusive rights is hard to estimate. In fact, there are counter pressures that might well lead to underinvestment under an unregulated open-to-entry regime.

[57] Another way of stating this point is to say that Pareto optimality does not necessarily require an outcome on the production-possibility frontier, so long as that frontier reflects only private goods exchanged through market mechanisms.

[58] The problem is that there is no agreement on a common unit of measure (or numeraire) by which the various costs and benefits flowing from the development of supranational institutions could be calculated, let alone one that would sustain the "interpersonal" comparisons required for the construction of a true social welfare function. For a clear discussion of this and related issues, see Dorfman and Dorfman (1977, pp. 11–13).

because the ISA will be able to cover its expenses from its own revenues so that it will not have to raise revenues from its members to sustain itself. This should certainly not be construed as an excuse to treat lightly the costs of operating the ISA. But it will eliminate contention surrounding scales of contributions which has plagued other supranational institutions like the United Nations (Stoessinger and coauthors, 1964).

Compliance

Assume that a functioning ISA is in existence and that it begins to make decisions concerning such matters as rates of use for manganese nodules, rules of entry for mining firms, and restrictions aimed at the limitation of social costs. What is the likelihood that the relevant actors will comply with these decisions? What recourse will the ISA have in dealing with actors that violate its decisions or fail to show clear evidence of compliance? There is no doubt in my mind that this a nontrivial issue. I do not find it hard to imagine the U.S. government lending support to noncompliant behavior on the part of its nationals if the ISA were to make decisions unfavorable to the American position on issues such as guaranteed access to nodule tracts (Samuelson, 1977a). Nor do I intend to single out the United States for special criticism. On the contrary, I have little doubt that many governments would exhibit even fewer scruples about lending support to violations of ISA decisions than the government of the United States.

All this means that the ISA would be faced with two distinct sets of questions relating to compliance.[59] To begin with, the ISA could choose to allocate some of its resources to programs aimed at eliciting compliance with its rules and decisions. It is easy to say that the agency should invest in such programs until the marginal revenues flowing from such investments (measured in terms of the gains attributable to a reduction in violations) just equal the marginal costs of the programs. So stated, however, this hardly constitutes an operational criterion. The development of such a criterion would require an extended analysis going well beyond the scope of this essay. My preliminary judgment is that the ISA would want to invest relatively heavily in the achievement of compliance. But this judgment rests more on the premise that mining firms would experience strong incentives to engage in certain violations than

[59] For a broad theoretical treatment of the problem of compliance, consult Young (1979 forthcoming).

on any detailed assessment of the costs of eliciting compliance in the realm of deepsea mining.

The other set of questions concerns methods. Assuming that the ISA decides to make some investment in the achievement of compliance, what sorts of compliance mechanisms would it find most effective in this realm? It seems clear that physical coercion will not be a viable alternative. I cannot see the members of the international community allowing the ISA to equip itself with a "police" force. Nor is it likely that a standby force composed of contingents from individual members will prove any more workable in this context than under the auspices of the United Nations (Bloomfield, 1964). Rather, I suspect the ISA will find it expedient to pursue compliance by employing nonphysical measures and concentrating on the behavior of the mining firms themselves. Various economic measures would be worth serious consideration. So, for example, the ISA could require each mining company to set up an escrow fund prior to the receipt of licenses to be used to cover potential fines or damages. Firms violating ISA rules could be prohibited from participating in subsequent license sales for new nodule tracts. Alternatively, firms compiling favorable records of compliance could be given various breaks relating to the payment of royalties or taxes. Beyond this, it would greatly simplify the compliance problems of the ISA if it could induce individual states to allow it to bring legal actions against mining companies through their courts. This would not only allow the ISA to pursue violators in an orderly fashion, it would also help to solve the problem of enforcement in specific instances. The response of individual states to this proposal is hard to gauge at present. No doubt the American reaction would be of critical importance since a high proportion of the firms engaged in deepsea mining would be corporations chartered under the laws of the United States (Eckert, 1974, pp. 144–151; Samuelson, 1977a, p. 1339). While such an arrangement might be favored by the Department of State, it would almost certainly be opposed by powerful interests in the business and financial communities. The American reaction would, therefore, turn on complex maneuvers within the domestic political system of the United States. Nevertheless, this discussion reconfirms my earlier observation that it would be desirable for the ISA to be accorded legal standing in the courts of the individual members of the international community.

REFERENCES

Allison, Graham. 1971. *The Essence of Decision* (Boston, Little, Brown).

Bailey, Sydney, D. 1961. *The General Assembly of the United Nations* (New York, Praeger).

Bloomfield, Lincoln P., ed. 1964. *International Military Forces* (Boston, Little, Brown).

Bell, Frederick W. 1978. *Food from the Sea: The Economics and Politics of Ocean Fisheries* (Boulder, Colo., Westview).

Bull, Hedley. 1977. *The Anarchical Society: A Study of Order in World Politics* (New York, Columbia University Press).

Christian Science Monitor. 1977. "South Pacific States Set Up 200-mile Limits, Oct. 25, p. 21.

Christy, Francis T. 1968. "A Social Scientist Writes on Economic Criteria for Rules Governing Exploitation of Deep Sea Minerals," *International Lawyer* vol. 2, no. 2, pp. 224–242.

————— and Anthony Scott. 1965. *The Common Wealth in Ocean Fisheries* (Baltimore, Johns Hopkins University Press for Resources for the Future).

Crutchfield, James. 1964. "The Marine Fisheries: A Problem in International Cooperation," *American Economic Review* vol. 54, pp. 207–218.

Dales, J. H. 1968. *Pollution, Property, and Prices* (Toronto, University of Toronto Press).

Demsetz, Harold. 1964. "The Exchange and Enforcement of Property Rights," *Journal of Law and Economics* vol. VII (October) pp. 1–26.

Devanney, J. W. III. 1975. *The OCS Petroleum Pie,* MIT Sea Grant Program Report No. MITSG 75-10.

Dorfman, Robert, and Nancy Dorfman, eds. 1977. *Economics of the Environment* (2nd ed., New York, Norton).

Eckert, Ross D. 1974. "Exploration of Deep Ocean Minerals: Regulatory Mechanisms and United States Policy," *Journal of Law and Economics* vol. 17, no. 1, pp. 143–177.

Furubotn, Eirik, and Svetozar Pejovich. 1972. "Property and Economic Theory: A Survey of Recent Literature," *Journal of Economic Literature* vol. 10, no. 4, pp. 1137–1162.

Gordon, H. Scott. 1954. "The Economic Theory of a Common Property Resource: The Fishery," *Journal of Political Economy* vol. 62, no. 2, pp. 124–142.

Hadwen, John G., and Johan Kaufman. 1962. *How United Nations Decisions Are Made* (Dobbs Ferry, N.Y., Oceana).

Hammond, Allen L. 1974. "Manganese Nodules I," *Science* vol. 183 (February 8) pp. 502, 503.

Hardin, Garrett, and John Baden, eds. 1977. *Managing the Commons* (San Francisco, W. F. Freeman).

Hardy, Michael. 1977. "The Implications of Alternative Solutions for Regulating the Exploitation of Seabed Minerals," *International Organization* vol. 31, no. 2, pp. 313–342.

Heggelund, Per O. 1977. "Japanese Investment in Alaska's Fishing Industry," *Alaska Seas and Coasts* vol. 5 (October) pp. 1, 2, 8, 9.

Hughes, Helen. 1975. "Economic Rents, The Distribution of Gains from Mineral Exploitation, and Mineral Development Policy," *World Development* vol. 3, nos. 11 and 12, pp. 811–825.

Kasahara, Hiroshi, and William Burke. 1973. *North Pacific Fisheries Management*, RFF Program of International Studies of Fishery Arrangements, Paper no. 2 (Washington, D.C., Resources for the Future).

Kneese, Allen V., and Blair T. Bower. 1977. "Standards, Charges, and Equity," in Robert and Nancy S. Dorfman, eds., *Economics of the Environment* (2nd ed., New York, Norton) pp. 217–278.

Lange, Oskar, and Fred M. Taylor. 1938. *On the Economic Theory of Socialism* edited by Benjamin E. Lippincott (Minneapolis: University of Minnesota Press).

Larkin, Peter A. 1977. "An Epitaph for the Concept of Maximum Sustained Yield," *Transactions of the American Fisheries Society* vol. 106, no. 1 (January 1977) pp. 1–11.

Miles, Edward. 1974. *Organizational Arrangements to Facilitate Global Management of Fisheries*, RFF Program of International Studies of Fishery Arrangements, Paper No. 4 (Washington, D.C., Resources for the Future).

Mishan, E. J. 1971. "The Postwar Literature on Externalities: An Interpretive Essay," *Journal of Economic Literature* vol. 9, no. 1, pp. 1–28.

Munro, Nancy. 1975. "OCS Development—What It Means," *Alaska Seas and Coasts* vol. 3 (April) pp. 1–4.

Nicholas, H. G. 1962. *The United Nations as a Political Institution* (London, Oxford University Press).

Nossiter, Bernard D. 1977. "Antarctic Nations Move to Control Fishing in Region," *Washington Post*, September 30, p. A22.

Olson, Mancur, Jr. 1965. *The Logic of Collective Action* (Cambridge, Mass., Harvard University Press).

Resources for the Future. 1968. *U.S. Energy Policies: An Agenda for Research* (Washington, D.C., Resources for the Future).

Rosenne, Shabtai. 1973. *The World Court* (3rd rev. ed., Dobbs Ferry, N.Y., Oceana).

Saila, Saul B., and Virgil J. Norton. 1974. *Tuna: Status, Trends, and Alternative Management Arrangements*, RFF Program of International Studies of Fishery Arrangements, Paper No. 6 (Washington, D.C., Resources for the Future).

Samuelson, Robert J. 1977a. "Law of the Sea Treaty—Talk, Talk, and More Talk," *National Journal* vol. 35 (August 27) pp. 1337–1343.

———. 1977b. "New Fishing Limits May Prove Big Haul," *Washington Post*, November 29, pp. D 7–8.

Sandler, Todd, and Jan Cauley. 1977. "The Design of Supranational Structures," *International Studies Quarterly* vol. 21, pp. 251–276.

Scott, Anthony. 1973. *Natural Resources: The Economics of Conservation* (Toronto, McClelland and Stewart).

Small, George L. 1971. *The Blue Whale* (New York, Columbia University Press).

Stoessinger, John G. and associates. 1964. *Financing the United Nations System* (Washington, D.C., Brookings Institution).

United Nations. 1971. General Assembly Resolution 2749 (XXV), 10 International Legal Materials 220.

————. 1976. Third Law of the Sea Conference. Revised Single Negotiating Text, A/Conf. 62/WP8/Rev 1/Part II (May).

————. 1977a. Third Law of the Sea Conference. Informal Composite Negotiating Text, A/Conf. 62/WP.10/Corr 1 (July).

————. 1977b. *U.N. Statistical Yearbook* (New York, United Nations).

U.S. Congress. 1872. "An Act to Promote the Development of the Mining Resources of the United States," 42nd Cong., 2nd Session (May 10).

————. Office of the Comptroller General. 1976. *Deep Ocean Mining Environmental Study—Information and Issues* (Washington, D.C., GPO).

————. Office of Technology Assessment. 1977. *Establishing a 200-mile Fisheries Zone* (Washington, D.C., GPO).

U.S. House of Representatives. 1977. *Report on the Deep Seabed Hard Minerals Act,* Committee on Merchant Marine and Fisheries, 95th Cong. Report 95-583.

U.S. Senate. 1977. *Report on the Outer Continental Shelf Lands Act* Amendments of 1977, Report 95-284, Committee on Energy and Natural Resources, 95th Cong. (Washington, D.C., GPO).

Washington Post. 1977. "U.S. Trims Foreign Catch." November 29, p. A3.

Young, Oran, ed. 1975. *Bargaining: Formal Theories of Negotiation* (Urbana, Ill., University of Illinois Press).

————. 1977. *Resource Management at the International Level: The Case of the North Pacific* (New York, Nichols).

————. 1979. *Compliance and Public Authority: A Theory with International Applications* (Baltimore, Johns Hopkins University Press for Resources for the Future).

Zartman, I. William, ed. 1976. *The 50% Solution* (Garden City, N.Y. Anchor Press/Doubleday).

Edwin T. Haefele

Political Applications of Social
Choice Theory

Social choice theory has been touted as a specific remedy for many ills of the body politic. It is said to be useful in choosing public policies, choosing processes or institutions that choose policies, choosing a constitution, evaluating all of the above, or selecting criteria that could do the evaluating.

No doubt the preceding paragraph is overdrawn, but the diversity of the papers in this volume provides substantial support to the wide-ranging nature of the activities that may go on from a social choice theory base, real or imagined.

In any event, social choice theory has been added to the Anglo-American political pharmacopoeia and is being prescribed more commonly than it once was. It is worth noting that other remedies in the same book have been historically, natural law, the common law, history itself,[1] reason or logical deduction and induction, and the rational models of behavior stemming chiefly from economics and related academic disciplines.

The earlier remedies were all algorithms for solving social choice problems, each having different definitions of fact and value, and a different method of reasoning from cause to effect. Social choice theory shares some of the characteristics of the economic algorithm (or paradigm) but as it is logically prior to economics, it must not be subsumed by economics. When it is, it loses most of its political applicability and much of its force.

---

[1] John Dickerson said at the Philadelphia Convention, "We must let experience be our only guide, for reason may mislead us."

I intend to illustrate that judgment by discussing with reference to a research agenda, three political problems that can best be addressed through social choice theory.

First, there is the problem of political aggregation rules. In 1800 Thomas Jefferson wrote, mainly for his own guidance in the Senate, his Parliamentary Manual. The Manual is regularly republished with every edition of the House and Senate Rules.[2] He compiled his manual, not from any a priori reasoning of how a deliberative representative body should proceed, but rather from English precedents of the House of Commons, "the model which we have all studied," as he put it.

Jefferson's manual bears little resemblance to the present rules of the House and Senate. It bears great resemblance, however, to the logical constructs of social choice theory, containing procedures that take account of "sophisticated" voting and cycling while allowing the "true sense of the deliberative body" to emerge. Standing committees on substantive issues were not allowed, on the very sensible dictum that they may well prevent the committee of the whole from being able to deliberate on certain measures. The whole House was forced to accept or reject a bill for review, a practice that allowed the House, as a whole, to set its own agenda. Any member could ask that a bill containing two separable issues be split, and the substance of any bill was considered separately from amounts of money (or any other quantity) by a process know as "filling the blanks." This last procedure was used, incidentally, by the Philadelphia Convention when it chose the number of executives under the Constitution.

Many of these procedures bear striking resemblance to certain social choice rules that have been explored in recent years by theorists totally ignorant of their long-standing role in political assemblies. Moreover, many of Jefferson's procedures have been abandoned, mostly for expediency's sake and in ignorance of the social choice consequences of abandonment.

I recommend Jefferson's manual to social choice theorists as a rich vein of high-grade research ore. Contrasting the manual with present-day House and Senate rules is a long overdue task that remains unperformed, to our mutual shame.

Second, there is a problem of political boundaries, particularly below the state level. Social choice theorists know that preference aggre-

---

[2] Sad to say, the manual was dropped in the 1978 volume of the Senate Rules.

gation rules start with the boundary question. Whose preferences are to be counted is as important as the aggregation rules, yet modern America struggles with local political boundaries that make no sense in political, economic, or social choice theory terms. While economists may instruct us on efficient-sized delivery systems, they cannot tell us *what* should be chosen for delivery. Social choice theory could say much about the boundary conditions for preference aggregation that would answer the *what* question.

We may need to reexamine the efficacy of territorial representation as the only means of aggregating preferences, particularly in light of the misapplication by the Supreme Court (no social choice theorists, they!) of the one-man, one-vote doctrine to upper house of state legislatures. Social choice theorists are peculiarly well equipped to explore, both historically and experimentally, other methods of representation.

Third, there is the problem of a social choice theory of Anglo-American history. The evolution of democracy in England and America can be charted in social choice theory terms as well as in economic history terms, and with much greater enlightenment to students of government. Indeed, a case can be made that the period from 1601 to 1787 represents the development of democratic social choice with the Constitution the peak of that development, and that the period from 1787 to 1978 represents a decline caused by increasing ignorance of the processes dictated in 1787.

The American Civil War provides a striking case in point, for during that war we made changes in rules and procedures, again for the sake of convenience, that had far-reaching effects on American government. The breaking up of the Ways and Means Committee in the House into separate committees on revenues and appropriations meant, predictably to a social choice theorist, that Congress would lose control of the federal budget. The establishment of the Federal Executive Bureau of the Budget in 1921 was a foregone conclusion and the newly established budget committees in both Houses a belated attempt to recover congressional control.

The present American infatuation with a nationwide count for the presidency is another manifestation of ignorance of the deliberately selected aggregation rule of the Founders. While they did not speak in social choice terms, they had easily perceivable aggregation rules in mind, rules that were, and are, much more subtle than the modern rules that are wanted to replace them. While political scientists, at least the good ones, know intuitively that the nationwide vote count is dangerous, it is the social choice theorist who can say why it is dangerous.

In summary, there is a whole host of political/institutional issues that are begging for attention by social choice theory. We have passed the 200th anniversary of the Republic without addressing them. Perhaps by the 200th anniversary of the Constitution, not so far away, we can do better.

James S. Coleman

Future Directions for Work
in Public Choice

If I am to comment upon future directions for "applied social choice," the term itself must be better defined than it has been in the papers of this conference. The meaning which I shall use is intentionally broader than that which is implicit in the uses of the papers, but it captures, I believe, the essence of the phenomenon in which we are interested. The definition contains inherently two elements: a certain kind of phenomenon and a certain orientation to the phenomenon. The orientation is one of rational action: we assume that individuals act rationally to gain their ends. But the phenomenon of interest is not the individual behavior, it is the social or collective result of that behavior. Yet it is not the collective result in the particularly simple and straightforward aggregation of individual action that is found in private goods markets where there are no externalities. The phenomena of interest are social outcomes unintended by any of the actors in a more profound sense than that implied by Adam Smith's invisible hand. Indeed, the outcomes are not only unintended, but in some of the most prominent instances of social choice, are perverse to individual intentions.

However, if it is the phenomena of interest which differ from those characteristic of economics, it is the orientation to those phenomena which differs from that in political science and sociology. That orientation is an assumption of rational action on the part of individuals. In short, the field of social choice has taken upon itself the difficult task of accounting for social and political phenomena by use of assumptions of rational action on the part of individuals—and in particular, those social and political phenomena that are not simple reflections of individual action (as, for example, total demand *is* a simple reflection of individual demand).

Now you may well ask why I have indulged myself so long in a rather ordinary, if cumbersome, definition of social choice. I do so for an explicit reason. The field of social choice or public choice began with the study of collective decisions, committee decisions, and legislative actions, which constituted formal structures for producing social action from individual action. The field has expanded somewhat, but it retains the marks of its origin. It still focuses to a large extent on voting, and on governmental actions; and it retains marks of the economist by often assuming that not only are individuals rational, it is money income, or material resources which may be priced in money terms, that individuals are maximizing.

If we once see the matter more broadly, it then becomes a short step to proposing that we examine, as the field of social choice, the full range of phenomena that it naturally includes. Concretely, what this means is studying phenomena that are at some distance from economics. I will mention some of these:

1. First is a panic of the sort that sometimes occurs in a crowded theater. The most puzzling question here is not why panics occur, but why their occurrence is so uncertain. In one situation, a panic will occur, as happened for example in the Beverly Hills Night Club in Covington, Kentucky, in 1977, when over 100 persons died. In other apparently similar situations, a panic fails to take place. Why? Another observation is that training, such as fire drills, is effective for certain kinds of panics, such as those initiated by fire. But training appears totally ineffective in other panics such as bank panics. Why the difference?

One reason I mention panics is that a panic is often explained as the product of "emotional," "irrational" behavior of persons under stress. Is such an explanation necessary? I think not; but if a rational choice explanation is to be given, it must answer the questions I have mentioned above; and it must outperform the "irrational" explanation in certain crucial tests. Empirical research can include both observation of naturally occurring panics and laboratory experiments.[1]

2. Another kind of phenomenon within the realm of social choice is a different kind of crowd behavior: the action of a hostile crowd in

---

[1] Ed. note: A reviewer has pointed out that panics are really not at any great distance from economics. Bank panics were a regular feature of nineteenth century America, and greater or smaller panics—both of buyers and sellers—still occur regularly on stock and commodity exchanges.

attacking a victim or an object of hostility. For example, around 1950, a black family moved into an apartment in Cicero, adjacent to Chicago. A crowd formed and milled around for a long time. Finally, a youth threw a rock and broke a window; suddenly the crowd was transformed into an active one, with rocks and firebombs thrown, and with police lines broken as the crowd surged toward the building.

Now this crowd behavior differs strikingly from that seen in a panic in a theater. Why this extensive period of "milling around"? How does the crowd get suddenly transformed from a passive, quiet, milling one to an active and aggressive one? Why does it seem inappropriate to think of training to avoid such outbreaks, in contrast to fire drills?

3. Still another phenomenon in this same general area, also within social choice, is the *absence* of action in social situations, for instance, the Kitty Genovese phenomenon where a young woman under attack died while at least forty persons were aware of the attack, but were somehow immobilized. More generally, the finding is that the chance that a person will intervene to aid a victim who needs help declines sharply with the number of other persons present. Indeed, there is some evidence that the decline is such that the probability that *someone* helps remains about constant as the number of persons present increases.

4. Still another collective phenomenon is that of fads, fashions, and crazes, which *may* involve money transactions (as in the tulip market craze in Holland in the eighteenth century, during which a single bulb sometimes sold for as much as a house), but may just as well not (as the craze among some boys for ducktail haircuts in the 1950s, or the collective madness that descended on some towns in the Northwest United States in which large numbers of residents were convinced their automobile windshields were being pitted by mysterious forces).

5. Systems of norms (for example, the whole set of sexual norms involving premarital codes, extramarital norms, homosexuality, and so on) provide another example. Some sociologists take norms as given, to explain behavior, but they obviously must themselves be explained because they are endogenous to society: they differ from time to time and place to place. And clearly the existence of a norm is in the interest of some persons. Norms are intimately related to prisoners' dilemma type situations, in which A and B are both better off if they can mutually constrain each other from acting in what would be to their individual best interest. But this raises more questions than it answers: just how do the actors circumvent the dilemma; how do they establish and enforce the norm? Only if we are able to specify the conditions under which

norms will arise if they do not exist or vanish if they do, and the conditions under which they effectively control action, can it be said that a system of norms has been "explained."

I have tried in outlining these problems to do violence to the current conception of social choice or public choice. I do so deliberately because I believe there is a serious danger that, because of the high proportion of economists among those who have defined their field of activity as public choice, and the near-absence of sociologists, the scope of public choice problems will be arbitrarily narrowed, and a field of extraordinary richness will be reduced to a promontory of economics, extending only a short way into politics and government.

I have picked these particular examples not randomly, nor because they are "sociological," but rather for two other reasons: first, because they seem initially to lie farthest from "rationality," being transient, emotional, concerned with intangibles. In addition, in my eyes, these phenomena have something in common. I believe that not only can they be explained as results of rational behavior, but also that they have in common a particular kind of rational behavior: that in certain situations, persons *transfer control* over their actions to others, fully or partially, and they do so both unilaterally (that is, not as part of some exchange involving another person) and rationally. They do so rationally in the same sense that persons make rational investments of material resources. I will not go into the explanatory scheme itself but only mention it in order to indicate that it may not be so outlandish to view these phenomena as within the province of social choice.

My intent is only partly normative. It is also predictive. That is, I believe it is likely that in the next few years, a major type of growth in the field of public choice will consist of an expansion into fields of social behavior that have until now lain outside its province. I have mentioned here a small sample of those fields.

Index

Index

Library of Congress Cataloging in Publication Data

Main entry under title:
Collective decision making.

  Papers presented at a forum held January 17–19, 1978
sponsored by Resources for the Future.
  1. Social choice—Congresses. I. Russell, Clifford S. II. Resources for the Future.
HB99.3.C64   301.1   79-16614
ISBN 0-8018-2320-X